9 Years on the 7 Seas with S/Y Nor Siglar

Anne E. Brevig

Published in cooperation with Halvor Nome, Nome Design & Publishing,
Halden, Norway

ISBN: 1497394635
ISBN-13: 978-1497394636

DEDICATION

To Martin

and the

People we met on the Way.

Dare to take the leap –
Dolphins will carry you

Honorine Hermelin

TABLE OF CONTENTS

	THE DREAM	**1**
1	**PART 1: VANCOUVER TO THE PANAMA CANAL**	**6**
	OUR BLUEWATER DEBUT	6
	MARVELLOUS MEXICO	11
	CHALLENGED IN THE GULD OF PAPAGALLO	16
	CHILLING DISTRESS CALL	24
	PANAMAS PACIFIC PARADISE	27
	ISLA PARADITA	27
	BAHÍA HONDA	31
	SALMONETE	34
	LAS PERLAS	37
	THE PANAMA CANAL	43
2	**PART 2. CARIBBEAN**	**48**
	SAN BLAS – HELP! DEAD MAN ON DECK!	48
	IN THE WAKE OF THE OLD PIRATES FROM PANAMA TO HONDURAS	58
	JUNGLE SAFARI IN GUATEMALA	63
	ISLAS DE LA BAHÍA	70
	TO SEE IT IS TO BELIZE IT	74
	CUBA	79
3	**PART 3. ACROSS THE ATLANTIC TO NORWAY**	**90**
	ANTIGUA	92
	BERMUDA	95
	THE AZORES	100
	THE HOMECOMING	102
	WINTERING ONBOARD IN NORWAY	106
4	**PART 4. NORTH SEA, MEDITERRANEAN, AFRICA AND THE ATLANTIC OCEAN**	**111**
	SOUTH TO WARMER CLIMES	111
	MEDITERRANEAN NEXT!	116
	ISRAEL	119
	TUNISIA	125
	WE SEEK REFUGE IN ALGERIA	130
	OUR MOROCCAN EXPERIENCE	138
	LONESOME ON THE ATLANTIC	150
	REUNION IN SAN BLAS	156

TABLE OF CONTENTS

5 PART 5 PACIFIC OCEAN **169**
PANAMA-GALAPAGOS 169
GALAPAGOS SLEEPLESS IN PARADISE 174
GALAPAGOS - MARQUESAS 180
FRENCH POLYNESIA 185
- MARQUESAS 185
- TUAMOTUS 189
- THE LEGENDARY SOCIETY ISLANDS 194
- TAHITI 194
- MOOREA 199
- RAIATEA 201
- BORA BORA 203
THE KINGDOM OF TONGA 206
FASCINATING FIJI 215
VANUATU 229
SOLOMON ISLANDS 233
IN THE WAKE OF CAPTAIN BLIGH 244

6 PART 6. SOUTHEAST ASIA **248**
AUSTRALIA 248
INDONESIA 250
AGROUND AGAIN 254
RITUALS, RITES AND REALITY 260
TROUBLES ON THE SOUTH CHINA SEA 265
SQUABBLES IN SINGAPORE 268
MALAYSIA THE INFAMOUS STRAIT OF MALACCA 270
THAILAND CHRISTMAS IN SPLENDID ISOLATION 273
THAILAND - THE MALDIVES 278
THE MALDIVES 282

7 PART 7. INDEAN OCEAN, RED SEA AND THE MEDITERRANEAN **287**
THE MALDIVES - THE ARABIAN PENINSULA 287
PROSPEROUS OMAN & IMPOVERISHED YEMEN 293
THE DREADED RED SEA 299
WARN-TORN ERITREA 301
DESTITUTE SUDAN 306
EGYPT – THE LAND OF PHARAOHS 313
ISRAEL – WE DID IT! 317

HOMEWARD BOUND – GIBRALTAR - NORWAY **321**
BACK TO TERRA FIRMA 325
ABOUT THE AUTHORS 328
ABOUT THE YACHT 330
EQUIPMENT 334
GLOSSARY 336
BEAUFORT SCALE 339
MORE ADVENTURE BOOKS 340

PREFACE

Anne and Martin

At the peak of their careers, Anne Brevig and Martin Vennesland made the decision of their lives: they chose freedom and a highly uncertain future on the high seas instead of secure jobs and the safety and comfort of life ashore.

In order to finance their dream, they sold their house and most of their belongings and moved onboard their 40-foot sailboat. It became their one and only home for 15 years. Neither imagined that they were going to spend 9 years on the 7 seas and journey more than 56,000 nautical miles. Back on terra firma, their once-in-a-lifetime adventure, which was packed with drama and excitement, was immortalized in a beautiful coffee table book, "9 Years on the 7 Seas". It quickly became a bestseller, and when it sold out in paper format, the adventurous couple decided to share their experiences with the world in the equally exciting "Seven Seas Adventures" Series, which is now available both in print and several eBook formats.

Anne and Martin's blue water adventure is not about breaking any records. Its main focus is meeting people from different backgrounds and cultures - encounters that take on entirely different dimensions when sailing off the beaten track far away from the traditional tourist routes.

Anne and Martin crossed the big oceans and visited 76 countries and island nations. They realized their dreams. Now, they hope that their books in the "Seven Seas Adventures" Series, which are saturated with enchanting encounters, danger and unique experiences, will inspire others to pursue their own dreams – whatever they may be. At least, to "dare to take the leap". The Series certainly gives a rare opportunity to live vicariously in theirs, and their beloved sailboat, "NOR SIGLAR'S" wake.

THE ROUTE

During her nine years at sea, Nor Siglar logged 56,000 nautical miles (a distance equalling 2,5 times around the world), visiting 47 countries and 29 island colonies on the way.

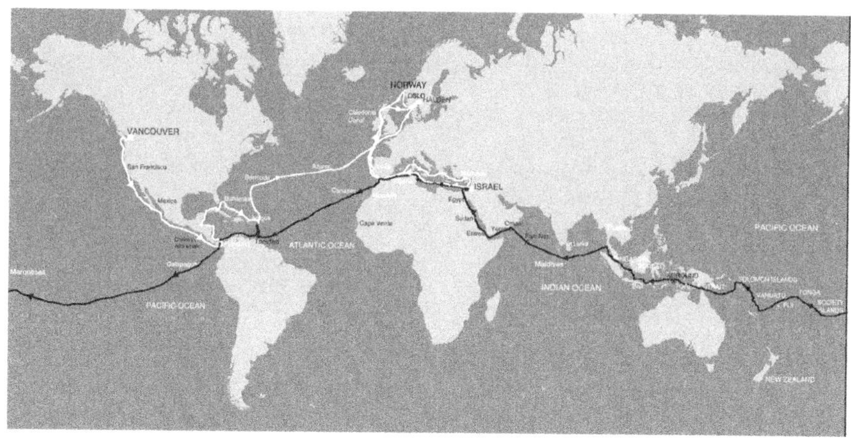

Our sailing route during the 9 Years on the 7 Seas adventure.

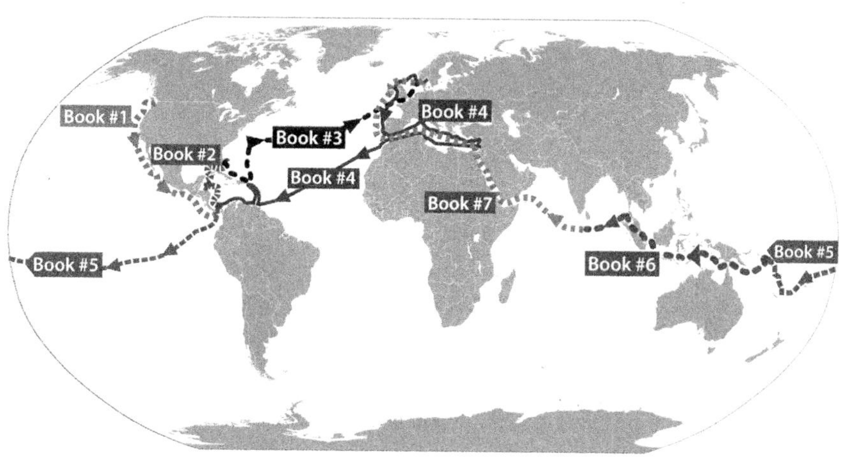

On the oval map, the "9 Years on the 7 Seas" Route is divided into seven parts, each corresponding to the 7 parts of this book, and the 7 books in the "Seven Seas Adventures" Series. The Series is available both in print, in Kindle and other popular eBook file formats, available for download from **www.sevenseasadventure.com**

THE DREAM

"I've just got to sell the boat, Anne!" He looked so despondent, this newfound love of mine, an avid sailor, born on the south coast of Norway with salt water in his veins. In my wallet I carry an old, crumpled black and white photo of a little blond boy in a hand-knit swimsuit complete with a sailboat on his chest. Time and again, Martin, whose hair was now turning grey at the temples, would reminisce about his happy childhood by the sea. Especially the time, when at the tender age of 12, he "borrowed" his father's 6-metre sailboat, took off without permission, ran into a full gale, was afraid to turn around and almost ended up in Denmark. Yes, indeed, the dream of sailing to distant and exotic shores on his own keel took shape very early in this young Viking.

"No way!" I exclaimed with fervour. The year was 1984; times were tough in Canada, especially on the West Coast, where the economy had hit a record low. In the mid 1950s, after Forestry School in Norway, Martin had emigrated to British Columbia where Canada's big forests were beckoning. Now, 30 years later, he found himself at the helm of one of the country's largest forestry consulting firms. His life had changed and he really should part with his beloved sailboat. "But Elysian is your sanctuary," I pleaded. "She is the only place where you can truly relax! If you get rid of her, how can you cope with all the stress you are under these days?"

It was Sunday afternoon. We were on our way back to the city after a perfect weekend in the Gulf Islands. In bright sunshine and an exhilarating fresh, northwesterly breeze, we sped home to reality and another workweek. Things aboard couldn't be better. Still, there was a feeling of despair in the air.

Martin began leafing through some nautical magazines, rather nonchalantly. "Look here!" he exclaimed. "This couple has sailed around the world. And not only that, before they left, they lived on board this little ketch for several years!" "What a great idea," I replied. "Why can't we do that too?" Little did I know then how that impulsive outburst was to change my life forever.

How I could come up with such a crazy statement is beyond me to this day. Little me, just a country girl, who having grown up on a farm, also in Norway but far away from the coast, had never set foot on a sailboat until I was 38. I was afraid of the sea, couldn't swim until I was 16, and more challenging still, became seasick easily. Had true love made me lose my senses? Had I gone totally mad? After 20 years abroad, working in various capacities within shipping, I had finally acquired a management position with an international company, which I really enjoyed. The work was interesting and well paid with excellent fringe benefits and a secure future. It was a dream job, the kind of job I had always wanted and worked so hard to get. But now, in a matter of seconds, it was a dream abandoned for new challenges and an uncertain future.

PREPARATIONS

The planning started right away. First, we had to decide what type of boat we should get for our once in a lifetime adventure. Although we loved our old Elysian, a 36-foot C&C, she was too small to live on while working full time and getting ready for going offshore. After some deliberation, we decided on a much roomier 40-foot Gib'Sea sloop, which we ordered new from the factory in France.

On a cold and wintry October day, Nor Siglar arrived on a freighter owned by the company I worked for in Vancouver for 17 years. A month later, after having sold the house and most of our belongings, save a few treasures, which kind relatives agreed to store in our absence, our carefully chosen "Northern Sailor" became our new home. At that point, neither one of us would ever have imagined that this space, barely larger than an average size kitchen, would be our home, our only home for 15 years.

Living aboard was essential in order to save as much as we could as quickly as possible. Besides, knowing nothing about boats, I had to find out if I could adjust to life onboard. I didn't dare quit my job before I was convinced of that. Just as important was for the two of us to see if we could function together in such close quarters 24 hours a day 365 days a year.

Nor Siglar arrives in Vancouver from the factory in La Rochelle via the Gearbulk frighter Charles L.D.

Outfitting a brand new sailboat for the high seas turned out to be twice as costly as we had thought. Therefore, to be able to finance our dream, we had to forego a number of things normally taken for granted in regular day-to-day life. Also, the preparations took much longer than expected. As the projects kept multiplying, the "to do" lists grew longer and longer. So it is really true: If you want to be 100% ready before casting off, you'll never get away from the dock!

It was a hectic time. We immersed ourselves in all kinds of nautical literature and attended seminars and slide presentations by experienced offshore cruisers. Although a veteran sailor and navigator, Martin still had to familiarize himself with the maintenance and repair of the engine and equipment. His biggest challenge, however, was to master the mysteries of electricity and the electronics onboard. It was truly mind-boggling for someone, who was already middle-aged before the advent of computers, to learn how to use all the modern gadgets we acquired. For me, everything was new; boat handling and equipment, navigation and communications, even the terminology. A long string of courses qualified me for a full range of nautical skills, as well as the coveted amateur radio licence. Both of us took courses in celestial navigation, radar and first aid.

Last day at work. Good-bye stress! Welcome freedom! It is only 10 minutes to downtown Vancouver from the marina where we lived for six years.

Martin quit his job nine months before departure. Even so, the last weeks were chaotic beyond belief. Hundreds of things had to be organized; we sold the car, renewed our passports and insurance policies, went to the doctor and dentist, met with our lawyer, accountant and bank manager, appointed a friend to have our power of attorney and to look after our bills and forward our mail. One week before cast-off, I quit my job, we got married, wrote our respective wills and were ready! The trial period was over.

Ours was not to be a circumnavigation of speed and impressive records. We had different goals. Because of our Norwegian roots, we wanted to go "home" first, to sail to "the old country" on our own keel. After many years abroad, we yearned to re-kindle and nurture relationships with family and childhood friends, now that we finally had more than a few short vacation weeks at our disposal. So instead of heading west, following the trade winds, the traditional route around the world, we chose to go east about first.

Originally, our plan was to reach Spain the following summer for Columbus' 500th anniversary in Seville and the Olympics in Barcelona. Then we wanted to sail in the Mediterranean, before heading north to the Land of the Midnight Sun and the Lillehammer Olympics. We did not realize the banality of it all until homesteaders on a beautiful island in Panama confronted us with the question: Why are you rushing through paradise?

Since then, we slowed down, smelled the roses and started to live for the moment. We met people and experienced things we otherwise would have missed. And it is these unique experiences we wish to share with you in our book, hoping that they will inspire other "ordinary people" like ourselves to pursue their own respective Dreams; Dreams that so many carry with them for a lifetime; Dreams that so few dare to fulfill.

PART 1

VANCOUVER TO THE PANAMA CANAL

OUR BLUEWATER DEBUT

Vancouver – San Francisco

There is no denying that I was quite nervous about my very first ocean voyage. Most disconcerting of all was the initial 1000 nautical mile passage to San Francisco. It was to be done non-stop and could take more than a week. There are few places to seek shelter along this exposed stretch, so it is quite customary to do this leg in one go. The prevailing wind is from the northwest, and in the fall, gales are frequent. Shipping traffic is heavy and the coast is often plagued by fog. So there were no lack of challenges for our offshore debut. Therefore, we decided to have a crew, and were very pleased when our friends Gerry Rolfsen and Erik Ollgaard agreed to come along.

Martin waves good-bye to family and friends

Our long anticipated date of departure finally arrived. We were actually leaving! Six years of dreaming, planning and preparations had come to an end. It was almost unreal. A wave of nostalgia rushed through me as we moved away from the dock leaving family and friends behind. We had worked so hard towards this goal, towards this very day, towards realizing our Big Dream. But when it was about to be launched, a sense of uncertainty suddenly emerged. A little voice deep inside me said: "What on earth are you doing? Taking off, just like that, quitting good jobs, leaving dear ones behind, leaving the safety and security of home, of the well known. How are we going to manage? Will we make it? Will we have any regrets? Be afraid? Lonely? Ill? Will the same people standing on the dock waving to us today be there for us when we return? Will anybody be missing? Have moved? Be divorced? Or dead? Will we lose touch with each other, or will distance bring us closer than ever? When will we see each other again?"

It was a moving occasion, one that brought back similar feelings from long ago, when I waved goodbye to my parents from the "America" boat in Oslo as I emigrated to Canada. But this time, as the figures on land disappeared in the distance, relief and joy soon replaced anxiety and sentimental thoughts. And as soon as the sails were hoisted and Nor Siglar on her way, there was only one thought in our minds: Finally underway!

It didn't take long before someone was hanging over the railing. And that was I. While Erik and Gerry grew paler and paler, quietly suffering, I succumbed to feeding the crabs – over and over again. Martin, who has never been seasick all his life, was OK, of course. The long and uncomfortable swells of the North Pacific didn't bother him in the least. So the first few days, while his crew were getting their sea legs, most of the chores were left to Nor Siglar's skipper. As long as we managed to crawl out on deck for our watches and the occasional sail change, he managed the rest with flying colours. Dinners had been prepared ahead of time with exactly this situation in mind. All he had to do was warm them up. So Martin didn't mind being the cook for a few days. Besides, there were hardly any dishes. He was the only one with an appetite.

We started the watch system right away; four hours on during the day, three hours at night. This way, with four people on board, everyone was able to get a good rest between watches. Galley duty was to be rotated so that each person would be responsible for cooking and cleanup once every four days. At least, that was the intention.

The night watches were lonely, but fascinating. At first, it felt spooky to sit alone in the low and shallow cockpit in the pitch black, exposed to nature's potent elements so close by. It felt as though I was all-alone in the whole wide world; just me, the boat, the sea and the horizon. It made me feel very, very small in a very, very large universe. And Nor Siglar just kept on going, ploughing her way steadily through the waves on a never-ending vast, open ocean. There was a pattern to the movements. Soon I began to anticipate every motion. It was an immensely powerful feeling.

Our blue water debut went beyond all expectations. Not only did we have the pleasure of the company of killer whales, dolphins and albatrosses along the way, we had steady following winds as well; mostly perfect fresh breeze to near gale. Only around Cape Mendocino, California's westernmost point, did we encounter a few hours of stormy gusts and short, steep seas. On the fourth day, when we crossed into California, our spirits were particularly high. After a shot of Gammeldansk, everyone had a good scrub, the first after leaving home, and we all felt like human beings again.

Major provisioning in San Diego before leaving for Central America.

So we were blessed with good fortune and great conditions and made it to San Francisco in good time, a little over six days. It was a wonderful feeling to sight Golden Gate Bridge after so many days at sea, and an enormous relief that both vessel and crew had mastered the challenge. The only visible wear and tear Nor Siglar sustained during the passage was a broken toilet seat! Overjoyed, we celebrated our first landfall with champagne and the cruising spinnaker flying under the famous landmark on our way to a well-deserved rest at the San Francisco Yacht Club.

Then followed a few weeks of relaxing day trips meandering down the coast, experiencing California's "carefree life", staying at some of the world's largest marinas and spending hours on end walking seemingly endless beaches, watching sandpipers playing along the water's edge and young and athletic surfers roaring down wild waves with great courage and skill.

As members of Royal Vancouver and Royal Norwegian Yacht Clubs, we were able to enjoy reciprocal privileges at some of the best yachting centres along the coast. Privileges included three days free moorage and access to all sorts of wonderful facilities. So we lived a few days in supreme luxury, enjoying life to its fullest, well aware that such comfort would be scarce in the open and exposed anchorages of Central America. In San Diego, we stayed put for six weeks while the hurricane season was nearing its end further south.

We cycled for miles on newly acquired folding bikes, took an intensive three week scuba diving course and worked on jobs which we had not had time to finish before we left. Of course we didn't complete them all, leaving plenty of chores for future stopovers. In early November, with the waterline raised by five centimetres, chock full of provisions and spare parts, Nor Siglar could finally continue south to eternal sunshine and warmer climes. The real adventure was about to begin..

MARVELLOUS MEXICO

The 900-mile stretch from San Diego to Cabo San Lucas on the southern tip of Baja California is known to sailors for its favourable conditions. The only exception is that an occasional hurricane moving north to Mexico could affect the area. But after October, this is unlikely. So a week into November, with old friends Sven and Althea Rasmussen onboard, we took off. After three lovely days with fresh breeze from the northwest, we were spooked to learn that hurricane Nora was moving towards us at a speed of 8 knots and wind strength of 100 miles per hour. If she continued with the same speed and direction, she would hit us before we could reach Cabo..

We had been heading out to Guadalupe Islands, but now changed course back towards land to seek shelter in Bahía Santa Maria. The night was rough and squally. Was Nora already making herself felt? By morning, however, it turned calmer, and much to our relief, Nora changed direction and blew herself out. But now our minds were set on spending a few days in the remote Bahía, so we continued there.

After seven days at sea, it was lovely to make landfall again. The entry into the bay was picture perfect with dolphins showing the way and local fishermen waving from dugout pangas. "Hola, Nor Siglar! Langosta?" We couldn't believe our eyes. Now was our chance to practice the Spanish we had studied underway. "Sí, sí", I tried. "Cuántos cuesta?" They stared at us with wide-open eyes. "Cigarillos, Señora?" Amazing. All they wanted was cigarettes! We gave them a package each. With trading in mind, we had provisioned lots of cigarettes in San Diego.

Lobsters! Chez Nor Siglar. Bartered for two t-shirts and a pack of cigarettes. "Muchas gracias amigos!"

The lobster was ours. But it would be nice to get a few more. "Ocho, por favor?" The fisherman pointed at Martin's T-shirt. Great! Just as planned. We had hoarded cheap T-shirts too and let them chose one each. They were visibly delighted. "Muchas gracias amigos! Adiós!" Our first impression of Mexico was just great, as we sat down to our first gourmet feast in Mexican waters. It was not to be the last. "Qué buena vida!"

A few days later, we rounded Baja's World's End, to arrive in Cabo San Lucas, a bustling resort surrounded by white, sandy beaches, rugged volcanic cliffs and an amazingly blue sea. We thought we had come to Paradise. The water was crystal clear, the temperature the same as the air. Restaurants were situated right on the beach, so you could sit and wiggle your toes in the sand while sipping margaritas and enjoying exotic cuisine. Balmy, tropical nights, a big moon and star-studded sky created a truly romantic atmosphere.

Cabo was also our first encounter with civilization in Mexico, this fascinating land of contrasts. With an economy largely dependent on tourism, its effects can be felt everywhere. We experienced this first hand at the many picturesque anchorages along the coast where large, luxurious hotels line the shores, and where piercingly loud Mariachi bands connected to powerful speakers kept us awake till dawn, at which time roosters took over with their incessant calls. Just a stone's throw away from these artificial playgrounds, ordinary Mexicans go about their daily lives, living in simple but airy palapa huts or brick houses, working to make ends meet. Domestic animals wander freely about, litter is abundant. The heavily perfumed air is a peculiar blend of tropical flowers and fruits, sewage and the unmistakable scent of animals.

Further north, the Sea of Cortés beckoned us with its world-renowned underwater paradise. But we really had to struggle to make it there. The 30- mile stretch around Punta Los Frailes to La Paz is exposed to the infamous Santa Ana, a strong and dusty offshore wind coming from the desert further north. By the time the vicious norther reaches the Gulf, it is often a full gale. We had to make four boisterous attempts before we finally succeeded.

No wonder so many sailors fight the elements to move up into this area. Diving is first class, fishing exceptional. Sports fishermen come from afar to test their skills. It is not unusual to get a 400-pound marlin on the hook. After losing our gear overboard to such a monster, we quit fishing for big game and started snorkelling instead. I was so fascinated by the wealth of colourful marine life that I forgot to be afraid. Was the childhood phobia of getting my head under water cured at last?

Unusual Christmas in Puerto Vallerta.

With Christmas fast approaching, we set sail for the mainland and Puerto Vallarta where cruisers from many nations gather to celebrate the holiday season. It was hard to get into the Christmas spirit in the 30-degree heat. On Christmas Eve, we joined a flotilla of 20 dinghies to serenade the Mexican Navy stationed in the harbour. The marines must have thought they were being invaded, as they put strong searchlights on us and piped all crew on deck! It didn't take long though, before joyous shouts of "Feliz Navidad" rang out into the night from the decks above.

After weeks on the touristy coast, we were keen to experience the real Mexico and decided to take a land trip. Wishing close contact with the locals, we travelled second-class. Squeezed in between colourfully dressed natives with their live animals and unconventional luggage, we rattled along on packed chicken buses, up and down incredibly steep and narrow gravel roads across the Sierra Madre and into the distant countryside. Our small, soft-spoken travelling companions appeared reserved at first, but were, in fact, just as curious about us gringos as we were about them. Stops were few and far between. When nature called, people simply asked the driver to stop, went outside and squatted right next to the bus in plain view of the other passengers.

We found what we were looking for; Mexico's rich history and fascinating culture, so evident at the many vibrant mercados and zokalos and the spectacular ruins from ancient civilizations, complete with ceremonial plazas for human sacrifices, temples and pyramids - all bearing witness to an extraordinary past.

We just loved Mexico. But the bureaucracy got on our nerves after a while. It was necessary to check in and out of every port. Usually, the offices were far apart, opened late and closed early. And then there was the Siesta in the middle of the day. It was impossible to get things done quickly. But there was no point in becoming excited. One might as well make it the entertainment of the day. If one should be so unfortunate to arrive on the weekend, one could expect even more delays and extra expense. In the sleepy, little town of Puerto Angel, we lost our patience.

It was late Saturday afternoon. We had just put the anchor down when two armed, visibly intoxicated marines boarded us with a pile of forms. But they were more interested in Playboy magazines and cigarettes than doing their jobs. Having neither, we gave them two baseball caps. Happy, they took off and left us alone.

Early the next morning, we woke up with a start. There was a loud knock on the hull. In no time, someone was in the cockpit. Martin grabbed the pepper spray. "No, no amigo! El Capitan del Puerto!" the fellow pleaded. "No problema!" He demanded our ship's papers and passports, and ordered us to report to his office immediately.

New forms, more delays. When all was done, the Port Captain slipped us a piece of paper under the desk with the number, 50,000 scribbled on it. "Pesos para mi, Señor!" he grinned slapping his chest. "Para servicios!" That was too much for Martin. "Bastante no!" he yelled, slamming his fist on the desk, suddenly speaking Spanish like a native. "Mañana vamos al officina del turismo!" he shouted, shaking his fist at him. Threatening to complain to the Ministry of Tourism did it. Suddenly, everything was in perfect order. The mordida was dropped without a word.

Locals trading livestock at the colourful market in Oacaca.

To calm our nerves, we spent the rest of the day on beautiful Zipolite Beach, a popular nudist retreat and backpackers heaven frequented by nature lovers from all over the world. No wonder. A hammock cost only a dollar a night. A small hippie style commune of the sixties had settled at the far end of the beach, living a seemingly carefree life away from it all. The outside world was easily forgotten in this hidden away paradise with its spectacular sunsets.

The overall impression of idyllic Puerto Angel was forever destroyed for us. Greedy officials and a petty theft of a loaf of homemade bread, compliments of cruiser friends, which we had left in the dingy while walking the beach, put a damper on everything. It was time for a change. It was time to leave Mexico..

CHALLENGED IN THE GULF OF PAPAGALLO

Just before arriving in Puerto Madero, our last port of call in Mexico, a Mexican destroyer called us up on Channel 16, ordering us to stop and prepare for a boarding party. A huge Zodiac was launched with two officers and six mariners who proceeded onboard for a friendly inspection. This was the true Navy, neatly dressed polite young men. It was a routine procedure in an area where drug smuggling is frequent.

The water in Puerto Madero was both smelly and dirty, so we hadn't had a swim for quite a while. As soon as we had cleared out from the authorities and were out in open seas again, it was tempting to take a dip. Martin went first. Suddenly, a yellow sea snake with a black zigzag stripe on its back wriggled its way towards him at lightening speed. "Watch out!" I yelled, and with the poisonous snake in hot pursuit, he took the ladder in one leap. That was the end of my bath. I settled for a safe cat wash in the cockpit instead.

The 600 nautical mile passage from Mexico to Costa Rica can be quite a challenge. First of all, because of unstable political situations in Guatemala, Honduras and El Salvador at the time, it was advisable to bypass these countries. That meant a 5-6 day continuous trip. Secondly, the area is affected by the notorious Tehuantapec and Papagallo winds, gale and storm force winds funnelled south from the Gulf of Mexico across the narrow isthmus through the canyons of Guatemala. It was strongly recommended to keep well inshore, not more than a mile or two off the beach, in order to escape the big seas generated further out by these vicious and unpredictable offshore winds, which can blow up without much notice. In fact, they come up so fast that they are rarely forecast in time. So cruisers are often caught off guard and clobbered by these adverse conditions, which normally last 3- 4 days. January and February are the windiest months. So why do the crossing in February? Because we were in a hurry at that point. We wanted to be in Seville and Barcelona by that summer!

For three days, we had the loveliest weather imaginable, flying the cruising spinnaker during the day and enjoying calm seas and full moon at night. The fishing was great. We hauled in one yellow fin tuna and Dorado after the other. It was exciting. But soon we had to stop. We couldn't eat it all.

Every so often, we heard strange thumps against the hull. The sound was a real mystery until we discovered a huge turtle glide by. She was well camouflaged in the water, and hard to see. Suddenly, aware of their presence, we realized that there were many more around. Although they can weigh over 200 kilos, there is no danger that they may hole a fibreglass boat.

There was no shortage of entertainment on this passage. Dolphins in abundance delighted us with synchronized shows of spectacular leaps and bounds. Always operating in pairs, they were fascinating to watch as they were frolicking around and darting back and forth. The brown boobies, on the other hand, gave us a lot of grief. They fell in love with the wind speed indicator at the top of the mast. We were worried that they would ruin the sensitive impeller and tried to frighten them with a slingshot. But their memory was short. No sooner had they been scared away before they were back again. We yelled and screamed and banged the mast with metal objects to get rid of them. But to no avail. Eventually, the impeller broke.

We thought that would be the end of their games. But then they discovered the fishing line we were towing. The shining lure was dancing on the water's surface. Suddenly, one of them got caught on the hook. The poor bird, squeaking and flapping its wings, couldn't get itself untangled. So we hauled it in as carefully as we could. Even though it had ruined our wind speed indicator, we felt sorry for the booby. We set it free. But it went right after the hook again! And got caught a second time! Again, we rescued the silly bird, which was now bleeding from two cuts. We put the line away. Then they went after the solar panels instead. We gave up. But without our attention, it was no fun any more, and they took off.

As we crossed the border to Guatemala, we discovered that we had forgotten to get the guest flags for the Central American countries. Fortunately, it was calm enough that I managed to get out the sewing machine to make them. We had a brochure with the flags of all the nations in the world onboard, but no fabric. The cloth from one of Martin's old t-shirts would have to do. The flags of Guatemala, Honduras and El Salvador are simple to make. All are blue and white, the design varying between vertical and horizontal stripes, with or without stars. Later, we purchased material in all colours so we could produce more professional looking flags.

At breakfast on day four, Martin recounted tales of an eventful night. First, he had been caught in the middle of a big fishing fleet, and had trouble keeping clear of the nets. Then, near dawn, a torpedo boat appeared out of the morning mist. It was the Honduran Navy. He had come too close to the coast, to within the international 12-mile limit. Ahead lay Golfo de Fonseca where it was important to hug the shore. We had escaped the Tehuantapecs earlier; however, if the Papagallos were to pipe up now, we could be blown out to sea. But it wasn't very pleasant to have cannons aimed at Nor Siglar's stern either, so he didn't really have much choice. He changed course out to sea.

Soon after breakfast, we noticed that the northeaster, which we had been enjoying, suddenly changed to an easterly direction. Just ahead, the sea turned dark, a sure sign of an approaching squall. At this latitude, the coast of Costa Rica swings eastward. Now, the wind was coming from that direction too. No sooner had the breakfast dishes been cleared away, than the wind was blowing a full gale.

So we weren't going to escape the brutal Papagallos after all. It had looked so promising. Oh well. Better get on with it. Three reefs in the main, the jib furled in to a small hankie. Waves were rapidly building, white caps forming all around us. It was just incredible how quickly it all happened. The temptation to fall off was great. Better not. We just had to stay close to shore.

At dusk, we were six miles from Corinto, a large commercial port in Nicaragua. It was very rough. Why couldn't we seek refuge there? At this point, I could risk just about anything for a quiet night somewhere. "Do you really think it is so dangerous in Nicaragua?" I tried. "All we want is to seek shelter from the elements. I am sure they won't mind." Seaports everywhere, political situations aside, must surely allow ships to come in due to bad weather?

Martin dug out some old charts. They were in bad condition. We studied the approach to Corinto. It looked very confusing. The navigational markers didn't make any sense. I grabbed the VHF. "Corinto Pilot Station! Corinto Pilot Station! Aqui el velero Nor Siglar, yate de Canada!" Long silence. Finally someone answered. A faltering dialogue ensued. My Spanish wasn't good enough. "May we come in and wait for good weather?" I asked as clearly as I could. "Momentito", the operator answered and disappeared. "Boss no here! You come mañana?" he reported after a long pause. Unbelievable! Here we were, just a few miles away, and were asked to come back tomorrow instead!

Suddenly, the boat took a big lurch, the sails were slapping and Jonathan, our Kiwi friend, who had been crewing for us for a while, cried from the helm: "Reef ahead!" We rushed into the cockpit. And there it was, just a few metres ahead, dark and scary, waves splashing way into the air. A flock of seagulls scattered in all directions, frightened away by the noise of the sails. "Good grief! That reef is not on the chart", Jonathan said. Swinging the boat hard alee, we managed to avoid the nasty rocks by the skin of our teeth. Stunned, we headed out to deeper water. "Costa Rica next", Martin announced. "I'd rather battle storms than uncharted reefs."

Now the wind was really howling. Poor Nor Siglar was bashed about like a nutshell, waves crashing across the bow and railing. It looked like we were going to have a rough night. I crawled into my bunk and dreamt of rustling palms and sandy beaches.

We made it through the night. But in the early morning hours, we discovered what we had feared most. We had been blown way out to sea. We just had to get back to the coast. At any cost. That meant battling a full gale head on. After a tiresome watch, I went below to rest. I was just about to drift off to sleep when a terrific crash sounded from above. "Anne!" Martin cried.

"Hurry! Jonathan is hurt! It looks bad." My heart pounding, I ran outside to find Jonathan lying in a bundle on the deck, one arm around the railing, the other clutching his leg. Neither he, nor Martin had their safety harnesses on. "Are you nuts?" I yelled. "I can't leave you for a minute and you take your harness off! Why do I always have to nag? It's a wonder he didn't fall overboard!" Now I was both angry and afraid.

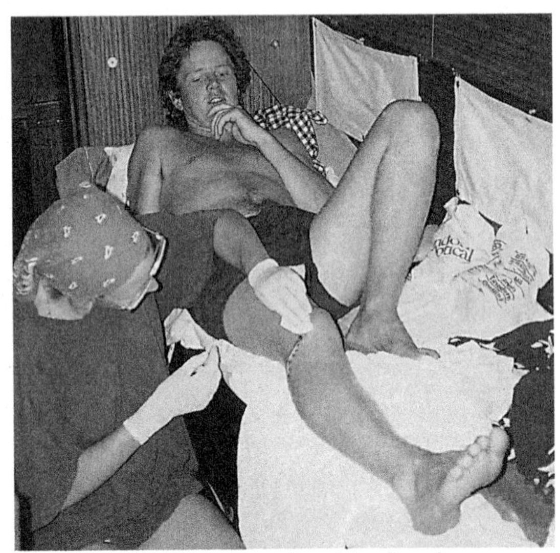

Anne administering first aid on Jonathan.

"Get a tourniquet, Anne! I think my leg is torn off ", Jonathan cried as I hauled him back into the cockpit. It felt as though my heart was going to explode. It can't be true. Why do we have to go through this? Blood was streaming through his fingers as he was holding a tight grip around his leg. "You've got to help me, Anne," he pleaded. I felt sick to my stomach. I looked at Martin. "Can you do this, please?" We had taken the same first aid course and knew roughly as much – or as little. "Come on!" he exclaimed. "I am better at keeping the boat under control. You take care of Jonathan."

I got hold of myself and brought out the first aid kit. The injury wasn't as bad as it first seemed. It was a deep, long cut on the upper calf, just below the knee, but certainly not life threatening. We managed to stop the bleeding. The wound should definitely be stitched. Did I dare try that in these rough seas? Stitching someone up for the very first time in a full gale? Being seasick to boot? We had the tools required, but would the patient and I be able to take it? That was the million-dollar question. "How long will it take to the nearest port, Martin?" I asked. "In these headwinds and waves, at least 24 hours", he replied. We decided on a temporary solution, taped the wound together with steri strips and hoped for the best. A doctor would have to fix it later.

The accident happened while moving the traveller down. The boom came charging over in a violent gust. Jonathan had hit himself badly. Martin lifted him down into the saloon where we made him as comfortable as possible. Then we continued as quickly as we could towards shore.

That evening, on the ham radio, we found out that the nearest doctor was in Bahía Salinas, 80 nautical miles away. We also got in touch with a hospital in Long Beach, which gave us assistance across the radio waves. It was reassuring to have this contact. We didn't feel so alone out there then. Cruising friends called us up to offer moral support. Two boats were waiting for us in Bahía Salinas. They would try to find some locals who could help us get Jonathan to the doctor as soon as we arrived.

While alone at the helm, things started to happen around me. Something strange was lurking on my port side. Suddenly, a long, black shadow broke the surface. It was just as long as Nor Siglar. Then I saw the spurt. It was a whale! It was only a couple of metres away. I froze. Instinctively, I thought about all the stories I had heard about boats mysteriously disappearing at sea. Take it easy. It will probably go away. It did. For a while. But then the depth sounder suddenly registered 4 metres, 3 metres, and then – WHAM! The whole boat shook like an earthquake. Martin was up in a flash. "What was that?" he called bewildered. Scared stiff, holding our arms around each other, we waited for the next bang. It never came. Spared again.

The closer to land we got, the more it blew. The wind speed was registering between 40-45 knots and the seas kept building. The night felt as if it would never end. Every time we tacked, we had to move our patient from one side to the other. And every time he whimpered. He was in bad shape. So we were overjoyed when we finally caught a glimpse of the lights of Bahía Salinas at 4 in the morning. Ever so carefully, using both radar and GPS, we navigated up through the large bay in the dark. Two hours later, we were safely anchored. What a relief.

But our problems didn't end there. We couldn't get the dinghy launched! We tried to hoist it over the railing with a halyard, but it just flew into midair. It behaved like a kite in the strong wind, which showed no signs of letting up, not even in the bay. We were just about to give up when we saw a local panga with two fishermen onboard on its way towards us. Soon it was alongside. In no time, they had lifted Jonathan into their panga and were on their way to the clinic ashore. Things were looking up.

Well attended by a local doctor, Jonathan was brought safely back to Nor Siglar within hours. Thereafter, our rescuers, Victor and Geraldo stopped by every day to see how the patient was doing and if we needed anything. The good Samaritans couldn't do enough for us. One day, they invited us home to their straw hut on the beach, where they served us a typical Costa Rican dinner: crisp deepfried fish and pinto gallo (rice and beans). We had already given them cigarettes and caps, but thought we'd better offer them some money for their help. After all, the two fishermen had lost a whole working day because of us. They declined. The only way they would accept money was if they could arrange a feast for us on the beach with their family and friends.

This was our first encounter with the considerate ticos, as Costa Ricans like to call themselves. It was also the first time we were in trouble and needed help on the trip. It became a heart-warming experience. According to our standards, the people of isolated Bahía Salinas have very little. But when it comes to generosity and kindness, their sources are inexhaustible..

A childhood dream come true.

CHILLING DISTRESS CALL

Our ham radio proved to be an excellent investment. We used it every day, reporting our position to the maritime mobile nets run by ham-licensed cruisers. Land based nets with volunteers who could patch phone traffic from vessels at sea, enabled us to make calls home. The amateurs would also relay messages from ship to shore and vice versa. In other words, these nets provided a wealth of services and information, while at the same time being very social. On the single side band, we were able to pick up BBC, Voice of America and many other useful frequencies. Other benefits included monitoring weather forecasts and being able to call for help. There was no need to feel cut off from the outside world.

Moving further south, we came within the range of Central America Breakfast Club, a particularly well organized maritime mobile net. It was assisted by two land-based operators, one in Costa Rica and one in Panama, who shared valuable information on local customs and conditions. The net was aired at 08:00 every morning. It was structured and followed a well-established pattern. Licensed sailors took turns running it. On my debut, I was thrown headlong into a serious matter.

"Any medical, emergency or priority traffic, please come now", I started. Normally, there was no response to this enquiry. Not today. "This is Gary on Nereid," a gravely serious voice answered. "At 4 o'clock this morning, two Mexicans boarded us. Both were armed. One of them threatened us with a machete while the other ransacked the boat. It took forever. When they tried to rape Pat, I managed to get hold of my gun. I killed them both. What do we do now?"

I was speechless. How was this to be handled? Before I could react, a senior net control and retired FBI agent took over, asking for suggestions. All sorts of ideas were launched; everything from heading into international waters as fast as they could – to giving themselves up to the police. Nereid was at anchor in Bahía Escondido in Southern Mexico. The last suggestion was not popular. Once behind bars, it would be difficult to get help. Also, it was rumoured that prisoners in Mexico may be tortured and even starve to death. It is the family's responsibility to bring prisoners food. No, Gary should definitely avoid being arrested.

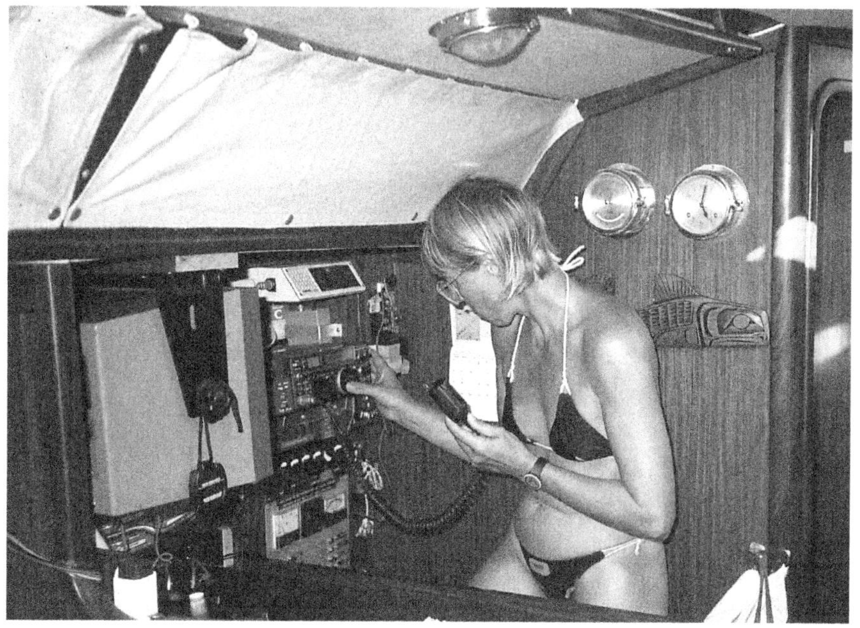

Anne keeping contact on the ham radio.

The conclusion was that the couple should contact the Mexican Navy. To everyone's relief, they received professional treatment. They were considered victims and given protection until a representative from the American Embassy arrived. The attackers were known to the police. They had many crimes on their conscience. In a few days Pat and Gary were free to cruise again. But Pat had become a nervous wreck and went home.

The episode frightened the whole sailing community. Safety precautions were reviewed. Intense discussions followed. Should cruisers have guns onboard or not? We do not carry any firearms on Nor Siglar. Maybe we are too naïve. But we tend to believe that most confrontations can be solved by peaceful means. If you have a gun, you must be prepared to use it.. We don't think we could do that. Nor do we have training in how to handle a weapon. The likelihood of being killed ourselves is far greater than that of the intruder. Also, weapons may transform a relatively innocent situation into a tragedy and end in death instead of injury. Most break-ins on sailboats are petty thefts performed by poor locals, who have no intention of killing anyone, and not by criminals, as in the case of Nereid.

Furthermore, a gun must normally be declared and handed in to the authorities on arrival in a new country. On departure, it must be collected again. The whole purpose of having a gun is gone. Besides, it's a time consuming, administrative hassle. Should one neglect to comply with the rules and be caught with a weapon onboard, the worst-case scenario is that the boat may be confiscated and the Skipper thrown in jail.

Our self-defence equipment consists of a couple of baseball bats, a few bottles of mace, a spear gun and a strong floodlight. An alarm system can be rigged up across the companionway entrance. If we should feel unsafe in a particular area, we will sail in company with others. Hopefully, none of this will ever be necessary.

PANAMA'S PACIFIC PARADISE
ISLA PARADITA
"Why Are You Rushing Through Paradise?"

The wealthy and powerful Aztec and Mayan civilizations did not expand their empires as far south as Costa Rica. Here, the tribes were much smaller and not as well organized. The Spanish Conquistadors met little resistance and obliterated them in short order. Therefore, Costa Rica's history and culture lack the grandeur of their neighbours to the north. And therefore, the little country cannot boast impressive remnants from the past. What it can boast, however, is spectacular nature: lush and green fertile highlands with expansive coffee, banana and rice plantations; numerous national parks with an exceptionally varied flora and fauna and rich wildlife including howling monkeys and lazy sloths, ancient looking iguanas and long beaked toucans, colourful parrots, jittery hummingbirds and many, many other species unknown to us.

Our month-long stay in Costa Rica also left us with recollections of sleepless nights in exposed anchorages with never ending swells rolling in from the Pacific, unbearable heat and muddy waters. Snorkelling was poor, so we only took quick dips to rinse off pouring sweat. March, being just before the onset of the rainy season, was incredibly hot and humid. We realized it would take time to acclimatize.

With the incident on Nereid fresh in mind, most cruisers chose to sail straight from Costa Rica to the Panama Canal without stop. Rumours were flying. Theft and violence were thought to be rampant along the thinly populated coast. Panama was an unsafe country, it was said, where people are largely uneducated and poor. We thought the arguments vague and unfounded, and decided to make a few side trips on the way. Are we ever happy we did! The experiences that awaited us brought us closer to the Panamanians than any other peoples we had met so far.

After the blistering heat of Costa Rica's southern port of Golfito, it was good to be underway again. An eventful overnighter peppered with thunder and lightning, squalls and lack of wind, caused us to halt for a rest in a delightful group of islands called Isla Parida. We anchored in the lee of the tiny islet, Isla Paradita. It looked deserted. So we got quite a surprise when the VHF started crackling. "Nor Siglar! Welcome to Paradise! Please come ashore and see us!" We became apprehensive. Could it be a trap? We were all alone. The only sign of life was the voice of this stranger speaking broken English over the radio waves. We locked the boat, launched the dinghy and rowed ashore.

A scantily clad, lean and muscular man with bushy hair and a long beard waved us ashore. Behind him stood a woman and a young girl. They had not seen people for a long time and were pleased to have company. Would we stay for dinner? Elan, Bella and Natalie were originally from Israel. After many years in New York City, they longed for a simpler life. Eventually, they found the pearl they were searching for. They settled down on uninhabited Isla Paradita.

The Jewish settlers were keen to show us what they had created so far away from civilization. Elan led the way through the bushes where he had cleared a narrow path with his machete. He was barefoot and moved like a native. Our tender soles could not have taken that. When we came to a clearing at the top of the island, Elan opened his arms wide and exclaimed: "Look at this! It's all ours! What more could you want on this earth?" We were spellbound. He was right.

Their dream consisted of a small straw hut, a vegetable garden and a fenced in area with a couple of shacks for pigs and chickens. It was just before sunset and the light threw a magnificent shimmer across the breathtaking landscape. It was exquisite. Still, I couldn't help but think of all the hard work and sweat that lay behind this romantic existence. Why did I always have to be so down to earth? Comfortable, in a hammock strung between two rustling palms, I was soon distracted from any such thoughts. "Relax!" Elan said. "Let us treat you to our island delicacy."

Elan split a coconut and poured the clear juice into an iron pot. He then grated the white flesh, squeezed the liquid into the juice and discarded the pulp. The juice had now turned into coconut milk to which he added rice and beans. While the dish was simmering on an open fire, we enjoyed the peace and idyllic atmosphere, sipping fresh juice from Paradita's exotic fruits and savouring the aroma from the crackling wood fire and the company of our interesting hosts. We quickly hit it off and tuned in to the tropical night. It was magic. The only thing that didn't jive was the Hebrew folk music in the background!

Elan and Bella loved Panama's Pacific Paradise. They couldn't fathom why so many sailboats bypassed it. "I guess you'll stay for a while? they asked after a perfectly splendid evening. Somewhat hesitant, we revealed our plans: Straight on through the Panama Canal, across the Atlantic to the world's Fair in Seville and the Olympics in Barcelona in half a year's time. Then on to Norway and the Winter Olympics at Lillehammer. That meant almost half a circumnavigation in only nine months. That said, it all felt terribly wrong.

The happy homesteaders scrutinized us in disbelief. "But why are you rushing through paradise?" they exclaimed appalled. "Isn't this what you are seeking? Happiness and freedom far away from stress and the daily grind, peace for the soul and mind? Slow down! Smell the roses! You can't rush through paradise and life like that!"

That evening, when we got back to Nor Siglar, we had a long, serious discussion. Elan and Bella were right. Wasn't this exactly what we had been dreaming of, what had made us decide to quit the rat race, cut all ties and take off after years in demanding jobs and an eternal fight against the clock? At last, we had the opportunity to do as we pleased. But what did we do then? Made another itinerary!

So it was this enchanting encounter that made us slow down and postpone the Atlantic crossing for a year. It took city dwellers turned homesteaders to convince us. Thanks to them, our focus shifted from the circumnavigation itself to the people we met along the way. Thanks to them, we were to experience things we otherwise would have missed, had we kept going at the same pace. And for that, we are forever grateful.

BAHÍA HONDA

A relaxing few days later, and a leisurely daysail further south, we chanced upon a jewel of a bay where we were welcomed by a real character with a big, toothless smile. "Domingo! El Capitán del Puerto! " the man introduced himself, lifting his crumpled hat as we shook hands across the railing. "Mi niña, Rosalind!" His daughter couldn't take her eyes off us. "Pescado, señora?" Domingo had worked in the Panama Canal when he was young and spoke some Spanish. We suggested a price for the fish. But he wasn't interested in money. Shops were few and far between, so food, clothing and practical items were more sought after. We agreed on sugar, salt and a couple of fishhooks. The jolly fellow was keen to trade and offered to bring us fresh fruit and vegetables from his finca. We saw the possibility of getting to see a genuine Panamanian jungle farm and suggested we come in and visit him instead. A bit risky, perhaps? We had no idea what to expect ashore..

Domingo, fisherman cum El Capitan del Puerto and his daughter Rosalind check us in to isolated Bahia Honda.

A group of Indians circled us in their dugout canoes. We were the only sailboat in the bay and very noticeable. The natives sat quietly in their hollowed out logs and stared at us. We sat down on the foredeck and stared back. When we smiled, they smiled too. When we were serious, so were they. It was almost comical. Then, one of them came alongside, holding up a large avocado. If we accepted it, the whole gang would, no doubt, descend on us. Yet, it was we who had invaded their territory, so it was important for us to develop a feeling of mutual trust. We offered him a bar of soap. Expressionless, he took it and handed us the avocado.

Then they came, one after the other. Three lemons, two oranges, a large papaya, mangoes and a hand of bananas changed hands for old t-shirts and shorts, milk powder and flour, sugar and coffee. A peculiar fellow made funny faces while rubbing his stomach and mumbling something about "mi madre". His mother obviously had a stomach ailment. We gave him some aspirin. His face lit up. "Only three per day", we explained. "Morning, noon and night". He looked puzzled. But his friend got the idea, pointing east for sunrise, up for noon and west for sundown!

Satisfied, the Indians disappeared with their loot. We hoped we were accepted. But alone, in such an isolated place, we felt rather insecure. So for the first time since leaving home, we rigged up the alarm system. During the night, we heard strange noises. A light flickered back and forth on the hillside. At times, there was a loud bang. What on earth could that be? It was impossible to sleep. We got up at first light. The Indians were all around us again. It was scary to think that they might have been there all night.

We were apprehensive about leaving the boat. But we had promised Domingo to come. We locked up, took the dinghy and ventured ashore. Domingo and his son, Kennedy, were on the beach waiting. Sporting razor-sharp machetes and baskets on their backs, they headed for the nearest coconut trees. It didn't take long before the baskets were filled to the rim. It was awfully hot. Kennedy cut the tops off some green coconuts so we could quench our thirst. The pipa juice was so refreshing!

Father and son led the way up a hill, which had recently been burned. Trees had been cut down for firewood and the jungle cleared to cultivate corn, beans and rice. The greenhouse effect is obviously not a concern to people whose number one priority is to feed themselves. Suddenly, a flock of wild pigs shot across the path ahead. With a sheepish grin, Domingo pretended to take aim and yelled: "Bang! Bang!" Aha! Here was the explanation to the mysterious sights and sounds that had kept us awake all night. It was our friend who had been hunting boars with flashlight and gun.

Domingo was growing corn and rice, fruit and vegetables on his little finca in the jungle. He also had a few dairy cows and pigs, some chickens and ducks, cats and dogs. The animals rummaged around in the mud. Their house was nothing but a room filled with hammocks hanging from the ceiling, the kitchen a simple corrugated shack. His wife and daughters were cleaning rice. Judging from their antiquated methods, the people of Bahía Honda must spend all their time just putting food on the table.

Rosalind handed me a ring carved from the shell of a turtle. "Para Ustedes," she whispered. It was a gift! From a girl who had so little! It was very touching. Spontaneously, I reciprocated with my earrings, little silver butterflies, which I had noticed her admire earlier. It is hard to say who received the most pleasure from the exchange, she or I. One thing is certain: I shall never forget the expression in Rosalind's eyes. I could have given anything for her thoughts.

Once again, we had experienced hospitality, warmth and trust from the locals. And back on Nor Siglar, everything was as when we left her. We couldn't help but think of all the cruisers who had chosen to sail to Balboa non-stop, avoiding this fascinating area. They should only know what they were missing.

Domingo invites us home to meet his family and to see a real Panamanian finca – their farm in the jungle.

SALMONETE

Domingo, Bahía Honda's self-appointed port captain was an informative fellow. Among other things, he told us about a little Indian village in the jungle, which he thought might be of interest to us. But it could only be reached by dinghy. It was not easy to find the river mouth, which was well camouflaged in the mangroves. After several blind alleys that just petered out in a swamp, we found an arm that seemed promising. When it looked like it would end, there was another bend around the corner. Sometimes, we had to lie flat in the dinghy to get through the dense, tropical vegetation. Sometimes it looked pretty hopeless. After 2 km, we were about to give up, when we suddenly thought we could smell smoke, a sure sign of life. We turned off the engine, which made an awful noise in the peaceful jungle, and rowed quietly on. And suddenly – there it was, in the thick of the jungle: The village of Salmonete. Curious children came running down to the riverbank. Wide-eyed, they stared at the strange, white people in their funny, orange inflatable raft. Women and the littlest ones observed us from a safe distance. We aroused a lot of attention. Pulling the dinghy ashore, I got out the goody bag. Instant success. Children everywhere love sweets. Excited, they swarmed around us with out stretched hands.

A strong, good-looking Indian approached us. "Tranquillo" he said barely audible, bowing his head. We wondered if he was the Chief. He only spoke the local dialect, so it was difficult to communicate. We pointed to a banana plant, indicating that we would like to trade. He waved us along to a simple straw hut where he introduced us to his wife, who was highly pregnant. They already had five children under the age of eight. We were offered the best seat in the house, the hammock where she had been sitting mending clothes. We opened our pack and brought out our trading goods. It caused quite a stir. Tranquillo fetched his machete and signalled that we should follow him.

The Chief of Salmonete greets us on the riverbank.

With what seemed like half the village trailing us, Tranquillo took the lead, pointing out the fruits he could offer. We selected a stalk of bananas, a pineapple and some cashew fruits. When we returned, his wife served us fresh papaya juice. My heart went out to the shy, little woman who looked very tired and surely older than her age. Judging from her husband, who was 33, she was likely younger than that, visible proof of the hard life women live in isolated jungle communities. Their hospitality was second to none.

We didn't say much, but had good contact all the same. It's amazing how much one can understand from body language and simple means. Tranquillo chose two of Martin's old t-shirts, his wife picked a cotton skirt and a pair of plastic sandals, the children wanted coloured pens and paper. Everyone looked pleased. As we prepared to leave, Tranquillo stood up. "Momentito", he whispered and disappeared. After quite a while, he returned with two eggs for me and a couple of stone axe heads for Martin. "Muy antigua" he explained solemnly. Could they possibly be from the Stone Age?

Moved by their kindness and generosity, we gave them a few more things from our pack.

Our visit was clearly a big event in the village of 150 natives, half of them children. When we left, it seemed like the whole tribe was on the riverbank to see us off. Downriver, we heard laughter and noise.

Visiting Tranquillo and his hospitable family deep in the jungle.

Around a bend, some plump and jolly women were loading their wooden panga with coconuts and bananas. The heavy working boat lay low in the water. We offered to take them in tow. They were going to Isla Talon, not far from where Nor Siglar was anchored.

With four big women trying to balance on top of an overloaded panga, we had problems taking the corners without them tipping over. But the cheerful women took it with good humour and looked like they were having a ball. We reached our destination in one piece. Curious onlookers helped us pull our crafts ashore. Again, we were surrounded by children, again the goody bag came out! The kids had just come home from school. They looked very smart in their white shirts, blue shorts and skirts. School uniforms seem such a good idea in poor countries.

Life in Bahía Honda was so peaceful and fascinating that we stayed much longer than intended. But finally, with our ship's hammocks overflowing with fresh fruit and vegetables, we set course for points further south in Panama's Pacific Paradise.

LAS PERLAS

To reach Las Perlas, a beautiful group of islands in the Gulf of Panama 250 nautical miles to the south, you have to round Punta Mala, a dreaded headland of nasty reefs that juts far out into the ocean, and where the Humboldt Current is particularly strong. A Dutch sailor had lost his boat going aground there recently, prompting us to study the charts with extra care before setting out for the area.

A fresh breeze from east-southeast soon increased to small gale. After a few hours fighting the headwinds, we abandoned our plan to sail the whole distance in one go and snuck in under Punta Naranjo to wait for better conditions. The anchorage was rough and uncomfortable, and we were up several times during the night to check that the anchor was holding. We didn't get much sleep, so when it was blowing just as hard the following morning, we settled down for another day in the bay.

It was Sunday and lots of commotion on the beach. A couple of strapping guys came out and asked us to come ashore. Christino and Clemente took us along in their canoe, which was carved out of a dark hardwood, probably mahogany. The oars were heavy, short and stubby. It was a sheer pleasure to observe the tanned, glistening muscular bodies handle their simple craft with such elegance and strength.

Ashore, we were met by a heavenly aroma of dried fish grilling on an open fire, and offered a welcome drink from a bottle of gin buried in the sand. Youngsters were listening to pop music and playing games while the elders lay snoozing in the shade of swaying palm trees. A young mother was breast-feeding her baby. The atmosphere was peaceful and harmonious. With the help of simple words, finger language and drawings in the sand, we all managed to establish a remarkable closeness despite external differences.

We wanted to return their hospitality and extended an invitation to open house on Nor Siglar. It was a popular gesture. The natives had never been on a modern sailboat before. To our surprise, books and magazines aroused most interest. They drooled over ads and pictures from the outside world. Everything was so expensive, they thought. It would take a lifetime for one of them to earn enough to buy an outboard engine.

Our visitors wondered how we had found our way safely in through reefs and rocks to a place we had never been before. Martin showed them Punta Naranja on the radar, turned on the depth sounder, which read 4 metres, and pointed out the contour lines and numbers marking reefs and shallows on the chart. They nodded and chatted amongst themselves. This was something they could understand. The young men knew every centimetre of Punta Naranja. They were virtually born and raised on these fishing grounds, inherited from their forefathers who had been fishing them for generations. The last guests to leave threw us a bundle of dried fish and a huge Sierra mackerel. Such nice people.

The Skipper has found his paradise.

After a pleasant delay, we managed to get around Punta Mala without any trouble. But the rest of the way was a challenge in full gale and big seas. With three reefs in the main and a tiny genoa, we were trucking in the strong wind. We stayed far out from land and did not notice much of a current, but were confronted with other problems instead.

Because of active drug smuggling, the U.S. Navy and Coast Guard keep a close watch on all vessel traffic, including pleasure crafts along the Panamanian coast. That afternoon, a helicopter appeared and hovered around us for a while. Later, we noticed a ship following us, hour after hour. We wondered what kind of vessel that could be. At 2 o'clock in the morning, Channel 16 suddenly came alive: "Nor Siglar! This is the U.S. Navy calling! May I ask you a few questions, please?" Quite a cross examination followed: "Where are you from? Where are you going? What is the maiden name of the Captain's mother? Ship's registration number, please? Finally, the interrogator apologized for disturbing us in the middle of the night and asked if we had any questions or needs. "How did you know the name of our boat?" we asked. "Our helicopter took photos of you earlier today", he answered. "Have a good voyage!"

Shortly after, Martin woke me up while hailing a freighter on the VHF. We were on a collision course. Nor Siglar had the right of way, but it didn't look as if they had seen us. Someone answered in poor English. Martin didn't get anywhere with him. The ship was getting awfully close. Terrified, we took the matter in our own hands and changed course. It was blowing hard and not an easy manoeuvre in the dark. We confirmed our new course on the VHF. "Oh no!" the fellow mumbled. "Me change too! You very dangerous!" Horrors! We were still on collision course! The huge monster was right behind us. We could hear its engines. By some miracle, we managed to turn Nor Siglar back onto her original course, just in time to stay clear. With no more than a hundred metres to spare, the freighter crossed our stern at a speed of about 15 knots. Closer to disaster we had never been.

We had heard talk of a German hippy couple, Dieter and Gerda, who had settled down on Isla de San Jose. Incredible stories were circulating about these characters and we decided to look them up. Having been at sea for a while, we had some nonbiodegradable garbage to get rid of, so we took it ashore and burned it behind a big rock on the beach. Suddenly, this Robinson Crusoe type character with long, flowing grey hair and a bushy beard, clad in scruffy, torn shorts came charging out of the bushes, shaking his fists at us, shouting: "Schtopp! Schtopp! Wass arrrr yooo doink on my island?"

There was no doubt. This was Dieter. He really let us have it. Burning was strictly verboten on his island. Asking where he got rid of his garbage, he replied: "Tse sea, of course!" Appalled, we explained why we would rather burn non-biodegradables ashore than throwing them in the sea, with the possible result of killing marine life. But Dieter wouldn't hear of it. His way was the only way, und tsaat waas tsaat.

Abruptly, he changed the subject: Did we have any rum for him? We had heard rumours of this addiction and were prepared. When he saw the rum, his tune changed. The tanned 60-year old waved us through a decorative drift wood portal with the inscription, Il Paraiso Bio Farm. We entered into Dieter and Gerda's realm. Here, yet another dream was being fulfilled.

Dieter led us through a drained swamp with grazing chickens and pigs past an old dug-out canoe filled with whale bones and animal sculls, shells, pottery shards and a variety of interesting artefacts. We continued through a large orchard of citrus and mango trees, along a cleared path to a shack on top of the hill overlooking Mona, a steep jungle clad rock resembling the head of an Indian, which jutted out of the ocean and dominated the entire bay. "Look!" Dieter exclaimed, stretching his arms wide. "This is all mine! And Mona is my God!"

This was all déjà vu to us by now. But this was Dieter and Gerda's paradise. Apart from the spectacular location and view, it didn't have much in common with that of Elan and Bella on Isla Paradita. All we could see was a dilapidated clapboard and corrugated sheet shack with a tin roof. No electricity, no running water, no sanitation facilities, no worldly comfort, no stores and definitely not very romantic, we thought. But Dieter and Gerda obviously didn't see it that way. Visibly proud and content, they served us the specialties of Il Paraiso: rum with fresh orange and cashew juice. Suddenly, Dieter grabbed his binoculars. Far in the distance, we glimpsed a tiny spot on the horizon. It was a sail. Rubbing his hands, the happy squatter exclaimed: "Gerda! Maybe we'll get more rum tonight!"

Dieter had fled from East Berlin in the mid fifties. 12 years ago, he had set out to sail around the world. Four years later, when he reached Las Perlas, he fell in love with the islands and sent for Gerda. When the opportunity presented itself, they moved ashore. Their 29-foot Seepferdchen was lying in the bay rusting.

The bohemian couple liked to talk and were most entertaining. They were completely preoccupied with themselves and their own life style. Not much outside their little radius interested them. They were at peace living in happy ignorance of what was going on in the outside world, and not the least bit interested in the magazines we brought them. Besides, they didn't like the media. A few years ago, a TV station had made a programme about them for which they received only twenty dollars. It was unfair that others might have made big money on them, while they were left with next to nothing. The Smithsonian Institute was more generous. They had interviewed them in connection with doing excavations on some ruins from the Stone Age. In appreciation of their assistance, the archaeologists taught Dieter and Gerda how to make rattraps. They were assured that it was not dangerous to eat rats; valuable information indeed, when you have to be self-sufficient.

Dieter and Gerda's closest neighbours was an Indian family on the opposite side of the island. But they had to admit that they did not have a very good relationship with the natives. Their dog, Zulu, had been shot and killed a few days ago. Gerda was devastated. Zulu was her watchdog. She didn't know how she was going to manage without him. Not only did he gather food for them, hunting wild boars, iguanas and rats. He kept snakes at bay as well. We shuddered at the thought of the sort of food they ate. But it was far to the nearest shop, so it was vital to be self reliant and capable of living off the land. The gun on the wall witnessed a tough existence. We hoped it was only used for hunting. But after hearing about the episode with the dog, we really wondered. Maybe their paradise wasn't so idyllic after all?

It was sizzling hot in the 35-degree heat, so Dieter and Gerda suggested a cool bath in their fresh water pool. It was not for the shy. A dip au naturel was as normal as could be to these originals. At least, it was much safer than in the anchorage, where we had seen a white shark, poisonous sea snakes and got a moray eel on the hook.

On our way back to Nor Siglar, we were allowed to pick oranges, papaya and lemons. Back at the portal, the weight was determined by putting fruit in one bucket and stone weights in another, hanging them both at the opposing ends of a long stick. Simple and functional. Normally, they had eggs for sale, but at the moment, they only had enough for themselves. Their only income, which was about 300 dollars a year, was derived from trade with offshore sailors. We couldn't help but wonder what will happen to Dieter and Gerda when they become too old to scratch out a living from their bio farm. They were happy now, and that's all that mattered.

Isla Contadora, the last island we visited in the Las Perlas archipelago, showed clear signs that we were nearing civilization again. The island is a popular resort complete with private villas and luxurious hotels frequented by wealthy jet setters that arrive from the mainland by private yachts and planes. All of this was a shock to the system after weeks in relative isolation amongst Panama's pleasant native population. Therefore, it didn't take us long to get away from this affluent island, where the Shah of Iran spent the last years of his life in exile.

THE PANAMA CANAL

The port of Balboa at the Pacific entrance to the Panama Canal is named after the Spanish explorer, Vasco Núñes de Balboa, who in 1513 was the first European to sight the Pacific Ocean after having crossed the Isthmus of Panama. Ever since, trade has flourished across the narrow S-shaped peninsula. It all started with rumours of a rich Indian Empire somewhere to the south. In their quest for gold and silver, conquistadors subsequently conquered the great Incas of Peru, plundering them for their precious metal, which was then transported on mule back across the Isthmus to the Atlantic coast. There are still signs of the old road, "Camino Real", along the jungle-clad shores of the Canal. The riches were kept in guarded treasury chambers until Spanish galleons came to bring them back to Spain. Piracy often interrupted their return voyage. British buccaneers, Sir Francis Drake and Henry Morgan, made history from their raids capturing treasures for their dear England, Spain's archrival at the time.

Things have changed. Today, about 13,000 ships per year transit the Panama Canal, which shortens the distance between New York and San Francisco by 19,000 km. The building of the Big Ditch, which this engineering feat is also referred to, started in 1882 and was completed in 1914. The monumental project was hampered by construction and management problems, lack of funds and terrible epidemics from tropical diseases caught in the dense and hostile jungle, which cost over 20,000 lives.

The Panama Canal is open 24 hours a day, 365 days a year. It has only been closed once since it opened; on the day of the U. S.

invasion of Panama in 1989, which resulted in the fall of Noriega's regime. The Canal is 82 km long from deep water in the Atlantic to deep water in the Pacific. It runs from northwest to southeast with the Atlantic entrance being 57 km north and 46 km west of the Pacific entrance. There are six double locks in the canal; three on each side of Gatun Lake, which separates the Pacific and Atlantic sides of the Canal. The man made lake is 45 km long and was created to feed the lock system. Ships are raised or lowered, as the case may be, 26 metres in chambers measuring about 33.5 metres wide, 305 metres long and a minimum of 13 metres deep.

Miraflores Locks. North America to port, South America to starboard.

A lot of paperwork and formalities had to be completed before we were allowed to transit. The boat was measured, the engine and 4 x 40 metre long mooring lines checked before we received our registration number and official admeasurement document. The ID Certificate was duly framed and placed above the chart table. Should Nor Siglar ever return, it would not be necessary to go through the time-consuming paper mill again. Also required were an official pilot and four line handlers. The tariff, which is calculated on the basis of tonnage, came to US$100.

Early in the morning of Good Friday, April 17, full of emotion and anticipation, we left the familiar Pacific behind. In the first three locks, we were rafted to another sailboat, and only needed two lines. Our nerves were quite on edge, but after a bit of practice, we were just fine. The pilot was helpful, and even though the line handlers ashore were rather nonchalant, we got through unscathed. Just one incident could have turned ugly, when a large tugboat squeezed ahead of us inside the lock, and we got caught in the turbulence of its propellers. Being tied alongside another boat, manoeuvring was difficult, and we nearly collided. The situation was totally uncalled for. It was rumoured that the local tugboat captains get a kick out of creating panic for the "filthy rich yachties."

We had to go full speed across Gatun Lake to make it to the other end in time to join a containership through the last three locks down to the Atlantic. While hovering around, waiting to enter, we discovered Gull Arrow, a freighter belonging to the company I worked for in Vancouver lying there at anchor! We made a little detour and called her up on the VHF. The Captain replied – and we knew each other! After a pleasant chat, he promised to send greetings to the office from Nor Siglar in the Panama Canal!

Gull Arrow saluted us with three blasts of the horn, dipped her flag and waved as we made our way into the next set of locks. The cruise ship, Sagafjord, was lying in the lock chamber parallel to us. Suddenly, our pilot, who was monitoring Channel 12, got a look of awe on his face. "The Captain of the Sagafjord wishes to speak to you!" he said, most impressed. "I see you are flying a Canadian flag, but with a Norwegian pennant under the spreader and a name like Nor Siglar, you've got to be Norwegian", the Captain said. He had watched the commotion with the Gearbulk ship and was curious. And believe it or not: Capt. Berntsen lived near Vennesla where Martin was born – and they had lots of friends in common! It sure is a small world! After another nice chat, Sagafjord too saluted little Nor Siglar as hundreds of passengers waived from the decks above.

The final descent also went well, and after a nine hour transit, when the last gate opened up into the Atlantic, spirits were high. "Atlantic! Here we come!" we toasted as the champagne was flowing. Full of excitement, we were ready for new adventures on a new and unfamiliar ocean. At the same time, we felt we had reached a milestone.

Fun encounter with Sagafjord and her Norwegian Captain in the middle of the Panama Canal.

We had managed to come all the way down the west coast of North America safely. We had passed the first test. Our blue water debut was over.

The time was ripe for reflection. A little less than eight months ago, we set out full of uncertainty and questions about the future and the project ahead. Now, we had some answers. How had we managed? Well, so far, we have mastered the challenges as they have occurred. Nor Siglar has also tackled hers. Strong winds, high seas, even collision with a whale, have not prevented her from bringing us safely from port to port. Yes, we can rely on Nor Siglar. She is fast and flexible. She is a good yacht.

Martin has proven to be a brave and capable Skipper. His seamanship and navigational skills are solid. As for me, I get seasick, as expected. However, I am able to do my watches and whatever is required when needed. I just have to. The alternative would be to give up. And that is unthinkable. So, all there is to it is to call upon that extra bit of will power, endurance and determination. Because without those qualities, this life style, which we have chosen and the adventures we seek, will never come to fruition. Nor will our dream.

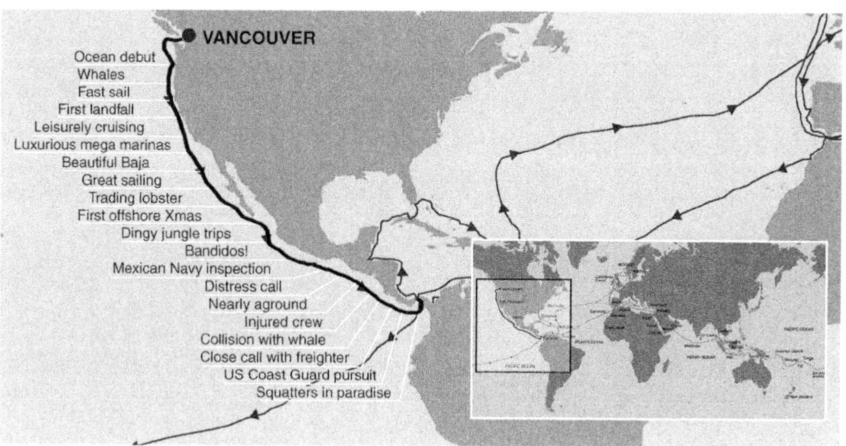

The end of Part 1 of the "9 Years on the 7 Seas Adventure", also published in print and as an eBook with the title **The Dream, the Plan and the Bluewater Debut.**

PART 2

CARIBBEAN
SAN BLAS – HELP! DEAD MAN ON DECK!

What? A dead body on Nor Siglar's deck? We must have heard wrong. The young Indian was gravely serious. "My uncle died this morning," he continued in perfect English, studying us with searching eyes. "We must get him to Carti before dark. Can you help us, please?" We couldn't believe our eyes. Was the little man trying to trick us? Sure enough, the natives of these isolated islands have a reputation for being aggressive. But wasn't this going a bit too far?

Chichime. An idyllic settlement in Kuna Yala

We had just anchored up in Cayos Chichime in beautiful San Blas, a group of 365 palm- clad little islands surrounded by coral reefs, located in the Caribbean Sea not far from the Panama Canal. San Blas is the domain of the Kuna Indians, the second smallest race on earth after the Pygmies. So far, they have managed to maintain their culture and way of life relatively intact. Theirs is a matriarchal society where men marry into the bride's family. Women are in charge of the finances and day-to-day activities, allocating tasks to the men, whose main responsibilities are fishing and the coconut trade with Colombia. "So watch out for the women," we were forewarned, "they are tough negotiators and extremely persistent."

Soon three women onboard a cayuko came paddling out to Nor Siglar. The dugout canoe was heavily laden with watertight buckets full of colourful crafts. In no time, they were alongside to peddle their treasures. But we had been told that we should hold off buying anything until we were ashore where the selection was better, and where we could be with these unique people in their natural surroundings.

Kuna come alongside to trade. They need money for a funeral. Could Nor Siglar transport the body to Carti for them?

"We'll come ashore later," we said firmly. "We are tired from our overnight passage and need a rest." The women looked puzzled. They only speak Kuna. "Please, my friends," begged our Englishspeaking ground, observing us from a distance. "We need money for the funeral. For coffee, sugar and rice. Could you buy some molas right away, please?" We looked at each other. They sure were persistent. But surely they wouldn't go this far in order to clinch a deal? The fellow noticed that we were in doubt. "It's true! 100% true!" he exclaimed, rattling off something to the women, who once again, showed us their crafts. "Not here," we repeated. "We'll come ashore to trade."

By the time we had launched the dinghy and rowed ashore, the women had hung their colourful molas on a clothesline between two straw huts. It was a spectacular display. Molas are the front and back panels of the unique blouse worn by Kuna women, the most visible proof of their identity. Each panel is made from several layers of cloth in different colours. The material is cut out in imaginative patterns and hand sewn with tiny stitches, using a special "reverse appliqué" technique. The result is wonderful.

Originally, the mola was only used as clothing. Today, the blouse, which has survived the many negative influences from the western world, is not only an important component of a very special dress, but a popular souvenir of primitive art as well. So nowadays, women are making them for sale, sewing day and night. In the olden days, only traditional, geometric patterns were created. Today, these are disappearing in favour of new, more contemporary designs inspired by visitors from afar, foreign magazines, household gadgets and motifs from nature.

Kuna women in traditional dress exhibit their molas outside their home.

The beauty, variety, artistic imagination and bright colours of the molas mesmerized us. It was difficult to make a choice. But were they ever pushy! "Here! Take this one, this or this," they insisted, pointing as they went along. We were flabbergasted. "Not now," we refused.

But, our modern Kuna, Braulio didn't give up either. "We need forty dollars for the funeral," he said. "If you buy two molas right now, we'll let you into our home to see the deceased!" That did it. We chose two beautiful blouses.

Only two families lived on the little island. In two small huts with straw roof, dirt floor and cane walls lived an extended family of 14 people and three generations. One hut was for cooking, the other for sleeping. It was into this sanctuary that we were cordially invited. And there, right in the middle of the room, we found the dead man lying in a hammock, fully dressed with his head and chin neatly tied in a pure white kerchief, hands folded on his chest. The man was tiny, tiny - and very, very old, they said. He wore an old, rumpled suit, white shirt and tie. His family had laid him to rest; a kerosene lamp was burning on the floor by his head, incense smoldering and candles flickering throughout the one-room hut. Children were milling about, playing quietly. It was all so very natural. The presence of the dead man didn't seem to bother them in the least.

There was no furniture in the hut. Nor windows. On the walls and beams hung a variety of clothing, hammocks, tools and gadgets. It was dark, cool and comfortable. The elders sat on low, carved stools along the walls, whispering amongst themselves, visibly moved. It seemed strange to be so near people of such a different culture, especially under such extraordinary circumstances.

"We are waiting for a big cayuko to transport the body to Carti for our traditional "Liberation of Spirit" ceremony," Braulio said. "But it is getting late and we are worried that they are not coming." The man had been dead since early morning. It was hot and high time to get moving. Carti was 10 miles away. It was 4 in the afternoon. At 9°N, it gets dark around 6 p.m. "If they really need help, we ought to give them a hand, Anne," Martin whispered. With the storm in Golfe de Papagallo fresh in our minds, where we had received help from locals, we didn't hesitate. "Of course we'll help you," Martin offered spontaneously. Braulio's face lit up. "But our charts are poor. And if we are going to make Carti before dark, we'd better get going right away." "Go ahead and hoist anchor," he replied. "We'll be right there."

It didn't take long before Braulio was alongside in his cayuko, the deceased still in his hammock, now wrapped in an old sailcloth tied to a long piece of wood, normally used as a mast. In a flash, the body was hoisted up on deck and lashed down under the boom together with an old beaten-up suitcase containing all his worldly belongings. It was very light.

The man's older sister also came along with his young, pretty niece and her five children, the youngest at her breast. The party clambered aboard in their native dress, bringing piles of stuff for their once-in-a-lifetime voyage, their first ever on a modern sailboat: plastic bags of clothing, bowls of smoked and dried fish, a burlap sack of coconuts, a large "hand" of green bananas, cans of milk powder, fresh water and an old, rusty propane bottle. The baggage appeared pretty dirty and smelly to us, and we couldn't help but think that if ever we were going to get cockroaches onboard, it would be now.

Braulio's mother creating a traditional mola.

They are really unique, these neat, little Kuna Indians, especially the women with their classic features, elegant posture and colourful dress. They wear the wealth of the family on their bodies; gold rings on fingers, in the nose and ears, their necks loaded with strands of beads, shells and silver coins that clatter when they walk. Beaded bands in geometric patterns adorn their arms from elbow to wrist and their legs from ankle to just below the knee. Their very special dress consists of a red and yellow cotton shawl, a black or blue wraparound skirt with yellow paisley pattern, and finally, the traditional multi-coloured mola blouse. According to ancient tradition, the women paint a decorative thin, black line on the bridge of the nose so that it will appear extra long, a sign of beauty within this tribe. They wear their hair short, use lots of rouge from natural sources and are normally barefoot. However, nail polish and plastic sandals are clear signs that modern civilization has begun to influence this isolated paradise.

In modern shorts, T-shirt and a baseball cap complete with pins, Braulio stood in strong contrast to his fellow passengers. Well underway, assured that he knew his way through the shallow waters strewn with treacherous rocks and reefs, we relaxed and struck up a conversation. Where had he learned such good English? "In California," he replied. "I lived in San Francisco with a Mormon family for three years and went to high school there. This is how I know your western ways." It was odd to sit and talk to an indigenous local who was familiar with two such opposing life styles. Having experienced our western civilization, Braulio instinctively knew what we would find interesting and strange, funny or hard to understand about his culture. He was more than happy to entertain us with tales of the many unique customs and ways of the Kunas. So not only did this crossing become our most unique passage ever, carrying the most unusual cargo we have ever had onboard, but it also turned out to be the most educational and fascinating two hours of our lives.

A Kuna girl with her mother's handmade molas.

"Our society is steeped in traditions and rituals," Braulio stated, "especially the many female life cycle rites. We celebrate everything from "Ear and Nose-piercing" ceremonies of newborn girls to "Puberty", "Hair-cutting" and "Naming" ceremonies. "Tell us about the "Puberty Ceremony"," I begged. "Sure," Braulio agreed, with the broadest smile we have ever seen. "When a girl reaches puberty, she is isolated in a small enclosure, painted black with the juice of the genipa fruit to protect her from evil spirits, and washed with salt water several times a day. This is an ancient purifying ritual. After four days, the isolation rite culminates in a 3-day "Hair-cutting Ceremony". Then the whole village celebrates her "Coming-of-Age" with song and dance, food and drink. When all is over, the girl is proclaimed an adult and ready to be married. In fact, this ritual is usually a prerequisite for marriage. You should try chica," Braulio chuckled. Barrels of this potent drink, which consists of sugar cane juice, corn and cocoa, are always bubbling and fermenting in Kuna villages, ready for use in their numerous celebrations.

"Marriage is a different story," Braulio continued with a sheepish smile. It was obvious that he enjoyed sharing his local knowledge with us palefaces. "Would you like me to go on?" We nodded. "Here in Kuna Yala, marriage is arranged by the parents," he explained. "The young couple may not be informed of the wedding ahead of time. That happened to me," he laughed, "so I know what I am talking about. Anyway, it goes like this: a group of young men appointed by the chiefs capture the unsuspecting bridegroom, carry him forcibly to the house of his equally unsuspecting bride, and throw him into her hammock. They then thrust the young woman on top of him, holding the prospective pair in place, while a burning brand is positioned under the hammock. When they are finally released, the man and woman flee the scene. This procedure is repeated three nights in a row. If the couple agrees to the match, they stay together the last night. At dawn, the bridegroom goes with his father-in-law to-be to gather two logs for his bride to place in a cross, creating a hearth. This done, the marriage is sealed.

"Pretty smart, don't you think?" Braulio chuckled while steering Nor Siglar with amazing ease. We were impressed and surprised at his sailing skills. Having grown up with the sea at his back door, he was obviously used to the water and an excellent sailor. But handling small, dugout canoes is quite different from a modern sailboat. The explanation was simple; he had been a deck hand on a schooner in California.

Braulio had always wanted to become a missionary. "But not possible," he admitted with great sadness. "I make big mistake!" He had left his wife and children after falling in love with another woman. So that was it. A missionary cannot be divorced. On the other hand, Braulio had a good chance to become a chief. So far he was too young. From what we could see, with the knowledge and experience he possessed, he would be a strong candidate. We thought he would make a magnificent chief some day.

The children were quiet and well-behaved, gazing at everything in sight with curiosity. So many strange things! We let them try the binoculars. Never ever had they experienced anything so amazing. Their straw hut, which was nothing but a spot on the horizon, was suddenly very near. How could that be? And when they discovered Nor Siglar's toilet, they couldn't believe their eyes. What on earth was that? Must be dangerous! What if water started flooding into the boat? It would fill in no time and sink!

The family of the dead Kuna underway on Nor Siglar to the neighbouring island for the Liberation of Spirit ceremony and burial.

This was something they understood and had great respect for. Their own little dugout canoes leak like sieves and must be bailed constantly. The children were deathly afraid of sinking. We demonstrated what the toilet was for. They stared at us in disbelief. How stupid! To prove his point, the bravest in the group climbed out into the cockpit and peed over the railing with a cheeky smile.

After two entertaining hours, Braulio, who also liked to call himself Frank, piloted us safely into Carti just before nightfall. As we approached the densely populated island of 2000, people came running down to the dock. It didn't take long before a cayuko was on its way with molas. Little did they know what kind of cargo we had onboard, until Braulio told them what had happened. The news spread quickly, and soon canoes came at us from all directions. Suddenly, there was great activity onboard Nor Siglar. The women changed into their Sunday best and started wailing, the very first sign of emotion. It seemed like a bit of a show for the villagers. Before we knew it, four guys jumped onboard, hoisted the corpse into their cayuko, sat down on top of it and paddled ashore, where women were crying and crossing themselves. Then, the funeral procession disappeared into the village. The wake could begin.

Sleek cayuko brings provisions for Carti.

The following day, el cacique sent for us. The ancient Chief welcomed us warmly to San Blas and thanked us profusely for our help. We were treated like VIPs and taken directly to casa de congreso, the very heart of Kuna community. The village gathering house, a straw hut similar to the others, but much larger, was full of benches. In the centre, strung from the beams, were several hammocks. Here, chiefs lay all day long, chanting and smoking their long pipes while debating and making important decisions on matters of the day. Every day at dusk, villagers met to deal with situations as they occurred. Village labour was organized, projects discussed and delegated, problems solved. If anybody needed help, assistance was granted immediately. In this way, neither problems, nor disputes became old before a solution was found. Maybe we have something to learn from this well organized, socalled primitive Kuna nation?

Braulio was the perfect host. We were invited to his home for dinner and met his mother who demonstrated mola stitching. He also gave us a guided tour of the local school and floating hospital, an old, derelict American merchant ship that served the larger islands. People nodded and smiled to us. We were the only white people there. So they knew who we were. Did we need anything? "No," we hesitated. "Although we would really love to attend the funeral." This time, however, it was we who were going too far. The funeral was definitely for Kunas only.

The old man from Chichime received his important "Liberation of Spirit" ceremony, before being escorted by a long cayuko flotilla to his burial. The procession left before dawn to get upriver before the women started their laundry for the day. There, deep in the jungle at dusk, he was buried according to ancient tradition, in his hammock together with all his worldly belongings – his little, old beaten-up suitcase.

IN THE WAKE OF THE OLD PIRATES FROM PANAMA TO HONDURAS

I was just about to drift off to sleep when I heard Martin's voice in the distance. "Anne! Put your harness on! We've got to get the sails down!" I didn't understand a thing. It was so quiet. He called again. "Quick! Hurry!" The rest drowned in roaring thunder. We were surrounded by dark, threatening clouds. Suddenly, sheets of lightening illuminated the sky and the floodgates of heaven opened wide. We barely got the sails down before the squall tore into us. Then, all we could do was wait - and hope for the best. I sent a little prayer into the darkness above. We were all alone on the open sea. The tall mast was definitely a high-risk target.

The rainy season was upon us. It was stifling hot and humid, so it was actually quite a relief with these regular squalls. They cleared the air. Despite potential danger, we looked forward to their cooling effect. It was so nice to take showers au naturel on deck. But you had to be swift. The heavy downpour would stop just as abruptly as it started. If we didn't rinse off quickly enough, we could end up with our hair full of shampoo. But it didn't really matter. There was plenty of water. Buckets and containers were replenished in no time. After a while, we got smart and rigged up a system with funnels and plastic hoses, enabling us to collect rainwater directly into the tanks. What luxury! Now we could use as much water as we liked every day!

After a brisk 3-day sail in a fresh breeze from the northeast, Isla Providencia appeared on the horizon, all by itself in the middle of nowhere. Although much closer to Nicaragua, the barely 8 x 3 km volcanic island belongs to Colombia. Its 3000 inhabitants are mainly descendants from the early pirates who discovered the island's strategic location, and were the first to settle. From here, they could attack Yucatan Strait further north. Henry Morgan has left numerous marks on the tiny island. Morgan is a common surname and several places are named after him. Morgan's Head, a rock formation which seen from the side resembles a man's head, is a well-known landmark to seafarers.

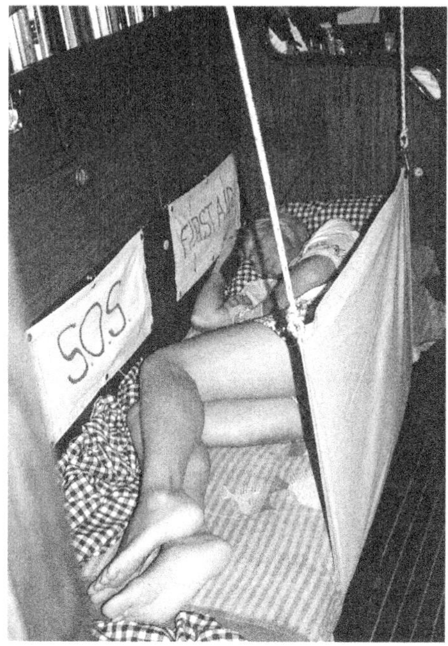

Anne sleeping on the settee.

After a short rest, we continued towards Cayo Media Luna, a convenient stop on the way north along the coast of Honduras. Sailing through the night under a full moon and listening to Mozart on the Walkman, time flew by. So did the miles. Before we knew it, we were there. It was still dark, so we lay a hull until daylight. But at dawn, the cay was nowhere to be seen. We checked the chart. Had we made a navigational error? No, the position was correct. We scanned the horizon. All we could see was water. A cruiser, who had tried to find it a few weeks earlier, reported on the net that he had had to give up. When he heard where we were, he broke into a sarcastic laugh and wished us luck.

With the GPS in one hand and his eyes fixed on the depth sounder, Martin motored slowly forward while I took up position on the boom to scout the crystal clear water for obstructions. With the sun behind and not a ripple on the water, I could see the bottom clearly. It was full of coral heads. But no cay. According to the GPS, we were right smack where it was supposed to be. And no kidding; a little further ahead, there it was, a tiny piece of rock sticking out of the water. We had found Cayo Media Luna! Around us lay the half moon shaped reef. The problem was, only 1% was visible, the rest being just below the surface!

We were really pleased to have located the cay, but also a bit worried about spending the night in such an exposed place without any kind of visible protection from anywhere. Finally, we dropped the anchor in five metres, about 100 metres northwest of the reef, assuming that if the wind picked up, it would come from an easterly direction with the prevailing trade winds. The reef would then protect us from the seas. It was, however, too low to shield us from the wind itself.

It was scary to be lying at anchor without land in sight in any direction. Only ocean - and one square metre of Cayo Media Luna! On the other hand, it was fantastic to have such a unique place to ourselves. We snorkelled all afternoon, but turned in early, being quite worn out from both the long swim and the overnight sail. At 5 o'clock in the morning, we were rudely awakened by a torrential squall. We rushed out on deck. Nor Siglar was pulling like mad on her anchor chain – and the wind was from the north! Suddenly we found ourselves in a precarious situation. The reef, which had offered protection so far, had now become a danger threatening us from behind.

"Turn on the depth sounder, Anne!" Martin yelled as he started up the engine. "I think we're dragging!" "Oh no! Only 2 _ metres!" We were shocked. Only 50 cm under the keel! The wind was howling, the rain pelting down. We couldn't see a thing. But we could clearly hear the breakers crashing over the reef astern and the anchor chain rumbling across the corals. "Run up to the bow and point me in the direction of the chain, and I'll try to motor up to the anchor", Martin said. "We must not get blown onto the reef. Too bad we can't move. But we'll never find our way through all the corals in these conditions."

A terribly long half hour followed. In the strong winds and just about zero visibility, Martin could neither see, nor hear me on the bow. Shivering and scared stiff, I ran back and forth showing him where to go. There had been no time to get dressed in the panic, and we were getting cold, even in the 30° temperature. Nervous, Martin motored into the wind and waves, trying to keep the boat snug up to the anchor, fully aware that Nor Siglar could be crushed at any moment, if we didn't have luck on our side.

All of a sudden, the nightmare was over. The wind and rain stopped just as quickly as it began. The sun came out. Nor Siglar had come through unscathed. We breathed a sigh of relief. But we had learned a lesson. Never anchor to windward of a potential danger. We had not been aware that squalls come from the north in this area. We should have been.

It was Tuesday and my turn to run the Central America Breakfast Club maritime mobile net. It went on the air at 0700. We had barely reanchored, when soaking wet and cold, I just managed to open it on time. I hoped nobody could hear my teeth chattering as I proudly announced that we had found Cayo Media Luna.

In Vivarillo Cays, 50 nautical miles to the north, we joined another cruiser already at anchor by a coral island teeming with birds. It was the nesting grounds for Man-o-war frigates and Yellowbilled brown boobies. The bird sanctuary was full of yearlings and fluffy, newly hatched chicks. When venturing too close to the well-camouflaged nests, we were met by fierce protests. The beaches were lined with piles of cleaned and discarded conch shells. Most were broken and had lost their lustre in the bright sun. The nicest lay under water, and we added a few to our growing collection.

Beach combing on a remote coral reef.

That evening, we joined the other cruisers, a Finnish Israeli couple and their infant daughter, for a wonderful crab feast. A small Honduran trawler with 30 fishermen onboard had given them ten crabs for half a bottle of whisky. The fishermen had warned them not to go west of Longitude 82°, because of a territorial conflict between Nicaragua and Honduras. They were squabbling over fishing rights. Honduran boats had been raided in the vicinity of Cayo Media Luna lately. It was scary to think that we had been so close to the disputed area.

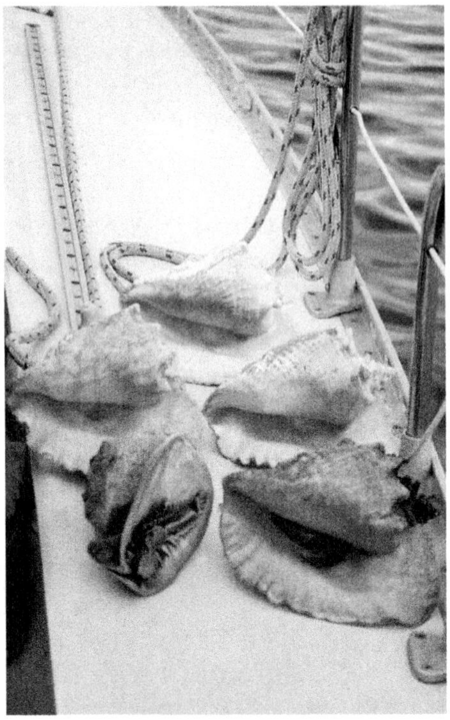

Catch of the day.

It was nice to make new friends in such isolated surroundings. Little did we know that we were going to meet again, and that next time, the young family would be four and that finally, when we arrived in Israel years later, they were there too! Unexpected reunions with fellow sailor friends are certainly one of the highlights of cruising.

JUNGLE SAFARI IN GUATEMALA
REALM OF THE MAYAS

"VE0 MCA! Victor Echo Zero Mike Charlie Alfa! This is Lima Alfa Three Uniform Lima calling! Do you hear me, Anne?" Unbelievable! A radio amateur from my hometown, Halden was on the air! He came through loud and clear. This was the break-through we had been waiting for, ever since we left Vancouver eight months ago. It was midnight in Norway. Even so, keen members of the local radio club were lining up to talk to us.

In Guatemala, it was 4:30 in the afternoon. We were at the entrance to Rio Dulce, waiting for high tide to proceed up the "Sweet River" to Mario's Marina, a popular hurricane hole in the Western Caribbean. Here, we could safely leave Nor Siglar during the hurricane season, explore the Highlands and take a quick trip home. It was an ideal arrangement. There was only one problem. To get there, we had to cross a shallow sandbar about 2 metres deep. There was a small tide difference of 30 cm. So the only way for us, drawing 2 metres to get across, was to do it at high-high tide. This occurred only twice a month. Thursday, July 9 was such a day. High tide was at 17:30 hrs.

We had been fretting about this moment for a long time. The tactics were well-known. Cross the bar in the late afternoon with onshore wind, current and waves from behind. We had arrived at the buoy, which marks the beginning of the sandbar a couple of hours early, to figure out the bearings for the narrow channel. Also, in order to make the boat as light as possible, we had emptied the water tanks and put fuel cans, spare anchors and chain in the dinghy. But on the first trial run, it crashed into the transom and hit the wind vane. Fortunately, our precious self-steering didn't break. We lengthened the towline to 60 metres and repeated the manoeuvre. Again, the dinghy came surfing down towards the stern. However, this time, it didn't catch up. We were ready.

Maya women weave spectacular patterns on simple looms.

It was hard to turn off the radio. Many amateurs were still waiting to make contact. I was really surprised when the voice of a childhood friend and neighbour boomed into the cabin. He taped a greeting for my mother and promised to visit her the following day. The conditions were perfect. We talked and talked. Martin was getting impatient. Even with earphones on, I could hear him in the cockpit. "You've got to quit, Anne! It's 5:30. Time to go!"

Reluctantly, we signed off. I was just about to hang up when I heard someone call my name. It was Kari Boye Young from Pitcairn! I had read her book, "The Last Mutineer". She was married to a descendent of Fletcher Christian, Bounty's First Mate and leader of the mutineers who fled to Pitcairn after the mutiny on the Bounty. It was exciting to speak to her. Martin became panicky. "Come on!" he yelled. "If we don't go for it now, we'll miss our chance."

We took a bearing from the buoy to the highest peak of land in line with a red roof on the riverbank. Holding our breath, we started to move. With our eyes glued to the depth sounder, compass and range line, we watched, as it was getting shallower and shallower. It was unnerving. Suddenly the depth measured 2 metres. Then 1.8. Nor Siglar slowed down. We could feel the keel ploughing through the mud. We looked at each other in despair. We were committed. "Full speed!" I begged. "There is no turning back now." Accelerating full throttle, pushed along by a big following wave, we just barely slid across the bar into deep water. "We made it!" Martin exclaimed with a big sigh of relief. "I haven't been this stressed since budget time at Reid Collins in the old days!"

Safe and sound in Livingston, a sleepy little Garifuna town overlooking the Caribbean, we could finally relax. Or so we thought. No sooner had we dropped the anchor when a terrific squall broke lose complete with thunder and lightening, torrential rain and winds gusting to 50 knots. In a matter of seconds, the boat spun around 360°. Keeping a close eye on the GPS, we sat anchorwatch way into the night. Before turning in for some much needed rest, we hoisted the dinghy on board and cleared the deck of loose items. Rumours had it that there was a lot of theft in the area. We forgot Martin's boat shoes in the cockpit. Sure enough, the next morning, they were gone, including a bucket of garbage. Not much of a loss, but it was unpleasant to know that we had had unwelcome visitors onboard while we were sound asleep.

Maya girls braiding colourful friendship bands.

Early the next morning, a delegation from Customs and Immigration came alongside to check us in, bringing with them the port captain and the local police chief. Jokingly, we reported the theft. With a serious expression on his face, the chief asked for the colour of the shoes and laces and promised to launch an investigation!

We received our three-month cruising permit and were free to continue up the 42 km long river to Lago Izabal. After ten months, mostly on open ocean in salty air, we welcomed a change. It was nice, but a bit weird, to be sailing into a jungle. It seemed so quiet. But we were mistaken. There were lots of sounds, only different. We were not accustomed to the voices of the jungle; a symphony of rustling leaves from monkeys swinging from the treetops, the singsong of tropical bids, high-pitched piercing tunes of the grasshopper, croaking frogs and squeaking creatures. It was all very intense, all very foreign to us.

We wound our way up through a spectacular gorge lined with sheer, 90 metre high cliff walls covered in lush tropical vegetation right down to the riverbank. Almost hidden by the dense foliage from overhanging bluffs, native Indians in dugout cayukos hugged the shoreline where the current was weaker. The air was sweet and heavy with the exotic fragrance of tropical flowers. And it was hot, searing hot.

Eight miles further inland, the river widened into a lake. Here, along the shores of El Golfete, palapa straw huts dotted the landscape, partially camouflaged by Mother Nature. In the door openings, timid women were gazing after us while excited children came running down to the riverbank waving. In a natural rock pool, a bare-breasted woman was washing her long hair, naked children splashing and frolicking by her side. The atmosphere was infectious. We were truly smitten by the tranquility of it all.

We found an idyllic little bay where we anchored and spent our first night in the thick of the jungle. A Maya woman came paddling up to us with a basket of blue crab, a local specialty. We picked out half a dozen of the small fresh water crabs, a feast for only 50 cents. The introduction to Guatemala was promising! And it was wonderful to have fresh water swims again. But we didn't feel too safe and stayed close to the ladder, not knowing what was lurking beneath the surface of the shallow, somewhat muddy water.

We settled down for a few days to get a feeling for the place; to observe, absorb and digest impressions. In the mornings, before it got too hot, we went exploring in the dinghy. One day, we came upon a little cafe hidden in the mangroves. The menu was simple: Chicken or fish with rice and salad. We chose fish. While the woman started cooking in her outdoor kitchen, her husband went fishing! In no time, he was back with his catch, which he cleaned on the dock while we were watching. Soon, the fish was sizzling in the pan. It couldn't be fresher. Nor cheaper. The bill was all of 3 dollars.

While reflecting on the seemingly peaceful and uncomplicated life of Cayo Grande, a gang of loud teenagers came crashing into the hut. They slung their schoolbooks in a corner, turned on the TV and ordered French fries with ketchup and coke. Dressed in T-shirts, shorts or mini skirts, they stuck their heads together, giggled and joked like youngsters anywhere. Maybe life in the jungle isn't so different after all?

But indeed it is. One of the girls had just a stump of an arm. She had been bitten in the hand by a poisonous snake when she was little. Her father had chopped her arm off just below the elbow with his machete. There was no doctor in the vicinity and he knew that it was only a matter of minutes before she would die. We saw many individuals with amputated limbs in the area. So we had the greatest respect for the jungle, for its dense vegetation and unfamiliar, maybe life-threatening - creatures.

On our way back to Nor Siglar, we stopped to watch an Indian carving a canoe from a log in the shade of a straw lean-to. Two boys were helping and learning. A woman big with child was watching from a distance. No doubt, she'll be having her baby at home in this region where infant mortality and illiteracy are very high.

Before we could tear ourselves away from El Golfete's fascinating surroundings, we arranged for a local to take us on a little jungle safari.

Rio Dulce. Maya Indian carves a traditional dug-out cayuko.

The Indian directed us down a narrow, winding tributary where we never would have ventured on our own. At times, we had to lie down to get in under the dense brush. We were jittery and easily spooked when strands of lianas tickled our necks. Stumps and branches in the water were enough to trigger our imagination. But we saw neither crocodiles, nor snakes on the excursion.

Miguel was both knowledgeable and informative. It was the Mayas who discovered chewing gum, he said. They were the first to chew chickle, a resin from the Sapodilla tree. So there is the origin of the name, chicklets. Almost in awe, he pointed out the giant Ceiba tree, the sacred tree of the Mayas. Our amigo had many old remedies to share: the blood red juice from the Sangré tree was, among a host of other things, good for stomach ailments. If we had understood each other better, we could probably have replenished our offshore first aid kit with medicinal plants!

We lucked out and saw macaws and toucans, howler monkeys and sloth close-up. The monkeys frightened us with their eerie infant like screams. The lazy sloth was more relaxing to watch, where it hung like a sack, upside down on a branch, barely moving. Apparently, it takes a whole week for the slowpoke to get down on the ground to relieve itself and climb back to where it started! Then the weekly cycle starts all over again. What a life!

Maya women put on traditional headdress, and Maya men in their Sunday best awaiting church service in Santiago de Atitlan, Guatemala Highlands.

After a week of solitude, we sailed the remaining miles up the river to Mario's Marina, a hamlet for offshore cruisers. Most had already arrived for the hurricane season. But there were some permanent residents there too; mainly hippy types from the 60's and Vietnam

War veterans who lived well on their pensions and unemployment cheques. The dollar goes a long way in Guatemala.

We were deep in the realm of the Mayas. In the early morning hours, fathers and sons paddled quietly about, gracefully casting their circular fishing nets. It was a peaceful scene. As though time were standing still. In the afternoon, the men came to the marina to sell their catch to the gringos. Mario's Marina was highly regarded by the Indians of Rio Dulce. Here, they could not only sell their products, but get a much better price than at their own markets.

The marina was often engaged in local projects. While we were there, an auction was held to raise money for Casa Guatemala, a local orphanage. The whole sailing community became involved, and enthusiasm grew with the project. When it was all over, we were pleased to hand over a cheque for US$1,500 to Dr. Helen, a volunteer at the orphanage. As a token of appreciation, she offered her services free of charge, knowing full well that many sailors had developed some form of stomach disorder. So the next morning, a whole dinghy flotilla made its way downriver with their respective samples for Dr. Helen to examine under her microscope. Martin had lost nine kilos in the last three months. He was feeling tired and lethargic and had trouble sleeping because of a rumbling stomach. So we were not surprised when Dr. Helen announced that he was anaemic. But we were not prepared for the rest of the diagnosis: Hookworms!

The cure worked quickly and we took off on our land trip exploring the Guatemala Highlands with its spectacular scenery, colourful native tribes and ruins from long ago. Highlights included the famous Chichicastenango market, beautiful Lago de Atitlan and Antigua, the old capital of Guatemala, rich in culture and baroque architecture, still evident after many devastating earthquakes, which have left parts of the city in rubble.

At the end of October, after returning from a quick visit home, the hurricane season was over and we could head back down Rio Dulce across the shallow sandbar and into the Caribbean again. This time, the bar was not a problem. The water level was higher after the rainy season. We welcomed the sea breeze and fresh air. It was great to be underway again.

ISLAS DE LA BAHÍA
HIDDEN ELDORADO OF THE BAY OF HONDURAS

After five months in the peaceful jungles of Guatemala, I had difficulty finding my sea legs again. The trade winds were a bit too strong for my liking. So it didn't take long before I hung over the railing feeding the crabs. When was I going to get rid of this inevitable seasickness?

Before heading north to Belize, we wanted to visit the remote Bay Islands a few hundred miles to the east. But that was easier said than done. After a few days of rough seas and wind on the nose, I begged, green in the face that we stop in Utila, the closest and smallest of the three main islands in the chain. Are we ever glad we did.

A pleasant atmosphere greeted us in Puerto Este, a charming little clean and neat town with a quiet main street almost devoid of traffic. There were only 4-5 cars on the whole island. White, freshly painted gingerbread houses with intricate latticework verandas and lush gardens lined the street, their windows filled with flowers, and lace curtains blowing in the wind. The majority of the 1500 inhabitants were descendents from British buccaneers who settled in the archipelago in the 18th Century. Surprisingly, the English language has survived. It was, however, difficult to understand, being a mix of Creole and the English spoken at the time. The people of Utila have little in common with their countrymen on the mainland. Even though Islas de la Bahía, as the islands are also called, belongs to Honduras, and the official language is Spanish, the population maintains its British culture. They are visibly proud of their heritage.

The Bay Islands lie in an arch, which curves northeast into the Bay of Honduras from the mainland. They are relatively untouched by tourism. So far, Hondurans have this secluded paradise more or less to themselves. It is still possible to find a place for a few dollars a night. Therefore, the area is popular with backpackers, who are also attracted by inexpensive scuba diving lessons in this fascinating corner of the globe, with its incredibly rich and varied marine life. Snorkelling was truly unforgettable through a maze of narrow channels and caves, amongst a multitude of colourful tropical fish and huge, sharp coral beds framed by pastel coloured ferns and plants waving gracefully in the underwater current. To preserve this fragile and precious eco-system, large areas have wisely been set aside for marine parks and nature reserves.

Not far from Utila, we found the idyllic Water Keys. As we were about to drop the hook, we noticed a young man waving and calling from the beach. It was impossible to hear what he said. But there was no doubt that he wanted us to anchor elsewhere. We rowed ashore and found him engaged in a lively discussion with a group of older men. "Why were you calling us?" we asked. The men laughed. "He likes to think of himself as the Port Captain!" they answered. On a walk around the 500-metre long key, we noticed quite a few individuals like him. Not so strange, perhaps, in such a small village of barely 300 people so far from civilization. No doubt, there was a lot of intermarriage in the community.

Pigeon Key, popularly called Suc-Suc, was another interesting and tiny, low-lying key. It was literally covered with clapboard houses built on pilings right out to the water's edge. They were constructed like this to prevent being washed out to sea during storms and floods. In strong wind, sand, bits of coral and shrubs blow ashore and pile up in huge heaps in the space underneath the houses, at times, leaving only a few centimetres between the floor and the pile. Under normal circumstances, the platform is the home's centre of activity. Here it is shady, well-ventilated, cool and comfortable. Here, children do their homework, women their cooking and laundry, men mend their fishing nets, play cards and snooze in hammocks strung below the low ceiling. Being elevated off the ground, insects, creepy crawlies, crabs and such won't get inside either.

Utila and the other Bay Islands are located on the outskirts of the hurricane area. Still, old-timers told us that they had experienced several during their lifetime. "How did you handle such a crisis?" we wondered. "Well," they said. "All you can do is board up the windows and doors and seek shelter on higher grounds. For us that means heading for the hills of Utila. Then, you settle down and wait - and hope for the best." It sounded awful having to abandon your home just like that. The answer was simple: you only have one life. It is precious. A house can always be rebuilt.

Our first impression of the idyllic spot was one of peace and harmony. However, walking around the island, we noticed a clear class distinction. The Spanish-speaking ladino colony lives on one side in small huts on stilts over the water, while the more well-to-do English-speaking population lives in cement houses at the opposite end. Electricity was a scarce commodity and a luxury for everyone. It was available only four hours a day. The male contingent prioritized TV over washing machines and electric appliances. Therefore, the generator was only turned on at night. This was not very popular among the female population, who seemed to be discriminated against. They had a tough life. To give birth, they had to go by open boat to the mainland, an often-rough four-hour ride. Some times, they didn't make it in time. It was obvious where the women found comfort. There were four churches in the tiny place.

We were really keen to see the other two main islands, Roatan and

Guanaja as well. But the conditions were far from ideal. For more than a week, we were holed up waiting for a full gale to blow itself out. It was only a day-sail further east. But to get bashed about in 30-40 knot headwinds was not very tempting. In the end we gave it a miss, and considered ourselves lucky to have seen Utila and the keys nearby. Besides, it was time to move on to Belize where our friend Nicole McRae was joining us.

TO SEE IT IS TO BELIZE IT!

"To see it is to belize it! That's our motto in Belize", some locals told us as we were making landfall in the outer cays. "But you'll soon realize that there is more to see below water than above in this little country of ours."

How true. For here, on the second longest barrier reef in the world, over 200 coral islands lie stretched like pearls on a string along a 250 km long chain, which runs parallel with the coast of Mexico in the north to Honduras in the south. Outside the reef, there are three separate atolls, the only ones in the Northern Hemisphere. Diving enthusiasts from afar come to explore this rare and beautiful unspoiled underwater paradise with its incredible visibility, flora and fauna. And it was in these waters that we were going to experience our most nerve-racking passages through treacherous coral strewn shallows and harrowingly narrow reef entrances. But everything is relative, because as we got used to it, we felt safe as long as we had a metre under the keel!

Our grand arrival saw us running hard aground. This was not an entirely unexpected introduction to Belize, where boats with more than 1.7 metres draft will encounter problems. Still, it was tempting to give it a try. But when the stress of avoiding the numerous and dangerous shallows became unbearable, we asked ourselves if it really was worth it. It was. The snorkelling was just as good, if not better than in the Bay Islands, which we had enjoyed so much. What's more, we even got to see eagle rays and nurse shark, hawksbill turtles and a docile manatee. And then there were all those sleepy little cays, where you could wander around barefoot on sandy roads with no traffic and Go Slow signs. Here, Creoles and Garifunas, Mayas and Ladinos had succeeded in creating a pleasant and workable community, accepting each other's differences and living together in peace. Magic tropical nights with exotic music and Latin rhythms completed an otherwise perfect setting.

Belizean fishermen show off their catch, teach us how to clean conchos and take us diving.

On Ranguana Cays in the south, we got talking to some young fishermen. They had just come in with their catch of the day. Four cayucos fully laden with lobsters and conchs lay side by side on the beach. "May we watch you clean the conchs?" we enquired politely, hoping they wouldn't find us too pushy or curious. "We have done a bit of fishing in Canada and Norway, but have no experience with conchs", we added. "But of course!" the fellows answered in unison. They were more than willing to demonstrate their skills. "No gringos have ever asked us that before," the most outgoing of the lot said. "It almost seems like they are afraid of us. No yachties ever come ashore here. They stay on their boats, have sundowners with each other and basically keep to themselves." The sympathetic fellow continued talking as he, quick as a whistle, removed the conch muscle from the shell with a small sharp knife. "Would you like to have a try, perhaps?" he asked handing me the knife. I made a real fool of myself. I didn't like the feeling of the live and slippery conch. They thought that was really funny and had a good laugh.

There was a small camp on the cay, where fishermen stayed during the lobster season. But these guys had erected their own lean-to in the shade of some rustling palms. That was all that was needed in this hot climate; just some protection against the sun, rain and wind. Once a week, a boat came out from the mainland to fetch their catch. At the same time, they brought fresh supplies of ice, water and provisions. The guys lived mainly on canned food. They were tired of fresh seafood. So when asked if they would trade with us, they didn't want any money. "Do you have any canned tuna, sardines, ham, or peaches onboard?" they asked eagerly. When we returned with a bit of everything, they were so delighted that they gave us a whole bucket of lobsters, conchs and a big snapper.

The strong dark skinned youths with kinky hair and Creole features were virtually bursting with energy and well-being. We couldn't imagine why cruisers would be afraid of them. Maybe they looked intimidating from a distance? We were glad we had ventured ashore. It didn't take long before we relaxed together with these mild mannered, polite young men. "Would you like to come diving with us tomorrow?" they asked. It was a deal.

The sun was barely over the horizon when they picked us up in a powerboat with a huge cooler amidships. We were off to the fishing grounds - four dugout canoes on the foredeck, four tanned Belizean free divers and two excited Viking yachties - ready for action.

With the mother ship securely anchored, the fellows launched their respective cayucos and paddled away in opposite directions. Raymundo took me in tow; Martin swam after Hector, holding on to his canoe. It was an unbelievable treat to watch these young divers in their element. Equipped with old-fashioned diving masks, flippers and snorkels, they jumped into the water and swam swiftly, pulling their cayucos along with one hand, scouting the water for prey. The banks were about 10 metres deep. Suddenly, Raymundo gave a mighty kick and dove into the depths. What for, I wondered. With a sweeping motion, he grabbed a clump of sand. Twirling around towards me, making the victory sign, he held up a big conch. Before coming up, he had caught two more. With one in each hand and a third under his armpit, he ascended slowly to the surface and threw the catch into his cayuco. I was speechless. I had not seen anything that resembled life down there on the sandy bottom.

Hector caught a giant lobster by free-diving to a depth of ten metres.

The three teenagers and their uncle carried on all day in the blistering sun, hardly taking any breaks. We found it unbelievable that they could keep going so long. Up and down, up and down. They did 10-12 dives an hour, staying under water 2-3 minutes at a time. Or so it seemed. They were like fish in water and clearly liked to show off. Their tools were primitive, their skills impressive. Imagine catching lobsters in sharp coral beds with only a stick with a hook at the end!

We wanted to give the youngsters something special for taking us along, and offered them some cigarettes and beer. Not a very good idea. "We must take care of our bodies", they said. None of them smoked nor touched alcohol. In actual fact, they didn't want anything from us at all. They had enjoyed themselves too. They were happy that we cared about what they were doing. However, if we really insisted, they wouldn't mind having a new mask or two. We were not able to part with our own, but promised to send a pair from Florida. We noted it on our list, exchanged addresses and left our new friends behind, who had given us such a special and rich experience.

A bit further north, in the Bluefield Range, we were awakened one morning by someone knocking on the hull. "God dag!" he called. "I see you are Norwegian!" The fellow was from a town near Oslo. After having sailed as cook on United Fruit Company ships for many years, he settled down in Belize, where he had been fishing for 20 years. The colourful character had five children with five different women in five different ports around the world. He never married. "I loved them all!" he said with a big smile.

The jolly fellow was also fond of something else. So when he heard that we had aquavit on board, we were immediately invited to dinner. We sent the bottle with him so he could put it on ice. A few hours later, when we sat down to eat, there was not much left in the bottle. Our countryman was really sentimental and talked exclusively about the good old days, speaking his native tongue as though he had never left. The conch soup was delicious. On leaving, he promised us fresh tortillas for breakfast. But the morning after, the man was nowhere to be seen. He must have gone to bed with the bottle and continued his trip into nostalgia land on his own till the wee hours.

We couldn't leave Belize without exploring Lighthouse Reef and the famous Blue Hole, where Jacques Cousteau recorded so many of his popular documentaries. It was poorly marked and difficult to find. But eventually, we managed to orientate ourselves from an old shipwreck on the reef. Suddenly, there it was right in front of us, this circular underwater cave, which is over 100 metres deep and at least as much in diameter. The visibility was perfect, so there was much to see on the edge of this enormous crater amongst colourful stalactites in an amazing, almost spooky underwater landscape.

It was not easy to leave this special place where we had had such neat experiences. The biggest highlight of this sea gipsy life of ours is decidedly the people we meet on the way. It is enormously rewarding to get close to people from different cultures and backgrounds, especially to take part in their day-to-day lives. And that is possible when sailing around on your own keel, visiting isolated places off the beaten track, far away from the traditional tourist routes. We feel privileged to be able to do just that, and consider these unique encounters the most genuine and valuable experiences of our adventure.

CUBA
CASTRO'S CARIBBEAN CREATION

It was difficult to get accurate information on the current rules and regulations in effect for visiting sailboats to Cuba. What we did know, was that because of the U.S. trade embargo, Americans were not welcome, and we were the envy of our U.S. sailor friends. So despite all the uncertainties, we decided to go anyway.

After two days in a strong current and fluky winds across the unpredictable Strait of Yucatan, we woke to a magnificent sunrise over the north coast of Cuba, dolphins frolicking around the bow. Otherwise, all was quiet, not a ripple on the water. Suddenly, the peaceful atmosphere was interrupted by a call from a big hulk of a ship, which appeared out of nowhere. It was the U.S. Coast Guard. There was no end to what they wanted to know.

We had a feeling of being under constant surveillance. But then we were in the Strait of Florida, where Cubans try to flee to the USA on all sorts of unsafe homemade rafts every day. Desperate, people risk their lives attempting to get across the 150 km wide strait. It was unsettling to be in such a dramatic area where so many tragedies occur.

While in Yucatan, we had tried to get a detailed chart of the Cuban coast, but without success. So on approaching Havana, we contacted Cuba Port Control and asked permission to enter. Hearing that we were Canadian, this was granted promptly, and since we didn't have any charts, a speedboat was sent out to meet us and escort us in to Marina Hemingway.

The check-in procedures with Customs, Immigration and Departments of Agriculture and Health went without a hitch. The paperwork was done onboard and finished within an hour. We received a three-week visa - they confiscated our passports. So the Cubans were efficient - but didn't seem to trust each other. The government officials operated in pairs. Not only that. Two representatives from Guardiera Frontera, Castro's border police, were keeping an eye on the proceedings from the dock.

Fidel's welcoming committee greets us with Cuba Libre.

We had barely fastened the mooring lines when a whole delegation headed by a sharp looking woman carrying a tray of Cuba Libre rum drinks came marching down the dock. She introduced herself as the Minister of Information of Cuba Tour, Castro's Department of Tourism. "On behalf of Fidel, I wish you Bienvenido a Cuba!" she announced, clinking our glasses. Then followed a long, well-rehearsed propaganda speech, frequently interrupted by toasts and laughter. Everyone was friendly and pleasant. We were relieved. After all, we had no idea what to expect.

There were only six sailboats in the marina, which had room for over 400 yachts. Construction of the huge complex, which included a hotel, shopping centre, swimming pool, restaurants and a park, was started during the Batista regime in the 1950's. Today, the project remains unfinished. The buildings are in decay. Solid cement docks and sturdy cleats suitable for large luxury yachts, bare witness to a grandiose playground intended for the rich and famous.

It didn't take long to realize that the marina was only accessible to the privileged few. Only tourists and staff were allowed inside the large compound, which was cordoned off from the outside world by high cement walls and guarded gates. Obviously, we had to venture outside this isolated oasis to explore the real Cuba.

At the bus stop nearby, we got talking to a chemist who had spent all morning trying to get hold of a roll of scotch tape. "Times are tough in Cuba these days," Guillermo explained in good English, which he had taught himself. "I am working only one day a week nowadays. Without proper supplies and government support, it's impossible to get any work done. Besides, I spend hours every day in line-ups to get food for my mother and myself. And she is sick," he sighed.

We had to wait an eternity for the bus. "There is a shortage of gasoline," Guillermo explained. "Besides, there are no spare parts, so maintenance is poor. Therefore, lots of buses are out of order. Since the fall of the Soviet Union, we are not receiving subsidies any more. Worst of all, we are not getting any cheap oil." There were lots of gas stations along the well-developed road system. But most were closed due to the rationing. In October, the allowance had been 30 litres per car. In November, none was available, except on the black market.

For ten centavos, i.e. less than a penny, we got onto a rickety old bus with broken seats and cracked windows. It was packed. Still, frustrated people pushed and shoved to squeeze themselves aboard. Some ended up hanging from the doors and windows, others crawled onto the running boards and the roof.

Our first priority was to obtain a ham radio licence for Cuba. Guillermo volunteered to accompany us to the Department of Communications. But nobody could help us there. The boss was away. Nobody had the authority to make decisions in his absence. No permissions could be granted without him. "Typical!" Guillermo muttered annoyed, shrugging his shoulders. "No wonder nothing works in this country."

We were interested in learning more about life in Cuba, and invited him to have lunch with us. There were lots of restaurants along Avenida de la Revolucion. "They're closed!" Guillermo announced frustrated. We protested. We could see several open ones along the beautiful treed boulevard. Shaking his head, he took us to one of them. The rundown restaurant was full of empty tables. A waitress served lemonade. Guillermo was right. There was nothing to eat. They had nothing to cook from. There was no electricity. No propane. "But you are more than welcome to come home with me for lunch", he continued. "If you'll accept beans. Because that's all we have nowadays." We were apprehensive. We had just met the guy. But he looked both respectable and sincere. We decided that it was an opportunity not to be missed.

Plaza de la Revolucion. Location of Castro's many famous marathon speeches attended by thousands of people.

Guillermo lived in a small apartment above the garage of an old rundown mansion with his ailing mother. Once inside, he felt free to talk - away from the scrutiny of the committees for la Defencia por la Revolucion, which were present in every neighbourhood with spies on every corner. The flat was sparsely furnished. We remarked on the colour TV. "Connections!" Guillermo smiled. "Family in Miami." His sister and aunt had fled after the Revolution. Thanks to them, he and his mom were better off than most Cubans. Their relatives sent money, toiletries and clothing from the U.S. to Cuba via Mexico. The practice was highly illegal. They could be thrown in jail if found out.

But without these supplements, they would really suffer. To prove his point, Guillermo showed us their ration book. We were speechless.

No wonder Guillermo looked skinny and drawn. He had lost 14 kilos in the last four months. Things had deteriorated significantly since the break-up of the old Soviet Union. Trade between the two countries was virtually at a standstill, and the financial aid, which Cuba had come to depend on, had been cut-off. People were oppressed by a system in which there was no room for initiative. They had grown apathetic and seemed incapable of helping themselves. We still had ample provisions in the bilges, and offered them the rest of our flour so they could bake their own bread, at least for a while. But they declined. It was no use, they said. They didn't have enough propane for the oven.

All around us, people seemed too small for their clothes, their cheeks were hollow, their eyes deep set. No one really complained, but they were thankful for handouts. We were particularly shocked when the wharfinger in the marina approached us one evening, enquiring whether we might have some soap and empty plastic bottles for him. There was a shortage of packing material at the moment. The bottles were for water, milk, coke and beer when available in bulk. He had a big family. They never had enough soap in their monthly ration. That explained, of course, why there never was any soap or toilet paper in the washrooms in the marina. The staff took it home.

Our chemist friend had not heard from his relatives in Miami for a long time, and his mother was worried about her aging sister. We offered to call her from the boat via a land based radio amateur in Florida. This way, at least Guillermo could get to hear her voice. But it was risky for him to come down to the marina, being off limits to locals unless they worked there. So we planned carefully how we were going to get him down to the boat.

The following day, two young men in shorts, t-shirts and runners strolled nonchalantly through the gate of Marina Hemingway where we were waiting. Guillermo and his friend, Marcos might just as well have been tourists. My heart thumping, I ran towards them and gave them a big hug. The guard must have thought we were old friends and waved us through. It took me a long time to calm down. Who knows what would have happened to us if we had been caught.

Since we had not been able to get a licence, we were not really allowed to use the ham radio while in Cuba. So when checking into the amateur net, asking for a phone patch to Miami, we reported that we were in international waters. Soon, TiaTina was on the air. "Hola?" Guillermo had written down what I was to say in Spanish. Still, Tia Tina didn't understand what was going on. Even though I conveyed greetings from her sister and nephew, there was no way she would accept a collect call from this Anna. Tia Tina could barely speak English, even after all those years in the States. She sounded worried. "No comprendo! Guillermo in Cuba! You no call me no more!" So the phone call to aunt Tina was a big fiasco. Surely, the radio amateur in Florida figured out what was going on. He had probably relayed similar calls before.

We had prepared a care package of milk powder and rice, sugar and lentils for Guillermo, Marcos and our marina wharfinger friend, who was hovering on the dock outside. We asked him aboard. Then their Spanish became too fast for us. But we understood the body language. They were clearly on their guard. Suddenly, they all broke into laughter, slapping each other on the backs. Guillermo and Marcos had suspected the wharfinger of being a DPR-agent, a spy for Castro's secret service. But they soon realized that he was just as innocent, hungry and poor as they were. He asked them to smuggle his loot out of the compound for him. If he were caught, he would surely lose his job. So this is how we became involved in the day-to-day life of Cubans. Nervous, with loaded backpacks and shaky legs, we accompanied our friends to the bus stop outside the gate. The guard waved us through. We obviously didn't look very suspicious to him.

The City of Havana is beautifully situated on the north coast of Cuba overlooking the Strait of Florida. It has a perfect protected harbour guarded by the impressive El Castillo del Morro, built by the Spanish in the 16th century. But the port was deserted. Apart from a couple of rusty, old freighters, there were no signs of the usual hustle and bustle from the loading and discharging activities in active harbours. Huge disintegrating warehouses on the docks were virtually empty.

It was sad to see how Havana, once a thriving metropolis has deteriorated. Old, stately mansions that used to belong to the wealthy before the revolution, now house squatters who have not looked after them since. The once beautiful buildings are totally run down, unpainted and dilapidated with dirty, broken windows and wash hanging from balconies, their tenants seemingly oblivious to their architectural beauty. The city is full of magnificent baroque jewels, the main cathedral of Old Havana being the most impressive. However, it has not seen any maintenance for 40 years. Valuable paintings were dusty beyond recognition; the stained lead glass windows cracked by tree branches piercing through the panes.

Havana's fashionable mansions reveal decades of neglect.

The boulevards and avenidas of La Habana were ideal for cycling, being wide with many lanes and little traffic. The Malecon, a 10-lane boulevard running along the seawall was the most impressive, but also rather strange being almost devoid of traffic. The few cars around were Russian, German and Japanese. But most noticeable were the American golden oldies from the 50's - remnants from an opulent pre-revolution era. Needing the exercise badly, we crisscrossed the capital on our folding mountain bikes. The locals all had heavy-duty bikes made in China. They had no gears. So ours caused a lot of attention, and more than once did we have a near crash when someone came a little too close to inspect the gears!

Being a Unesco Heritage Site, Havana is destined for a massive renovation project. So far, only a few of its original spots have been preserved, the most famous being Ernest Hemingway's favourite bar,

La Bodeguita del Medio. This is where the writer, who spent so much of his colourful life in Cuba, drowned his sorrows in mojitos, a popular rum and lime drink with mint. His signature is eternalized for everyone to see in a frame over the bar. Hemingway is enormously popular in Havana, and many places are named after him.

As we didn't have time to sail around the island, we decided to take a 17-hour train ride to Santiago de Cuba on its southwestern shores. We got the tickets, which Cubans themselves must order way in advance, in one day. Everywhere we went we were hustled to the front of the long lines. It was hard to take the preferential treatment offered tourists. It didn't feel right. But the locals didn't seem to care. We admired their patience. But there was a definite look of apathy in their eyes.

The horse taxi provides public transportation in Castro's idyllic realm.

We were assigned soft seats in a special coach for tourists only. Contrary to general belief, the air conditioning worked the whole way, so we just about froze to death in our shorts and t-shirts. We would have starved to death too, if we hadn't been told to bring a lunch. There was no guarantee that there would be any food available on the 600 km long trip, which was known for its poor service.

We were keen to see the countryside, but most of the trip was during the night, and in daylight we found the windows to be so dirty that we could hardly see through them. We wondered if it was intentional. Still, we got a feeling for what the interior of Cuba is like. Most notable were the miles and miles of tobacco, coffee and sugar cane plantations swaying in a rolling landscape. The scenery was quite lovely. The villages, however, left a depressing impression of shabby looking primitive bohios - square, little unpainted wooden shacks with straw roofs.

In Santiago de Cuba, there were propaganda posters everywhere. An election was coming up, and with only one party in power, the outcome was a foregone conclusion. Si por Cuba slogans signed by Fidel were plastered on every conceivable wall. Every morning, we could hear children at a school across from the hotel recite poems by the great father of all revolutions, Jose Marti. In the evening, the TV program, which started at 6 PM, opened with a 15-minute propaganda show. Historical events were relived and heroes riding beautiful horses applauded, always concluding with excerpts from one of Castro's many fiery marathon speeches.

Safely back in the marina, after a hair-raising return on a derelict Russian propeller- driven plane from the 50's, we discovered that we had had uninvited visitors onboard. Our flag was gone. The line was cut. Who in the world would do something like that?

It was time to leave Castro's beautiful pearl and head north to the land of the free. After having given away most of our provisions onboard, we were looking forward to shopping in well-stocked stores again and to enjoying a life without so many rules and regulations. However, one thing is certain: we were happy to have had the opportunity to visit Cuba when we did, but equally as happy to be able to leave when we wanted to. We were also fortunate to develop such a close relationship in such a short time with the two Cubans, Guillermo and Marcos. Thanks to them, our stay became unusually interesting and meaningful. We learnt a great deal which we otherwise would have missed as "ordinary tourists" on our own.

The end of Part 2 of the "9 Years on the 7 Seas Adventure", also published in print and as an eBook with the title **Exploring the East Coast of Central America**

PART 3

ACROSS THE ATLANTIC TO NORWAY

Before setting out across the Atlantic, Nor Siglar needed a thorough overhaul and renewal of some of her sails and equipment. After a year and a half, mostly in the harsh tropical sun, and with 10,000 nautical miles under her keel, she was showing signs of wear and tear. So we spent two busy months, January and February, in Fort Lauderdale getting Nor Siglar ready for her biggest test to date..

There is no denying that we were quite apprehensive about the upcoming challenge – a distance of 5,000 nautical miles and our longest passage yet. So a lot of planning went into how we were going to tackle it. We had endless discussions with sailors who had done it before and immersed ourselves in the Atlantic Crossing Guide and Jimmy Cornell's World Cruising Routes, where we found the best times and routes for the transit.

Based on this research, the departure was set for May 1 from English Harbour, partly because we wanted to be in Antigua for the popular Race Week, partly because this would work well with the rest of our plan. This way, we would have time for a couple of weeks in Bermuda before the start of the hurricane season, and in the Azores before the final stretch to Norway in July.

For me, it was a great relief that the crossing could be done in stages; the first one to Bermuda, the second to the Azores and the third to Norway. We were both happy that we had been able to get friends to crew for us on the various legs. With that in place and Nor Siglar ship shape again, we settled down for a couple of months of leisurely cruising in the Caribbean.

ANTIGUA

The stressful atmosphere surrounding the prestigious Race Week didn't agree with us, and we soon longed for the solitude of the open ocean again. Nor Siglar was ready and so were we. After a few months of carefree cruising in the Bahamas, Dominican Republic, Puerto Rico and the Virgin and Leeward Islands, we felt rested and reasonably well prepared, both physically and mentally, to set out on the first 1,000 miles of our transatlantic challenge.

It was getting dark as we rounded the south coast of Antigua, changed course to the north and caught the trade winds over the starboard quarter. Under double-reefed main and the working jib half- furled, Nor Siglar made her entry into the open seas helped along by a favourable current. Her crew settled down and started to count miles. Above, high in the northern sky, the Big Dipper was beckoning. It was going to guide us all the way to the old country.

The dark nights, the loneliness and the close exposure to the often-rough elements, which I had found so frightening on our Bluewater debut, didn't bother me any more. I had grown accustomed to the motions of the boat. Nor Siglar had proven that she could handle her part. I felt safe and was much more relaxed. By now, we were getting to be old hands at sailing in the dark. Even so, we never tired of the night watches. I was always looking forward to this special time on my own. In an environment conducive to reflection. My thoughts would wander. It was natural to philosophize about the meaning of life, about the mysteries of the universe. I was captivated by the magnificence of the star-studded night sky. Could there really be other civilizations hiding amongst the constellations up there?

"Never stare into the wake of your boat, Anne!" Gearbulk's old flagship captain warned when we left. But the temptation was great and my curiosity got out of hand. Completely spellbound by the phosphorescence, which sparkled and shone like fireworks astern, I felt as though I was being drawn into it. So that was what the old salt had meant. It was a spooky sensation, and my imagination went wild in the mysterious waters of the Bermuda Triangle.

Knowing full well that I wouldn't be of much use in the galley the first days out, I had prepared a few dinners in advance. Martin looked after the meals and also took longer watches until I gradually found my sea legs. Then, we fell into a comfortable routine with equally shared duties.

The watch system of four hours on, three off during the day and three hours on, three off during the night, works well for us. After some practice, we have found out which shifts suit us best. Martin likes the after dinner turn from 19:00-22:00 and the dogwatch from 01:00-04:00. I prefer the 22:00-01:00 and 04:00-07:00 shifts. The day watches are less structured and basically organized around the meals and radio schedule.

The sails required minimal adjustment in the steady trade winds, so it was easy to stay on course. Day after day, night after night we were charging ahead on starboard tack in an exhilarating 15-25 knot breeze. Sudden squalls kept us on our toes. For when the squalls strike, you have to be quick. The jib was easy. With its furling mechanism, it can be rolled in very fast. The main sail, on the other hand, is more of a problem and often gets roughed up in the squalls.

Without lazy-jacks, the old, original sail was slapping uncontrollably from side to side every time we lowered it. So we were more annoyed than surprised when it ripped all the way from the luff to the leech in a particularly nasty squall. Thoughts went to heated discussions in Fort Lauderdale, where we had argued about whether it should be replaced before the crossing. Diplomatically, nothing was said about that matter. For now, the important thing was to do the best we could with the situation at hand. We soon discovered that we had actually been lucky in our misfortune. The tear was just above the first reefing point. That was easy to remedy. Putting in another reef, we could continue without a problem. But we were unable to maintain our 150-mile per day average.

Torn mainsail! Every offshore sailor's nightmare.

Crossing the Tropic of Cancer, we had reached the halfway point. It was getting noticeably cooler and we had to dig out warmer clothes. On the sixth day, when we sighted the Longtail, the graceful national bird of Bermuda, we knew we didn't have far to go.

BERMUDA

Bermuda is a heavenly place to be – but a hell of a place to get to is a famous saying by Mark Twain. Dangerous reefs circle the islands as far off as thirty miles. Also, the reefs are so low that they cannot be seen until very close. Mariners are often plagued by stormy weather and poor visibility and many ships and lives have been lost in this notorious ocean cemetery, especially during the old sailing ship era.

So we were prepared for the worst. And sure enough: In the early morning hours of the seventh day, when we had only 20 miles to go, we still hadn't seen land. And literally, out of the clear blue, we were hit by a strong gale from the north. There had been no such warnings on the forecast, and since the easterlies had been so steady, we had not made allowance for such a drastic wind change. Hitting us square on the nose, we had to fight our way into it for ten hours to make the last 20 miles. We took on more water in the cockpit during those hours than on the whole trip so far. We thought we'd never make it in before dark, but in the 11th hour, we managed to sneak in through the narrow Town Cut into St. George's Harbour. Wet, tired but happy, we congratulated each other on the completion of leg number one.

We had barely finished checking in, before an old acquaintance, the ex-Postmaster General of Bermuda was on the dock welcoming us with a bouquet of fragrant hibiscus and a generous supply of rum and ginger ale. Naturally, the occasion had to be celebrated with Dark & Stormy, the national drink of Bermuda! With such a reception, it wasn't long before the crew was nodding off, and peace and quiet descended upon the good ship Nor Siglar, in quaint and beautiful St. George's harbour.

Bermuda is like an enormous botanical garden sprinkled with world-class golf courses and pastelcoloured English Country style homes with whitewashed roofs designed to collect rainwater into private cisterns. Tourism is the mainstay of the economy, so people are extremely friendly. It's a great place to bicycle as the island is only 35 km long and the speed limit a mere 35 km per hour. Although the roads are narrow and often obscured by beautiful blooming hedges, we never felt in danger, as the motorists were polite and the traffic limited by one car per household. Population density and living standards are high in this charming archipelago, which originally was populated by shipwrecked colonists on their way from England to Virginia in the early 1600s.

It's nice to have something to hold onto when swimming mid-Atlantic with 4000 metres depth under the keel

We spent three enjoyable weeks sightseeing, doing the usual boat maintenance and psyching ourselves up for the next leg. With the first stretch behind us, we were not as worried about the next one, even though it was twice as far. However, monitoring Bermuda Harbour Control and the U.S. Coast Guard was rather nerve-racking. They were searching for five missing racing yachts on their way from Antigua to Jersey who were caught in a full storm a few hundred miles east of Bermuda. Eventually three of the boats sank. All sailors except one were rescued. According to our original schedule, we were destined for the same area at the same time. But luck was on our side. Due to a broken shroud and the first tropical depression of the season, our departure got delayed by a week.

Finally, on June 3, with our new crew and old friend Hubert Bunce onboard, we were ready for the Azores, a distance of 1,800 nautical miles, which, depending on the wind, was expected to take 2-3 weeks. Because of the Azores High, we were more likely to get too little than too much wind. It started out nicely, and for more than a week, it blew steadily from the southwest, and we could record 150 nautical miles per day in winds rarely stronger than 20 knots. The wind vane looked after the steering. Our faithful styrmann is never hungry, never tired, never complains and steers just as well as we do, if not better.

The feeling of being needed is just as important on a sailboat as it is at home. It is vital to have specific duties, to feel that you matter, that you contribute to the well being of the crew and the operation of the ship. One of my responsibilities was communication. It gave me a sense of importance, as well as pleasure, to keep in touch with the outside world, to be in charge of the weather forecasts and to keep track of the news on CBC, BBC and Radio Norway. At sea, it is nice to have contact with other boats in the vicinity. But nicest of all, is the schedule with keen radio amateurs around the world. During this crossing, hams in Norway and Holland noted our position every morning and evening. Faithfully, they tuned in at a predetermined hour to follow our progress and keep our families oriented. The radio contacts became the highlight of the day. It felt good to know that those at home knew exactly where we were at any given time, something that gave me the sense of security and moral support I seem to need.

The best weather prognosis came from amateur meteorologist,

Herb from Southbound II in Bermuda. Every night without exception, he recorded the positions of the cruisers, who in turn reported their wind strength, wave height, barometric pressure and cloud cover, which he then compared against satellite pictures and weather faxes from official channels. Combined with the detailed information collected from the boats at sea, he could then analyze each individual area with great accuracy. It was amazing how correct his predictions were. Very soon, we came to rely on his judgement. By following his advice, we managed to avoid bad weather systems as well as the big highpressure areas with no wind.

Wedding anniversary in the middle of the Atlantic Ocean!

June 10 was a big day onboard. Our anniversary. It was completely calm and we took a day off bobbing up and down in peace and quiet. The ocean was like a mirror, sparkling under a clear sky and bright sun. Now was our chance to swim in the middle of the ocean, in waters of dizzying depths of 4,000 metres. After a refreshing dip, we dressed up and celebrated in style with champagne and smoked salmon, chicken vol au vent and strawberry cheesecake. It's amazing what you can come up with from a variety of dried and canned goods – and a bit of imagination.

Friday the 13th came and went as superstitious sailors might expect. For what seemed like an eternity, a scary waterspout was hovering on the horizon. Then, a terrific squall broke loose, complete with pouring rain, lightening and thunder. So I was not at all surprised when I woke to a loud bang, followed by a flood of roughneck logger's language from happy days in Canada's big forests. It was the main sail again. But this time, it had torn above the top reefing point. All we could do was lash it down around the boom and continue under jib alone. The only good thing about the day was that we had reached the three-quarter mark to our destination.

THE AZORES

As we were closing in on the Azores, the weather became more and more unstable. So we were just fine without the main, which none of us had the energy to repair. Even so, we managed to maintain the speed, and five days after the mishap and 15 out of Bermuda, we made landfall on the green and fertile island of Faial. The busy port of Horta has been a popular stopover for sailors crossing the Atlantic going back to the days of Columbus. He was blown into the Azores by a terrific storm on his return to Spain after his first voyage to the "New World".

The dock in Horta is covered with boat graffiti. It is bad luck for visiting yachts to depart without leaving a painting behind.

Martin immortalizes Nor Siglar's visit with the help of local teenagers.

Horta Marina is famous for its "wall" filled with graffiti by visiting sailors from around the world. It is bad luck to leave without making a contribution. So literally thousands of paintings from the 700- 800 boats that call per year, adorn the marina.

The days went by with the usual maintenance and repair, sightseeing and rest. Like Bermuda, Faial is wonderful for biking, albeit much more strenuous in a hilly and rolling landscape. But we needed the exercise and even climbed Pico, the highest mountain in Portugal, on the nearby island of Pico. On July 2, we had a change of crew, with Hubert signing off and my nephew, Jim Brevig and his wife Anne Ziffer signing on for the last and longest leg to Norway.

THE HOMECOMING

A huge high-pressure system prompted us to steer a northerly course in order to pick up the westerlies around 45° N, instead of taking the shorter great circle route to England. A prudent decision, as those who followed the more direct rhumbline got caught in the doldrums. The first days, a pleasant moderate breeze filled our cruising spinnaker. At 47° N, half way to Lizard Head, we finally caught the northwester, which provided us with wonderful sailing all the way to the English Channel.

Having crew on a long passage feels so much safer than being only two. If one should get hurt, the other is not alone to cope with everything. With a team of four to share watches and cooking, we got plenty of rest and could enjoy the experience. The Skipper, who is always on standby, was even exempt from galley duty for a change.

Having towed a fishing line for days without any luck, I was about to open a can of tuna, when we got the big catch we had been waiting for. The monster was so heavy and unruly that we had to winch it aboard. The cockpit looked like a battlefield by the time the 20-kilo tuna was pacified and gutted. So not only the can went overboard, but the contents of my tender stomach as well.

At the entrance to the Channel, the visibility was poor, the current strong and traffic heavy. Even so, we tried not to use the radar, as it takes so much electricity. But after some hair-raising incidents with crossing ferries, we left it on around the clock. Thereafter, we had two on watch; one glued to the radar screen, the other at the helm. Three days later, after having transited the Channel without seeing land on either side, we steered out into the North Sea.

The North Sea! Almost home in the old country! We're getting excited, the crew impatient. Our progress is sooo slow! The normally rough North Sea gives us nothing but a gentle breeze. It is tempting to start the engine. But the Skipper is adamant. Why, we're sailors, aren't we? So we settle down, slowly passing oil platforms and fishing banks with familiar names.

Skagerak! Only 200 miles to go! We enter the waters between the south coast of Norway and the north coast of Denmark, having covered 2,000 nautical miles in 18 days. Finally, the wind picks up. But from the wrong direction! We tack and we tack. Kristiansand, Martin's hometown ahead! Hooray! Martin becomes nostalgic. For he has sailed these waters before. Once again, he recalls the time when he, barely 12-years old, "borrowed" his dad's 6-metre without permission, ran into a gale, was afraid to turn around and ended up almost in Denmark. "Imagine coming back here all the way from Vancouver on my own keel!" he mused. "Talk about a boyhood dream come true!"

Keen radio amateurs are pressing us for an exact time of arrival. Nor Siglar must receive a proper welcome, you know! It occurs to us that others are just as excited about our homecoming as we are.

Koster! The treacherous rocks marking the Swedish border with Norway appear ahead. Hvaler! Norway! We are too early! LA9 QJ, who has been following our progress from his cabin at Sandøy, comes on the air. "You're welcome to spend the night at our Yacht Club dock, if you like! Here you may rest up for your big arrival in Halden tomorrow!" As we are escorted into the calm harbour, the guest flag of Norway flies aloft. It is a tired, but happy crew who kiss terra firma and invite stunned club members to a celebratory anchor dram aboard the proud vessel Nor Siglar.

Logbook entry Friday, July 23, 05:00 hrs: "We're wide awake. Jim shaves his beard; the two Annes explore the island; Martin polishes the brass." With boat and crew ship-shape, we set out on our final stretch. At 11 o'clock, I catch the first glimpse of Svinesund, the landmark bridge between Norway and Sweden. A chill runs down my spine. Childhood memories come alive: Summer jobs at the border café, picnics in Sponvika, family outings and swimming at Isebakke, seasick on the open section of Sekken. Never in my wildest imagination had I dreamt that one day I would be coming home by sea from the other side of the globe on my own boat.

Only when we see our amateur radio friends with video cameras and flags on the bridge do we realize the fuss we are causing. Journalists and photographers meet us in their tenders and climb aboard. It is such a surprise, yet very touching to be the cause of so much attention. We really want to come in under full sails, but the strong current and fluky winds in the Ringdalsfjord make it impossible. Suddenly, Fredriksten Fortress looms to starboard. It looks different from this angle. At Sørhalden, we pass Verven, my great grandfather's shipyard. At the turn of the 20th century he built sailing ships which operated in regular service between Norway and Sweden. My grandfather was a ship's captain, my father a farmer. For the first time ever, it occurs to me, who has always considered myself "just a country girl", that maybe it isn't so strange that I should end up on the high seas – and actually enjoy it.

Aslaug Brevig, aged 88, welcomes her daughter home.

We poke the bow around the last bend, and there it is - my birthplace, Halden - surrounded by familiar hills and landmarks. Then, everything happens all at once. The mainsail is dropped, mooring lines fastened and fenders hung over the side. I see lots of people on the dock. It's hard to concentrate. Good thing there are many to catch the lines. Because I've got the shakes and virtually stumble ashore to hug my dear 88-year old mother, who heads a delegation of family and friends, welcoming us with flowers and ribbons in national colours.

It feels overwhelming to be the source of so much attention. The contrast from the solitude at sea is enormous. The local radio wants an interview. There are many questions. It's difficult to give simple answers. Experiences are many, impressions strong. Our maiden tongue is marred by years abroad. We stumble on words and sense that we are making fools of ourselves on the air.

From the Customs Building across the street, officials are watching the commotion on the dock. Suddenly, we remember that we must check in here too, as everywhere else, and hurry up to the office to apologize for the delay. "Not at all!" a softspoken officer replies. "We don't want to disturb your festivities! It's not everyday that a sailboat coming all the way from the Azores calls on little Halden!" "But we'd like to stay for a whole year!" we declare in our Sunday best Norwegian, concerned that Canadians on a Canadian sailboat may not be allowed to remain that long. "We can't imagine that will be a problem for you two. Relax! And welcome home!"

The first goal of our dream has been achieved. It is good to be home again. Now we are going to resurrect old friendships. Family ties and relationships neglected during years abroad shall be strengthened. There are reunions and anniversaries to attend. Our native tongue shall be revived. And last, but not least, it will be great to get to know our motherland again.

WINTERING ONBOARD IN NORWAY

"What do you mean? Live aboard all winter? You can't be serious." The family was shocked. Ice had started to form on the fjord, the temperature was already way below zero and it was only the middle of November. Little did we know that the winter we were planning to spend onboard Nor Siglar in Norway was to be one of the coldest in a long, long time.

Relatives came with tempting offers. But we declined. For we were experienced live aboards, you know! We could boast of six winters in Vancouver. Besides, we didn't want to inconvenience anyone. Nor Siglar had been our home for half a dozen years; we were used to living on her and preferred to be on our own. But were we really prepared for a winter so far north, at about the same latitude as the southern tip of Greenland and only 800 km south of the Arctic Circle? Winters in Norway were not what they used to be. The basin in Halden's inner harbour hadn't frozen in years. Time and again, we were reminded that Norwegians no longer are born with skis on. Why, children can't even ski any more due to mild winters and lack of snow.

Early in the morning of November 29, we were aroused from a deep sleep by a loud noise. We peered out from underneath Mum's warmest eiderdowns, stepped on to ice-cold floorboards and rubbed the frost off the windows to see what was going on outside. It was an icebreaker! It was running back and forth breaking up the ice all around us. A thin layer of snow adorned the Fortress. It was time to evacuate. Guided by a pilot boat, we moved to the mouth of a river nearby, where the current runs strong and there was no danger of getting stuck in the ice. Here, we remained for the whole winter, snugly moored in lee of a big cabin cruiser, whose kind and thoughtful skipper let us use his boat's warm salon and watch TV if and when we so desired.

We resurrected our old diesel furnace, which hadn't been used for a long time, installed an electric baseboard heater and acquired a portable one to be moved around as required. In the forepeak, where we sleep, it was freezing, so we put sleeping bags along the bulkheads and pillows in the bow to keep our feet warm. Bundled up in flannel pyjamas and layers of eiderdowns, we could leave the hatch above us ajar all night. Then we covered the floorboards with rugs and put insulation in the bilges. We were ready! Warmly dressed in long johns and several layers of wool, we managed to keep nice and warm during the long and dark winter days and nights. Flickering candles made it extra cozy below.

Christmas on Nor Siglar in Halden Harbour.

Actually, our biggest concern in the freezing temperatures was not our own comfort, but that the engine might freeze. Starting it up with regular intervals and protecting it with extra padding and a heat lamp did the trick. Bursting seacocks was another concern. Should we close them or not? We decided to leave them open. But this was nerveracking, especially when we were away from the boat for longer periods of time. And that was often. Although we had declined living accommodations ashore, we never refused the loan of cabins in the mountains. So we skied miles and miles in superb conditions and the most fabulous winter wonderland. We even got to see some of the winter Olympic games at Lillehammer, another dream come true! And yes, the seacocks were just fine. Even at -20 C°.

At Christmas, we decorated Nor Siglar with ribbons and sheaves of wheat, freshly cut pine branches and a tree from the farm. Martin played the accordion and as he got the hang of the carols a Christmassy feeling descended upon the ship. People walking by in the dark winter nights were surprised to see life onboard at this time of year. Hearing music, someone knocked on Nor Siglar's deck. Before long, our visitor was thawing out over a shot of rum carried all the way from the exotic Caribbean, and being dazzled by dreams, memories and tales from tropical climes.

Such was our first meeting with Bengt Sørensen, who was to turn our sailing adventure into something very special for us. A local optician, he gave us the idea of donating used eyeglasses to the poor in places off the beaten track. He is a man of action, and he sent with us the very first shipment of glasses, a gesture for which we are so grateful, as it was to give our circumnavigation a whole new dimension.

Before we knew it, the year in the old country was coming to an end. It was tough to say good-bye to family and friends, and touching to be escorted down the fjord by young sailors, who were dreaming of following in our footsteps some day. We were greatly moved when the young sailors, turning back to Halden, hailed us. They dipped the Norwegian flag to Nor Siglar, wishing us well as we continued our quest. For six weeks, we meandered through beautiful fjords, hiked spectacular mountains on the wild and rugged west coast of Norway, visited bird sanctuaries and marvelled at relics from the past: Stone Age rock carvings and runic inscriptions, historic sites from the Viking era, stone churches and monasteries from the Middle Ages. Last but not least, we could never get enough of watching the sun set and rise with barely an hour's interval, in this wonderful Land of the Midnight Sun. Then, at 63° N, we headed out to sea again, following the wake of our ancestors, the Vikings, to the Shetlands and the Orkneys, Scotland, Ireland and points further south.

Nor Siglar's crew live aboard in Halden during the coldest winter in a long time.

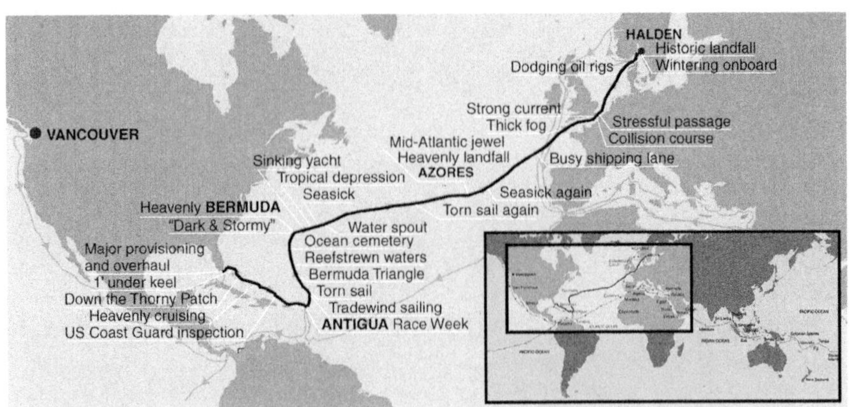

The end of Part 3 of the "9 Years on the 7 Seas Adventure", also published in print and as an eBook with the title **The Atlantic Crossing Challenge.**

PART 4

NORTH SEA, MEDITERRANEAN, AFRICA AND THE ATLANTIC OCEAN

SOUTH TO WARMER CLIMES

"What if I'm washed overboard?" I worry anxiously as I sit exposed and alone in the large shallow cockpit while Nor Siglar barrels down the west coast of Portugal in a full following gale. Bashing around like a cork, she surges ahead on breaking wave tops at record speed. We register 12 knots before the waves sink away and leave us in a sea of foam and bubbles. The next one will end up in the cockpit for sure. But no, Nor Siglar is like a ballerina, dancing with great ease and skill in the big seas and the cockpit stays dry.

"You're looking great!" a freighter captain calls with envy in his voice. His ship is barely visible in the rough seas. "Would you like to trade places with me?" We keep up with him for quite a while.

Since we left Norway a month ago, we have explored the isolated Shetland and Orkney islands, transited the canals and lakes of the beautiful Scottish Highlands and visited some of Ireland's famous old yacht clubs, pubs and castles. But the whole time we worried about the challenge ahead. The infamous Bay of Biscay. We wanted to get across before the autumn storms set in. That meant having to cut our stay short and miss England. Impatient, we left at the tail end of a gale, a move that has often proved to be a wise decision for us. And so it was. Except for the first day out, we had benign conditions and the crossing went remarkably well. So it was a happy and relieved crew that after seven days at sea could report to keen radio amateurs back home that Nor Siglar had arrived safely in Porto. What we did not report, however, was that the bread was mouldy, the milk sour, the fridge on the blink, the head leaking and the aft bunk soaked with salt water. But such is the joy of cruising.

And now we are on our way further down the unprotected coast. It's midnight and change of watch. Exhausted, I collapse into bed. I am feeling really miserable so Martin puts a patch behind my ear. Lying down, the boisterous sleigh ride feels like a carousel gone wild. Sleep does not come easily. It's fitful and restless. My brain is working overtime, thoughts popping in and out of my head. I recall a Christmas greeting we received long before we set out on our adventure: "are you two still intent on going ahead with this oft-mentioned circumnavigation of yours?" Now, three years and 20,000 nautical miles later, still plagued by seasickness, the question arises time and again: Why in the world am I doing this?

"It's love, of course!"an old childhood friend exclaimed, as simple as that. She is right, of course. But only partly. Had I not met Martin, the sailor, none of this would have happened. Still, there is no way he could have forced me against my will to leave a good job, the comforts of home and a safe existence on land. So there is definitely something much deeper behind a motivation, which makes someone voluntarily cut all ties, to chance, even to embrace, a totally new and uncertain lifestyle, filled with totally new and possibly extreme challenges.

Why then would someone want to expose oneself to so much danger and discomfort? The reasons are many. Pure adventure is, of course, the obvious one. New challenges – both physical and mental – and the satisfaction of mastering them, is another.

Could it be the need to prove to yourself and others what you are good for? Or a strong desire to test and get to know yourself in a new and unfamiliar situation, to see what else you are capable of beyond the regular day-to-day grind? Maybe it is a fascination for the fight for survival? The fight against the elements? Against the conventional? Against the clock? Or is it simply the quest for freedom? For a new and meaningful lifestyle? Certainly alluring is the dream to run away from it all. From the rat race, routine and restrictions, to seek something better elsewhere. It just might be that the grass is really greener on the other side of the fence – or the horizon in our particular case. One thing is certain: It feels wonderful to be FREE, to be independent, self sufficient and a bit crazy – at least for a while.

Lying in a daze, I meditate and ponder my situation. Did I regret what we have done? No, not for a moment. Although, after the first month, when it hit me that we didn't have to go back to work, it felt rather strange. My colleagues predicted that I would miss my job, be sorry, change my mind and want to come home again. "And you of all people!" my boss exclaimed when I handed in my resignation. "You, who worked so hard for equality! How could you possibly abandon your career just like that, to become a subordinate on a small sailboat? You, who are used to being in a management position making important decisions every day? No, Anne. This will never work!"

Portuguese Woman in traditional dress laying out fish for drying.

But it has. And why? Because there is no power struggle onboard Nor Siglar. First priority at sea is to reach your destination safely. To ensure that, the person in charge must have complete confidence and control. Regardless of size, there is only room for one captain on a boat. And there is no doubt who is the best qualified on Nor Siglar. Martin is a born sailor. He has been around boats all his life. He never gets seasick and reacts automatically when something happens. Sailing is in his blood. What is second nature to him is far from natural to me, having learned the ropes as an adult. Besides, seasickness gets in my way. So relinquishing this power to my soul mate has never been an issue.

Still, power struggle and dissatisfaction are typical problems on a small yacht. So why have these conflicts never afflicted us? An important reason is that we were already used to living onboard and existing together in an area barely larger than a normal size kitchen. We had already tested our relationship and knew that we were able to function well in close quarters day in and day out. We discovered that we did not need our own space. We like each other's company and enjoy being silent together. Quite simply, we don't get on each other's nerves. Besides, we are usually on the same wavelength and move at the same pace. Basically, we have common goals and seldom disagree. In fact, we are quite similar. We are best friends.

Cala Coticcio, Sardinia. One of the most beautiful anchorages of the circumnavigation.

So it comes as no surprise to us, who seldom disagree ashore, that we don't do it onboard either. At sea, where you are completely dependent on each other, it is absolutely vital to cooperate – to play on the same team. We feel that we have become such a team. We have found a balance that suits us. We are comfortable with our roles and responsibilities. Things get accomplished with few words and little kafuffle. But there is no doubt that in order for this kind of undertaking to succeed, it is absolutely necessary to be patient, flexible and understanding, and last but not least, respectful, considerate and kind to one another.

Still, it is obvious that living together so closely may be stressful. And at sea you can't escape or take off when you feel like it. Therefore, it is important to deal with the issues as they arise. It is important to speak up the minute something bothers you. Keeping things bottled up inside only leads to more frustration. So conflicts must be solved right then and there. There is no use sweeping the problems under the carpet. And never ever go to sleep as enemies.

Being an optimist at heart and blessed with a good sense of humour makes life a whole lot easier. Fortunately, neither one of us is pessimistic. Martin may, however, consider me overly cautious at times. He thinks I worry too much. In my defence, I like to think that I am just being realistic. I am obsessed with safety onboard. So when my fearless skipper doesn't want to reef, wear his safety harness or be as careful as I would like, the atmosphere can be pretty tense for a while.

My ponderings are rudely interrupted by a sudden racket above. "Anne! Help me! Hurry up!" The genoa sheet has come undone and the sail is flapping uncontrollably in the strong wind. Martin, minus harness, has been trying to bring it in while falling off the wind. But Nor Siglar just won't cooperate. Even with the main reefed right down and the traveller to leeward, she keeps pointing into the wind. We are not used to our new main sail yet, which we had made in Norway. It is much more powerful than the old one. Eventually, we manage to furl the genoa.

As the sun peaks over the horizon, we round Cabo de São Vicente on the south-western tip of the European continent – once considered the end of the world – and set a new course for the Strait of Gibraltar and the Mediterranean.

MEDITERRANEAN NEXT

Somehow we had thought that you could sail in the Mediterranean year round and had only planned one season there. The fact is that the winter is not particularly pleasant on this weather-beaten inland sea and sailors stay put between December and April. So we started to look for a place to winter. It had to be safe for Nor Siglar and interesting for us.

On December 21, we left the Atlantic Ocean behind and headed up the Guadalquivir River. We wanted to spend Christmas in Seville before settling down for the winter, probably somewhere on the Costa del Sol. In order to make the 85 km long stretch upriver in one day, one has to take advantage of the incoming tide. Otherwise you risk having to stay overnight in the middle of the river, where traffic is heavy and there is little room to swing on the anchor. Our calculations worked and we made it through the harbour lock just before it closed for the day. Once inside, we were signalled into the marina by someone flashing a light from the quay. "Why, isn't that Anne and Martin?" we heard in the dark. We couldn't believe it. In front of us was Voyager, the Finnish boat that hosted a fabulous crab feast in Honduras a couple of years ago! At that time the couple had an infant girl. Now, they had another baby boy!

Not only did we spend the holidays in Carmen's beautiful Seville, we wintered there as well. It was impossible to tear ourselves away from such a vibrant, typical Spanish city, virtually void of tourism at that time of year. We celebrated Christmas Norwegian style with traditional food and drink. Radio Norway International provided familiar carols and amateur radio friends passed greetings to the family. I had a good cry and then we opened our gifts, reminisced and got homesick for our loved ones.

Cala Covas, Menorca. Landlocked harour surrounded by hils full of ancient caves.

During our four-month stay, we had ample time to get to know the other blue water sailors who also had found their way into the heart of Andalusia. We met Patton, a self-proclaimed American general who loved to share unbelievable tales about his boys and battles; Diego, a dashing Sicilian with Mafia connections; a soft-spoken Dane, three times divorced, because he couldn't seem to get his boat ready for the big adventure; a 70-year-old retired New York banker, who was having a break from his circumnavigation due to recent hip and knee replacements; a dirt poor hippie couple from California, who had fallen in love with flamenco and everything Spanish and will probably never leave, and finally, a German who had planned his voyage to the minutest detail and had everything under full control. No, it certainly wasn't a boring group!

In April, our journey continued through the Strait of Gibraltar to the Mediterranean and the spectacular anchorages of the Balearics, to mountainous Corsica, picturesque Sardinia and historic Sicily. In Greece, Martin's son Nils and his friend Eric Stockner joined us as

Nor Siglar island hopped in the wake of Homer's Odyssey exploring the ancient waterways of the cradle of civilization. Mid October, our journey temporarily ended with another winter ashore, this time in Turkey, our first encounter with the Muslim world and the mysteries of the exotic East.

ISRAEL
SIGHTSEEING THROUGH THE BIBLE

"Cancel the rally?" The Turkish organizer looked puzzled. "Isn't it too dangerous to go to Israel right now?" we hinted. "There is so much unrest on the Lebanese border. Don't you have an alternate plan in case of war?" "But Madame!" he exclaimed, visibly perturbed. "This is the Middle East! This is life!"

A few days later, the 7th East Mediterranean Yacht Rally took off. Together with 120 sailboats from 20 countries, we crossed the starting line in Antalya. Normally, we shy away from crowded events. But we wanted to visit Israel at the end of our one-year sojourn in the Mediterranean, and didn't have the nerve to sail there on our own. This way we could do it in company with a large, well organized group.

In Bozayazi, our last port of call in southern Turkey, the fleet split up. Half set course for Syria and Lebanon, the rest for North Cyprus. Two weeks later, the participants joined again in Israel to continue the final leg to Egypt together. For safety reasons, the Turkish Coast Guard escorted both groups to Israel.

We must admit that we were somewhat apprehensive about our visit to the Turkish part of Cyprus, a beautiful but conflict stricken island claimed by a multitude of peoples over the ages. Today, the Greeks and Turks are vying for power. Both have deep roots, both are just as idealistic in their cause.

The port of Girne, previously called Kyrenia, was incredibly idyllic. But there was not enough room in the little horseshoe shaped harbour, so we had to tie up below the steep fortress embankments outside. It felt as though we had stepped a thousand years back in history, being moored in exactly the same spot as Richard Lion Heart's fleet during the third Crusade in 1191. We were truly following in the wake of the crusaders.

We encountered only friendly people and did not detect any problems in the picturesque town, which was adorned with magnificent Moorish architecture from the Ottoman era. After a short but memorable stay, we continued towards Israel. The fleet set out before sunrise in order to complete the 170-mile crossing to Haifa before dark the following day. Colourful spinnakers flew aloft in an exhilarating following breeze. It actually felt like a proper race for a while. But the night was stressful. Being surrounded by rally boats, the Coast Guard and other traffic, we didn't get much sleep.

At dawn, as we were nearing the Lebanese border, things started to happen. Two dark spots on the horizon started closing in on us: a police boat and the Israeli Navy. They required notice of arrival within 50 nautical miles of the coast and we had been calling them since early morning. On the VHF a sailor was cross-examined about something he had thrown overboard. "It was just a banana peel!" he replied annoyed. "How can we be so sure of that?" a shrill female voice snapped. "This is Israel!" The episode had nothing to do with pollution. It had everything to do with location. In these waters, they were obviously prepared for the worst.

Helicopters circled us in the skies above. Fighter jets zoomed by. There was no doubt. We were in a war zone. BBC reported that Hezbollah had fired rockets across the border from Lebanon. Israel had retaliated. It was only a few months since the assassination of Yitzhak Rabin, and the election campaign between Netanyahu and Peres was in its final stages. The Middle East was tense, as usual. We couldn't help but think of the organizer's comments. Now it was too late to change our minds. But in the company of EMYR, we felt safer than on our own.

Before being admitted into Haifa harbour, the Navy called us up for the usual details about boat and crew. Then, with a cheerful: "Shalom, Nor Siglar! Have a nice time in Israel!" we were given green light to proceed to the dock.

In Carmel Yacht Club, efficient good-looking women in uniform took care of the formalities. Did we want our passports stamped? Unfortunately, we had to decline. We were planning to visit Muslim countries later. With all papers in order, everyone headed for the showers. Everything was modern, clean and tidy. And in working order! This had not been the case lately. Then we were treated to ice-cold beer and falafel. Maybe this wasn't going to be so bad after all…

The yacht club was well organized, the atmosphere positive. The members were clearly used to teamwork. Each club member was assigned a rally boat and brought their respective guests home. Our hosts were originally from Morocco. They chose Nor Siglar because they had lived in Montreal. It was an unforgettable evening complete with traditional Jewish food and drink, music and stimulating discussion. Holy sites were put in living perspective through a combination of historical facts and present day reality generated by religious complexities. We acquired a deeper understanding of the conflicts in the Middle East during this short evening than we had to date. There is no better way of getting to know one another than within the walls of one's home, the Jews say. They are right.

The family lived in a high-rise in a new settlement on the hills overlooking Haifa, the Mediterranean and the Crusader town of Acre near the Lebanese border. Were they not worried about living so close to the war zone? No, they had been through this so many times before. And generations before them. During the Gulf war, they had experienced bomb attacks every day. They spent long hours in their little emergency shelter, an airtight room in the middle of their apartment where they had first aid equipment, oxygen and masks, water and emergency rations, radio and a cell phone. In the corner, on a small table with a white lace cloth, were a Menorah candleholder, the holy Torah, a yarmulke scull-cap and a beautiful prayer shawl. "You won't survive long in here," Yusef said shrugging his shoulders. "The oxygen will only last a couple of days." During the Gulf war, the windows in the apartment were blown out. Other than that, they escaped with a scare. "I guess it wasn't our turn!" the Moroccan Jew concluded.

After Haifa, we visited the ports of Herzelia and Ashkelon, both sporting new marinas with room for 800 and 600 boats respectively. Luxurious facilities were reminiscent of California's deluxe yacht harbours. As a matter of fact, many things in this fertile little oasis, turned ultra modern state, reminds one of USA. Except the location, of course. In the middle of a desert – surrounded by enemies.

From Herzlia and Ashkelon the rally organized excursions to the

Holy Land, the highlight everyone was waiting for. And what a bizarre experience it was! At the front of a packed bus, our guide, with a microphone in one hand and the Bible in the other, read scriptures to the accompaniment of the Hallelujah chorus blaring over the speakers. Lessons learned way back when, came alive as we made our way to the town of Nazareth and the Church of Annunciation, to Tiberius on the Sea of Galilee and the Mt. of Beatitudes, site of the Sermon on the Mount. We passed fertile kibbutz communes founded by Russian Jews a century ago, and the Golan Heights, which are fought over to this day. We wandered through Capernaum in the footsteps of Jesus and swam in the river Jordan, where he was baptized. I couldn't help but think back to my elementary school teacher. How would she have reacted to all this? Nothing was anywhere near what she had led a small soul to believe.

Jerusalem. Ultra orthodox Jews pray at the Wailing Wall

Did it ever feel odd to go sightseeing through the Bible, to come face to face with holy sites introduced through one's mother's milk; sites, which might not have been perceived as real; sites, which were sort of associated with holidays and family traditions only; sites which do in fact exist: In Jerusalem, we explored the Garden of Gethsemane and the Mount of Olives, strolled up cobble stoned Via Dolorosa littered with gaudy souvenir shops, stood in lines for the

Church of Holy Sepulchre and the Al-Aqsa Mosque, visited Temple Square and the Wailing Wall on the Sabbath, no less, watching ultra orthodox Jews in deep concentration over their Torah. Signs of instability were evident everywhere. Armed guards were posted on every corner. Soldiers with machine guns were patrolling in pairs. Ambulances and military vehicles were ready for action. A teacher, on an outing with his school class, had a firearm slung across his shoulder.

Jerusalem. An armed teacher with his class at the Wailing Wall.

The Palestinian towns of Judea and Bethlehem were only accessible through roadblocks. On Manger Square, we joined a stream of tourists eager to enter the Church of Nativity to pass a marble star in the floor where Jesus was born. Again, nothing resembled images formed in the mind of a child from the frozen north.

We had long been wondering whether we should continue our circumnavigation east about down the Red Sea and across the Indian Ocean. However, after some research, we decided against it. We would encounter an awful lot of adverse currents and winds. Timing, which is so important on a circumnavigation, is more complicated when sailing in an easterly direction. In order to avoid hurricane and cyclone seasons, one has to be at the right place at the right time.

Sailing “the wrong way”, it is more difficult to find hurricane holes and the most favourable time for the various crossings. It is better to have the trade winds astern. We decide to take a few more years on our adventure and point the bow west, back out of the Mediterranean again.

Clutching the coveted EMYR-plaque, we left the rally in Ashkelon. Little did we know then that we were going to be back in four years – as full-fledged circumnavigators.

East Mediterranean Yacht Rally pirates Party in Turkey. The Vikings take second place!

TUNISIA

It's humming, buzzing and vibrating throughout the boat. We have been invaded. There are insects everywhere. In the head, under toolboxes, in shoes and bunks. I panic when a huge bug lands on my face as I am trying to fall asleep one night. When we discover cockroaches as well, I sit down and cry. Our African experience becomes a battle against beetles.

It is always exciting to make landfall in a new and foreign land. When it lies on a new and foreign continent as well, it is particularly exciting. Yet, it was with some trepidation that we approached Tunisia, our first encounter with an Arab land and the African continent. Even so, we had never thought in our wildest imagination that we would receive such an unpleasant introduction.

Other than that, we could not complain about our reception. We had barely finished docking when a hearty "Bon Jour!" sounded from the quay. "Permission to come aboard?" a tall good-looking man called. "First time in Africa?" "Yes, Sir. That's correct," we confirmed. "Here in Northern Africa, we consider ourselves almost European", the Port Captain continued. "Tunisia was a French protectorate, you know."

"Do you have any fire arms, liquor or cigarettes onboard?" he asked, glancing across the interior. "Just some wine and liquor for our own consumption", we replied. That was the end of the formalities. "Bien venu au Tunisie!" he greeted warmly, shaking our hands. "I hope you'll like our country. But you'll probably notice a lot of poverty here. Tunisians don't have as much material wealth as people in the West. However, money isn't everything!" the jovial man smiled. "We Muslims prioritize other things," he concluded, touching his heart.

We apologized for not flying the Tunisian flag. I hadn't been able to make it ahead of time. "Pas de problème! The Harbour office will look after that. Follow me!" The Moorish whitewashed building was identified in both Arabic and French. Once again we were cordially welcomed. We received prompt attention, and on top of that, were given a brand new guest flag for free.

A few days later, we complained about the huge black beetles that had invaded us. The Port Captain roared with laughter. "They're not at all dangerous", he assured us. That might be. But we thought they were awful. In fact, I thought I was going crazy. So when we heard about a three-day desert safari for only 135 dollars, Martin insisted I take a break from both beetles and boat. He himself didn't dare risk a 1000 km drive in a bumpy Land Rover on rough roads. His back had been bothering him for a while and he wanted to give it a rest. The Atlantic crossing was coming up pretty soon and he just had to get better.

The chauffeur, who mad a bold pass at Anne

A Berber woman spinning wool the traditional way.

A safari! An unattainable dream for most people. And what an adventure it was: picturesque Berber villages and the holy cities of Islam, underground cave dwellings and strange lunar landscapes, fertile oases with thousands of date palms, golden sand dunes and the

Partially camouflaged for the desert.

obligatory camelback ride at sunset in the endless Sahara.
But it sure wasn't easy for a woman to travel alone in an Arab country. There was no shortage of exotic propositions. First, our guide Mohammed, a genuine Bedouin, proposed spending the night in the sand dunes under Sahara's star studded sky. Next, our chauffeur Ali made alluring suggestions of the most intimate kind in the privacy of a rustling palm grove. And nally, it was the Berber, Nori, who wanted to see the little sailboat, which brought a middle-aged couple around the world. Safely back in Monastir, I asked him aboard to meet le Capitaine. While Martin was showing him our travels on the globe, I suddenly felt a hand on my thigh under the table. "Does your husband speak French?" he asked with an intense look in his eyes. Shocked, I shook my head. "Well, then – why don't you join me for a walk on the beach?", he continued. "Just you and me – after sunset." Martin jumped high when I suddenly slammed my fist in the table and yelled: "Non, non, non! Absolument non!" On that note, the charmer stormed ashore and disappeared down the dock never to be seen again.

A week later, our journey continued north. We shuddered as the mainsail was hoisted and beetles, cockroaches, grasshoppers and cicadas drizzled onto the deck and shot out from coils of rope, fenders and the dinghy. We were actually thankful for a proper gale for a change. In the wind, we might get rid of the intruders – at least for a while.

Safe anchorages were few and far between. The east coast was exposed to the sirocco, a hot and dusty southeast wind from Sahara. The north was open to the mistral, a cold and squally northerly wind that blows down from southern France. There were not many marinas either. So if one wanted to sail by day only, one had to resort to fishing harbours where yachts were not always welcome. So when we wanted to seek refuge from a mistral in Hergla, we wondered what kind of reception we would get. It was a positive experience. As soon as we were inside the jetty, people came running to take our lines. The officials were professional and polite. We didn't even have to pay moorage. Similar receptions were repeated along the entire coast. The harbours were not particularly attractive, often soiled by oil spills, rubbish and a bad odour. But for us, these stopovers allowed us a glimpse into the real Tunisia.

Hergla was full of fishing boats sporting proud names like Fatima, Hannibal and Saddok, also waiting for the mistral to abate. We struck up a conversation with a group of men relaxing on one of them. They were passing a bubbling water pipe around. "Would you like to try, perhaps?" "No thanks. We don't smoke." "But shisha is nowhere near as harmful as cigarettes!" They were clearly disappointed when we still refused. "In that case, you must at least have a cup of nana with us!" Water for the fresh mint tea was already boiling in a small enamel kettle in a bucket of glowing embers. The mint felt soothing for my sore throat. A large plate of couscous was placed in our midst. There was no cutlery. I declined because of my cold. That was obviously no reason to refrain from using the fingers. It was delicious. But I couldn't help but wonder if anybody caught my cold afterwards.

We reciprocated by inviting them onboard Nor Siglar. The fishermen had never been on a sailboat before. They were full of questions and discussed amongst themselves when they saw something they were not familiar with. Suddenly, a Garde National officer appeared on the dock and ordered the gang ashore. They were not to bother the tourists. "Damned police state!" the guys muttered annoyed as they left.

When the gale had blown itself out, we continued to Hammamet, Kelibia and finally, Sidi Bou Said, the home of the oldest and most luxurious marina in the country. Outside the gates, taxis offered 8-hour excursions for only US$50.00. We concentrated on Tunis and the capital's 1000- year old medina with its magnificent mosque and myriads of souks and labyrinths. Within its ancient kasbah walls, there was bustling activity, loud street vendors trading with veiled women and tourists alike in narrow alleys and colourful bazaars overflowing with brass and wrought iron ware, carpets, mosaics and tiles, the exotic scent of perfume and aromatic spices permeating the air. Here, there was ample opportunity to test one's bargaining skills. A Berber cross for 50 dinares? We got it down to ten. Sterling silver, he said? Here, no one seemed to have a bad conscience. Not even with the Muezzin's call in the distance.

A typical Berber village with homes built from sun dried clay.

Saturated with new impressions, we set sail for Bizerte to check out and provision for the passage to Gibraltar. Already behind schedule, we planned to do it non-stop. Unsafe Algeria did not appeal to us, and we did the Balearics last year. Friends, who wanted to join us for the Atlantic crossing, needed to know when and where to meet. Reluctantly, we set a date for December 1 in the Cape Verde Islands, hoping that nothing would delay us in between. The pressure was on.

WE SEEK REFUGE IN ALGERIA

We are anchored in the lee of Cape Farina in the Gulf of Tunisia to scrub the bottom. With a clean hull, the speed will increase by about one knot per hour, thereby reducing the passage to Gibraltar by 24 hours. We are behind schedule and plan to do the 750-mile passage non-stop. At 120 nautical miles per day, it should take us six days.

I have eaten something that doesn't agree with me, so Martin has to do most of the scrubbing. Even though the water temperature is 25C°, it gets cold after a while. Every 15 minutes or so, he climbs onboard to get warm. When we finally weigh anchor, he feels poorly too. We figure it is the same stomach upset as I have, so there is no point in delaying the departure for that reason.

The forecast is for a high across the western Mediterranean. That's great except for the westerly winds. Gibraltar is due west, i.e. wind right on the nose. We start out slowly in a gentle breeze. After 24 hours we can log only 91 nautical miles. 20 miles off the mountainous coast of Algeria, the wind dies. We must resort to the iron horse. Martin is feeling lousy. A few hours later, when I report to my evening watch, he is doubled over with pain. His face is ashen. He is cold-sweating and retching. "It must be kidney stones," he moans. "I had an attack when I was young and recognize the symptoms". I get him some painkillers. But he can't keep them down. We have no suppositories onboard. Martin is desperate. "Give me some regular tablets. Who knows? Maybe they can be used the same way."

I am scared. Martin must get to a doctor. Fast. I study the chart. Algeria is only four hours away. But do we dare go in there? No, it's too risky. Our safest bet is Tabarka in Tunisia. That means backtracking 60 nautical miles, which will take at least 12 hours. But it is the only sensible solution. We turn around and head back.

After a while, the pain subsides and he falls asleep. It starts to rain. Visibility is poor. Traffic is heavy. I must be alert. We don't have an autopilot, so I have to hand steer as long as the engine is running. At midnight, the wind increases just enough to fill the jenny, so I can engage the wind vane and take a break. It helps my state of mind to be under full sails again. To be at the helm for hours on end is tiring. I set the alarm to ring every 20 minutes and feel like a proper single-hander. Isn't this how the big boys do it? The solo sailors? I realize that I shall never have such ambitions.

At 4 a.m. Martin pokes his head out of the companionway and throws me a package. "Happy Birthday, dear! I bet you'll never forget this one!" He is feeling much better. "You know, Anne, I think we should go back on course and continue," he proclaims happily. But I won't hear it. It's more than 600 miles to Gibraltar. Lots can happen in that time. We must find out what's wrong. Tabarka it is. Martin capitulates, grabs a sandwich, drinks lots of fluids and goes back to sleep.

It's a long night. I struggle to stay awake. Suddenly, in the middle of a catnap, I am aroused with a start. Nor Siglar takes a violent lurch to starboard. We've been hit by a nasty squall. The sky is black. In seconds, the wind pipes up to full gale. It's a struggle to get the genoa furled and the main down. The last few miles become a battle against steep seas and fierce winds. Finally, I see the entrance. It's difficult to dock, but I manage. We have been underway for almost 48 hours, have covered 138 nautical miles and are only 50 closer to our destination.

Martin feels just fine. He wants to take off right away. "Otherwise we have to check in and out with the authorities again! It's such a bother", he complains. "No way!" Now I am really angry. "We're not getting out of here before you've seen a doctor!" "Have you been cold, lately?" the Arab physician enquires. "No, I don't think so," Martin replies. "Come on! Don't you remember how cold you were when you were scrubbing the hull the other day?" I interject. "Voila! You've got a urinary infection, mon ami. That's all it takes," the pleasant doctor confirms, while asking a mere $3 for the consultation.

Despite an unpleasant start, the day ends with a nice birthday dinner at a quaint little café in one of the town's many narrow back alleys. The street is full of men, sipping mint tea and watching a soccer match. The TV is hanging high in a tree for everyone to see. The reception is poor, but the atmosphere great. We strike up a conversation with a young Belgian couple, originally from Algeria. Their parents fled to Belgium after the coup in 1962. "Are there any safe ports along the Algerian coast where one can seek shelter?" we ask. "Hardly," they reply in unison. "Although Skikda, the previous Philippeville, could be a possibility. But only in an emergency," they stress. "We're afraid we must warn you strongly against visiting our native land. Fundamentalists kill innocent people there. Even tourists are not safe."

The medication works and we get a green light to continue. It's Friday. I am superstitious and beg to wait another day. But we are already several weeks behind schedule and Martin wants to leave right away. Even a low across the Balearics producing gale force winds from the west cannot stop him now. Nor another front moving in from the Atlantic. Locally, we are promised a fresh breeze shifting to southwest and increasing by morning. "Perfect!" he chuckles. "Let's go!"

A boisterous passage towards Gibraltar calls for an emergency stop in Algeria.

We set out on our second attempt to reach Gibraltar. Initially, we make good progress, but at sunrise, we wake to a falling barometer and a blood red sky. I can't help but think of the saying: "Red sky in the morning, sailors' warning." And sure enough, shortly after, a storm warning is issued for the entire Western Mediterranean.

In no time at all, the wind is howling and short, steep seas pound away at us. 24 hours later, we record a miserable 108 nautical miles. And not only that. A contrary current has forced us 58 miles off course. We are only 74 miles closer to our goal, a pathetic average of 3 miles per hour! The low is stationary over the Balearics. We change course towards the African coast, hoping to find gentler conditions there. "There you go – we should never have left on a Friday!" I whimper.

Even with two reefs in the main and the genoa half-furled, we are flying. But in reality, we are getting nowhere. We are not able to point high enough into the wind. And the current is relentless, pushing us further and further away from our course line. After two days, we are only 90 miles closer to our destination, a depressing 1.9-mile per hour average. At this rate, the passage will take us twice as long as expected. So when the wind is blowing 40 knots steady, gusting to 50 and showing no sign of abating, Martin suggests that we run for shelter. "We're not making any headway. There is no point in carrying on like this." But this time, we don't have to return all the way to Tunisia. It's 50 miles back to Skikda. We'll give ole' Philippeville a try.

Falling off and running with the wind, we are much more comfortable. In the early morning hours of the third day, we notice a band of flickering lights in the distance. It must be hotels lining the long, beautiful beaches. But no, this is not Costa del Sol. The lights turn out to be flames from hundreds of oil refineries dotted along this hostile and deserted coastline. Not luxurious resorts like on Spain's crowded shores.

At last, we pick out the contours of a city. I make an anxious call on Channel 16: "Skikda Port Control! Skikda Port Control! This is Canadian sail yacht Nor Siglar, VD3296. We are caught in a bad coup de vent and ask your kind permission to seek shelter in your harbour." The answer is prompt: "Pas de problème, madame! Vous êtes bien venue ici á Skikda!" We are instructed to proceed to the old port while a pilot boat is dispatched to meet us and escort us to the dock.

After some confusion, we are allocated a berth directly across from the Port Authority, squeezed in between two huge tugboats alongside a very rough and rickety dock lined with black tires. The surface is marble, well worn from the Roman Era of old Numibia. Skikda turns out to be a large, commercial port. It is bustling with activity from fishing boats and ferries, tankers and freighters, police and pilot boats, tugs and barges. There are no facilities for pleasure craft; in fact, Nor Siglar is the only sailboat there.

The first person aboard is the Port Captain himself. "Don't worry. We'll look after you", he assures us. "I don't know what is known outside Algeria's borders," he continues with a grave look on his face. "We have serious problems with certain groups in this country. These fanatics have killed over 50,000 people in the last four years. So far, Skikda has been fairly safe. But you never know. We'll do everything we can to ensure your safety while you are here. But we can only take responsibility for you within the safety of the port. Therefore, you are not to leave the compound. If you need anything, we'll get it for you."

A steady stream of public servants proceeds to board us. It is impossible to tell who they all represent. Many are from the police – that's for sure. Everyone is polite. Everyone promises to take good care of us. We complete a pile of forms. Our passports are confiscated. "Do you have any weapons onboard?" the Port Police asks. The answer is negative. He doesn't appear to believe us. The boat is carefully searched. Everything is bon, bien, trés bien.

When the formalities are finally over, we climb into our bunk and fall sound asleep. We are dead to the world and don't come to until the early morning hours, when we hear a knock on the deck. "Monsieur! Madame!" It's the Port Captain. "Ca va?" he smiles, handing us a fresh baguette still warm from the oven. "Bon appétit mes amis!" There is no doubt that we are in good hands.

People want to talk and we learn lots about this oil rich country, which is almost half the size of Europe and the second largest in Africa. 85% is covered by desert. Only a narrow strip along the coast is fertile. This is where most of the population lives. With considerable natural resources, Algeria has the potential to be a prosperous country. Still, there is high unemployment and a big gap between rich and poor.

"I am proud to be Algerian," a sympathetic young man declares. "Algeria is a beautiful country. But the government is no good. The rich become richer, the poor poorer. But in general, we have a good life here. We have enough to eat, warm clothes and a roof over our heads. Lack of security is our biggest problem. The fundamentalists want 100% Muslim rule. To accomplish this, they attack innocent people. Nobody is safe here. I have two children and worry about them. Could you help us emigrate to Canada, please?" We get many such requests during our short stay.

That evening, two armed soldiers take up position by Nor Siglar. They are barely 18 years old. However, in combat fatigues with Kalashnikovs slung over their shoulders, you wouldn't want to mess with them. "Is it because of us that you are here?" we ask. They nod. We are to be guarded around the clock – for our own protection.

That night, we don't sleep at all well. Having a machinegun just a few feet from your head isn't exactly relaxing, even if it's meant to be for your own protection. At 2 a.m. we hear voices outside. We peek under the curtains. The soldiers on the dock are talking.

Nor Siglar under 24-hour surveillance in Skikda.

Now they are four. At 4 a.m. we hear another noise. This time it's much closer. The boat is moving. There is someone onboard! My heart thumps. Slowly, ever so slowly, we hear the companionway hatch slide open. It's pitch black. A silhouette appears on the ladder. "What the #$%^&* is going on?" Martin yells, jumping out of the v-berth. The shadow stops dead in his track. There is complete silence.

Then, a barely audible whisper: "Cigarettes, monsieur?"

We turn on the lights. It is one of the soldiers from the dock. He seems more embarrassed than dangerous. But having an armed intruder onboard in the middle of the night in a country like Algeria is no joke. So what do we do now? We try to make light of the situation. "I'm afraid we don't have any cigarettes, but we can offer you a coke," I suggest. The boy appears genuinely relieved. There is no doubt that he was looking for something quite different from cigarettes. We decide not to make a big event of the episode. After all, the soldier is supposed to protect us. We better stay friends. We dress, serve him cookies and coke and chat for a while. Then he steps back ashore and continues his watch. The other soldiers have gone. We refrain from reporting the case. You never know who is in cahoots with whom in this place.

When the muezzin wakes us with his first prayer call of the day, there is a change of guard on the dock. The fellows seem a bit older. "I have been in the contras for five years and have lots of experience," one of them says. Skikda is situated on a hill overlooking the harbour. "Everyone knows there is a foreign sailboat here," he smiles, pointing at our tall mast. We suddenly feel extremely exposed.

People ask us time and again if we need anything. Food is not a problem as we provisioned well in Tunisia. We'd love to get some cheap diesel, though. At 10 cents a litre it's a real bargain. Our request produces feverish activity. After much ado, we are told that it is possible. But we must pay with local currency. That means we have to go to the bank, which again means that we have to leave the safety of the harbour.

Wheels are set in motion to obtain a shore leave. It takes a whole day before all the papers are in order. We may now go to town, but not on our own. Two plainclothes policemen with 9 mm semi automatic pistols under bulletproof vests turn up to accompany us. I am instructed to cover my arms and legs. A woman lends me her shawl for my head. The situation is much more serious than we ever imagined.

We are driven directly to the bank, dropped off right in front of the entrance and ushered past a long line-up straight to the teller. While being served, our escorts don't let us out of sight for a moment; one standing guard at the counter, the other at the exit. The transaction is completed in no time. "Anything else?" they enquire.

"Well, if we are leaving tomorrow, we really should get some bread." I reply. We are whisked off to the bakery. Once again they watch us like hawks. One comes with us inside, while the other slowly backs up the street, his eyes fixed on the entrance. Mission completed, I ask if it is possible to make a quick stop at a bookstore as well. "We'd love to get some post cards and a book or two from Algeria," I plead. But that was pushing our luck. "Non, madame! No more chances now. We don't want anything to happen to you. We'd better hurry back to the safety of the harbour."

After three days we get the weather change we have been waiting for. We check out, get our passports back and ask for the bill. There is nothing to pay. We make up a parcel of old clothes, various and sundry, which we hope will please these friendly people who have been so kind to us. When we enter the Port office to deliver our gifts and say good-bye, it is so quiet you could hear a needle drop. We peek behind a door, which is ajar. And there – right in the middle of the room, the Port Captain is on his knees praying. He is completely absorbed by what he is doing and doesn't sense a thing around him. We are about to leave when his assistant motions us to wait. Prayer is a normal part of the Muslim day. So when the Port Captain gets up and sees us there, it is business as usual. We feel we have witnessed something very personal. He doesn't seem to think anything of it, accepts our gift and walks us back to the boat.

When we are ready to cast off, we hear on the radio that a car bomb has exploded in a busy market near the capital killing 20 and injuring 80 people. Our faithful friends from the port, who have indeed looked after us so well, come running to help us with the lines. "May I come with you?" a young fellow pleads. How painful it is to leave these nice people behind with their serious problems and uncertain future. Algerians certainly leave a strong impression on us.

On our third and last attempt to reach Gibraltar, Poseidon blesses us with benign conditions. Five days later, we are back in Sheppard Marina where we started our Mediterranean cruise a year and a half ago. A huge mail parcel is awaiting us. It's quite an occasion, as we haven't had any mail from home for a long, long time. So there is much to be happy about and to celebrate in this fascinating, fortified bastion, so steeped in history from its "once upon a time" important strategic location under its unmistakable landmark, the Rock of Gibraltar.

OUR MOROCCAN EXPERIENCE

Nor Siglar is in Gibraltar getting ready for the Big Atlantic crossing. She is not alone. There is hectic activity in Sheppard Marina as sailors from all over the world frantically prepare themselves and their vessels for the upcoming challenge. Everyone is anxious to get underway. Everyone has long Maintenance & Repair lists. Nerves are on edge – the atmosphere is tense.

"Replace the standing rigging" is the first item on our list; not a simple task, even under normal circumstances. And especially not for Martin, who has a bad back and is unable to do the job himself. We have to rely on someone else's expertise. So when the rigger arrives and sends his apprentice up the mast, while he himself shouts orders from the deck below, we lose our cool. We realize that the job will take forever. It may not even get properly done. We are already delayed far behind schedule, and voice our concerns. "Yes, but he's got to learn some time," the rigger exclaims visibly annoyed. "Of course!" we counter. "But not on our boat."

We keep going from early morning till late at night. The wind generator, which is completely eroded, is replaced with solar panels. The life raft receives its annual inspection, the emergency beacon and bilge pumps are checked, the engine overhauled, a new toilet installed, the first aid kit replenished, health and boat insurance renewed. We also invest in a new whisker pole for the trade winds ahead, renew emergency lights and flares, stock up on batteries and bulbs, blocks and shackles and spares for every conceivable purpose.

When we think we have covered everything, we suddenly remember something else. To relieve the stress, we ride our bikes every afternoon; either around the famous Rock, or across the airport runway to Spain, where we copy charts for next to nothing and provision at La Linia's colourful outdoor market. The boat is virtually turned inside out and reorganized from stem to stern to make room for new purchases and provisions. We pack and stow, stow and pack, move things from their usual spots, forget where we put them, become miserable and get on each other's nerves.

Celebrating Martin's birthday abeam Europe's westernmost point.

Our two-week stay soon becomes four. At the 11th hour, we trade our Mediterranean cruising guides and charts for those needed in the Caribbean and note the coordinates of a small port in Morocco, in case of emergency. Finally, on October 30, the Skipper's birthday, we're as ready as we'll ever be. But Martin's back is painful. "You ought to take a few days rest," I plead. But no way. "It's my birthday, so I should be able to do as I like, don't you think?" We cut the lines, hoist full sails and set out to sea. The current runs strong in the Strait. But that doesn't prevent a school of playful dolphins from giving us a wonderful show, a lovely start to a long anticipated journey.

As we round Europe's southernmost lighthouse, the birthday boy is celebrated with canapés and gifts – and a tiny shot of aquavit. We like each other again. Things are back to normal. Almost.

For when it's Martin's turn at the helm that night, he needs help to tie his shoelaces. And when he signs off at 0100, the pain is so intense that he can barely climb into the bunk. I keep watch until the sun peeks over the horizon, so that he may have a long rest. But, when I call him, he is barely able to get up. Fortunately, the weather is still good, so he can lie down in the cockpit with pillows under his knees, while the wind vane takes care of the steering. The situation is not encouraging. We consider aborting the passage to the Canaries and deviate to Morocco. There is only one problem: Our small-scale chart is not at all suitable for entering a harbour.

The second night out, Martin's back seizes up completely. He can't get up for his watch. The night is long and lonely. I am not keen to continue alone like this for another 3-4 days with an incapacitated skipper onboard. The following morning we admit defeat. I find the notes from Gibraltar, where someone recommended a small yacht club just north of Casablanca. We check into the British Maritime Mobile Net. The coordinates for Mohammedia are confirmed. It is reassuring to talk to someone who has been there before. "The coast is clear and free from obstructions," radio amateur ZB2IO declares. "Just find the breakwater and go straight in." What a moral support these ham nets are! With an amateur licence and a short wave radio onboard, you are never alone. Help is only a phone-call away, which is an enormous relief at sea, far away from civilization.

The visibility is poor. The air is full of dust from Sahara. Soon a thin layer of orange desert sand covers the boat. I get a fright when I discover the lower spreaders drooping downwards at a strange angle. The shrouds are slack. The so-called experts in Gibraltar have failed to put clamps at the ends of the spreaders. I hesitate to tell Martin. He wouldn't be able to do fix it anyway and would only worry. It helps to tighten the turnbuckles a bit. Fortunately, there is hardly any wind so I can lower the sails and continue under motor minimizing the stress to mast and rig. Only six hours to go. I struggle to stay awake. It's hard when you don't have a horizon to concentrate on. The coastline is low and we can't see land until we're virtually on top of the breakwater. Thank God for GPS and reliable coordinates!

Ever so slowly, I poke the bow around the jetty into a big, open bay. Without a proper harbour chart I have no idea where to go. A fishing boat comes steaming by. "Messieurs! S'il vous plaît!" I call out. "Could you tell us where the marina is, please?" The men ignore me. "My husband is sick," I continue. "Could you help me find a place to dock?" That does it. "Bien sûr, madame! Follow us!"

The fishermen escort us past a large petroleum refinery to a small marina full of cabin cruisers, a few sailboats and the Moroccan Coast Guard. As we approach, two guys suddenly start waving like mad. "Non! Non! Privé!" they yell at the top of their voices. "Excusé moi! The captain is ill," I call back in despair. The mood changes tout de suite. "Ahhhh madame! Venez ici!" We are given a prime spot alongside the Gendarmerie.

Rumours of a Canadian sailboat with a sick captain onboard spread fast in the harbour. People come flocking down to see us. Everyone is kind. Everyone offers help. But there is no space available in Yacht Club de Mohammedia. "How long are you staying?" the Club Manager asks, looking at Martin who can barely move. "As soon as I am mobile," he answers. The next day, a member's boat is put ashore to make room for us.

So there we were. In an unfamiliar little port in Morocco feeling sorry for ourselves. Our mood improves a bit, though, when we discover that we are in good company. King Hassan II has two of his yachts moored right across from us. "You are safe here," a very pleasant Harbour Master states as he clears us in. Genuinely concerned, he enquires about Martin's health, and assures us that we can stay as long as we want. "There is no need to worry," he reiterates. "Since the King has his yachts here, the compound is heavily guarded around the clock. All traffic must enter through a checkpoint."

We receive preferential treatment from day one. The night guard accompanies me to the pharmacy, brings us flowers and mint tea. Suddenly, out of the clear blue, a physiotherapist appears. But after four treatments, Martin's condition takes a turn for the worse. He has lost the feeling in several toes. The pain is excruciating. We send for a doctor. The diagnosis comes as no surprise. "You have a slipped disk which exerts pressure on the sciatic nerve," Dr. Nezha, a young, pretty female doctor confirms and orders complete rest. "Oh no! We don't have time for that!" the Skipper exclaims with impatience. "I've got to get well fast! We have to pick up crew in the Cape Verde Islands 1000 nautical miles from here in less than a month."

In order to speed up the healing process, the doctor decides to give Martin a cortisone shot once a day for two weeks. We enjoy her morning calls onboard. She always brings us goodies; figs and dates, almonds and homemade bread. And she always takes the time to chat. This way, we learn a lot about the people and life style in this country, whose King is said to be a direct descendent from the Prophet Mohammed. We learn that Morocco doesn't have such severe problems with fundamentalists as their neighbour, Algeria. "But what about poverty?" we enquire. During conversations with marina staff, we have been led to believe that poverty is a big problem in Morocco. "Not at all! It isn't as bad as it looks," Dr. Nezha, a typical representative of the monarchy's small elite insists. "It's hard for you foreigners to understand, but the poor in Morocco live quite well. We Muslims are obliged to help each other. It says in the Koran. Therefore, nobody has to go hungry or be destitute in our society. We look after the sick and needy and respect the elders. Nobody has to end up in an old folk's home here. The extended family ensures that nobody is lonely. For us, religion and family are more important than money and material wealth," this very modern Arabic doctor states, while criticizing the western world's treatment of the older generation. Dr. Nezha definitely strikes a tender, guilty chord. We can't help but ask if she also prays five times a day. "Mais bien sûr!" she exclaims surprised. "It's just as natural for me as brushing my teeth."

When the treatment is over, Dr. Nezha exclaims with a bright smile: "Now only rest and Allah's help can get you back on your feet!" But even Allah can't get us to Cape Verde in time for our rendezvous. Our crew is informed and invited to join us after Christmas instead.

Days turn into weeks, weeks to months. Martin shows no sign of improvement. "You must come with me to hammam, capitaine!" an upbeat Abdelhak, YCM's jovial night guard suggests one day. "A healthy Turkish bath! That's all you need.

Then you'll get well in no time. We Arabs don't like doctors. No, we place our trust in a hot and steamy hammam, natural herbs and remedies, not to mention a proper Moroccan massage. And Allah, of course."

He is just fabulous with us, this young man who works 14 hours a day 7 days a week and supports an extended family of ten on a salary of $170 per month. Night after night he brings us dinner from home.

The night guard, Abdelhak makes fresh mint tea onboard.

"Since you're not able to go out and eat good Moroccan food, my wife and mother will ensure that you get proper, healthy nourishment as long as you're here with us," he states with a smile. But Abdelhak won't let us pay for the meals. "It's not us who are doing this for you. It is Allah!" We understand that it is important to be on a good footing with Him. We also understand that if Muslims accept money for a favour, it is no longer considered a gift but a service. It won't count when the points are added up on Judgement Day.

We try to figure out how we can reciprocate this endless generosity without hurting their feelings. There are no laundry facilities in the yacht club. Maybe we could ask them to do our washing for us? Then we could pay them for the food indirectly by giving them a little extra for the laundry. We know they are poor. In addition to his two children, his wife and mother, who, by the way, is also his wife's aunt, Abdelhak has three unmarried sisters and two unemployed brothers-in-law to support. Our laundry comes back clean as a whistle, nicely folded in a large prayer shawl. But there is no way he'll let us pay for it.

One evening, Abdelhak is not his proper self. He has a toothache. "I must pull five teeth," he moans. "But I can't afford it. Besides, I am too scared." We send him off with a jar of aspirin. Suddenly, we get a bright idea. Martin makes a terrific drawing of Abdelhak in the dentist's chair, complete with his trademark Los Angeles Raiders baseball cap. Below, he draws five ugly molars and the amount, 100 dirham each. Then we put the drawing together with 500 dirham in a mayonnaise jar, wrap it in some old T-shirts and hide it amongst the pots and pans that he picks up in the morning, after his customary cup of coffee onboard.

When Abdelhak turns up that evening, he is overloaded with plastic bags containing a veritable gourmet feast. The money is not mentioned with a word. As he is about to leave, we ask if he found anything unusual amongst the dishes that morning. Somewhat embarrassed, he admits that his wife, Saiida discovered the jar first. "She was so delighted that she ran straight to the souk and bought a live chicken and seven types of vegetables before I could stop her! Had I found it first, I would have returned it to you," he insists. We can't help but grasp the opportunity. "Well, you know, Abdelhak, it wasn't us who gave you the money. It was Allah!"

Many more drawings and dirhams found their way into jars hidden amongst used clothing and goodies for the family. We shall never know who received the most pleasure from this game and the relationship that ensued. One thing is certain: For us it became an incredibly meaningful experience, an experience so touching that we shall never forget.

Our dear Abdelhak had only two molars extracted. "But why?" we wondered. We could see that he felt uneasy. "I was afraid," he replied with a sheepish grin. We suspected that he had something else on his mind. Then it came, barely audible: "My neighbour died this morning." The family needed money for the funeral. And since Abdelhak had the cash, he gave it to them. So there went the rest of our money. To pay for the funeral of a complete stranger. "But Abdelhak!" we said rather perturbed. "The money was for you! Not for someone we've never met! You were supposed to use it on your teeth!" "Mais monsieur et madame!" Abdelhak countered meekly. "I had no choice. It says in the Koran: Muslims are obliged to share their wealth. Today I had the cash. Next time it may be me who needs it."

This is how we realized why Abdelhak would never borrow anything from us. He could not guarantee that he would be able to return it. Martin had offered him the use of his raingear as long as we were in Morocco. But non-merci! If someone needed it more than him, i.e. a sick, old man, he would have to pass it on. Now we had the explanation of why the dinner pots some times were half-empty when he arrived at night. He had given some of our food to hungry guards on his way to work.

Seven weeks later Martin's condition is still unchanged. We become more and more depressed. It looks like he may have to have an operation. We discuss the situation with some French-Moroccan yacht club members. They have nothing complimentary to say about the local medical system. "Don't ever let yourself get admitted to hospital in this country", one of the richest members of the club warned. "The standard is shocking. We expatriates go to France when we need an operation."

Couscous with our Muslim friends

We must get home somehow. But how? Martin's radius is limited to a hobble from the forward bunk to the head and back. And what should we do with Nor Siglar? There is no way we can leave her in YCM. Even though people are both kind and helpful, we cannot rely on them to look after our beloved home in our absence. A few days ago, a powerboat sank right next to us. If we could only put her ashore! But the travellift in the marina can't handle sailboats. Maybe we could sail back to Gibraltar and put her "on the hard" there? But then there is the question of weather. December is not a good month to sail north. Not a good idea with a helpless skipper onboard. Day in and day out, we are racking our brains to find a workable solution. The dilemma gets more and more complicated as time passes by and Martin doesn't get any better.

Just before Christmas, his condition deteriorates. He has developed a bedsore. Something has to be done. "Is it possible to have a cat scan

here in Morocco," we ask Dr. Nezha. "Yes, of course!" she confirms. "At a private clinic in Casablanca." An elderly French Moroccan widow, whom we have befriended, offers her help and becomes our chauffeur for the rest of our stay. And what's more – Madame Lili de Bridieu de Chateaubriand lived in Anne's hometown after the war! "This must be fate", she announces. "When I was in Halden, it was me who needed help and a kind family looked after me there. Now it's my turn to help someone from Halden here!"
"This is an emergency! Your husband needs an operation right away. We can do it tomorrow!" the Arabic doctor concludes after the examination. He can sense our hesitation. "We've heard so many horror stories about Moroccan hospitals and are really scared! We'd like to get home," I plead. "Oui, madame, I understand perfectly," the sympathetic surgeon replies. "But under these circumstances, such a long trip is too risky for your husband. Clinique Anoual is a private clinic. All our doctors are educated in France and well acquainted with the latest in technology and procedures. Your husband is in good hands. I'll perform the operation myself." Dr. Amrani is Professor of Neurology at the University of Casablanca. The clinic looks neat and clean. The staff is professional and polite. Martin looks 100 years old where he sits doubled over with pain in his wheel chair. "Let's get it over with," he whispers with resignation.
The operation takes place the following morning. When I visit the patient in the afternoon, he is surrounded by beautiful Berber and Arabic nurses. A dozen red roses adorn his bedside table. They are from the clinic. The foreign sailor receives VIP treatment. He loves every minute of it. The operation is successful, the pain is gone and three days later, the day before Christmas, Martin is released from the hospital.

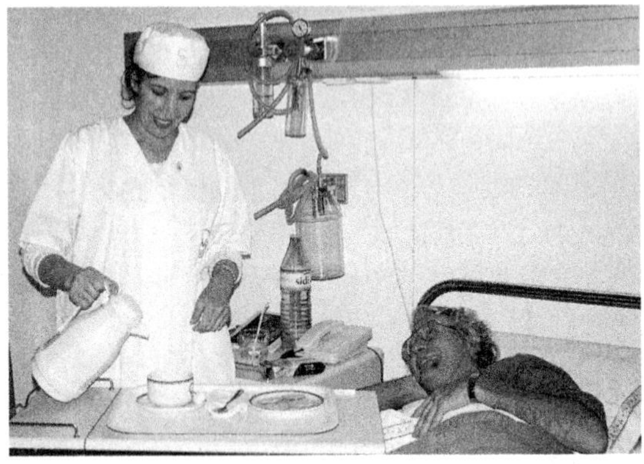
The foreign sailor gets TLC from beautiful Arab nurses.

And what a Christmas it is! Our dear friend, Abdelhak brings us all sorts of delicacies from home, and together with Madame Lili, our chauffeur, we celebrate an unforgettable Christmas onboard Nor Siglar. Abdelhak is in his glory as he surprises us with gifts galore: a nicely framed scripture from the Koran, purple velvet slippers and beautifully embroidered one-size-fits-all underpants for madame, a djellaba and white pleated balloon breeches for his beloved capitaine. And how could he afford all this? Well, it was thanks to the Christmas bonus we had given him, hidden in a jar the day before.

Our dear Abdelhak buys us gifts with the Christmas bonus we gave him.

Martin improves rapidly. As soon as he is well enough, we accompany Abdelhak and his wife, Saiida to the hammam; one for men, one for women and children. The huge public bath is piping hot and steamy, full of stark naked women in all ages, shapes and sizes. Saiida finds an empty spot for the two of us. She then proceeds to wash my hair and entire body with loving care; gently massaging me all over before rinsing me with buckets full of warm water collected from huge tubs with continuously running faucets.

Saiida treats me like a queen. "Ca va, madame?" The look in her eyes is both inquisitive and tender. "Are you ever beautiful," I think. "And what a shame that your husband can't see you now." Saiida is truly a sight to behold, like a sensuous painting, as she gracefully, almost passionately shampoos her long, black hair with exquisite poise. After the bath, we go home to the Sitaf family. We even stay overnight in their humble quarters where the kitchen is nothing but a shack and the toilet a hole in the cement floor. We feel a curious, yet intense closeness toward these strangers, as though we've known them forever. And it is truly unique to be able to observe them as they go about their daily chores. Everything is so different from what we are used to. I never thought it possible to squat all day long cooking for a family of ten on a single burner propane camp stove.

Madame Sitaf squats all day long, her grandchild on her back, cooking for a family of ten on a one-burner stove.

"Is it really true that Abdelhak beat you when you were newly married, Saiida?" I ask, as I watch her preparing the traditional couscous. He had told us on the boat that when they met, she didn't know how to cook, so he had to beat her till she could. "Oui, madame," she answered earnestly. "It's true. I really didn't know how to cook."

A few days later, as we celebrate Ramadan with our doctor and friends from the elite, the contrast between rich and poor feels enormous. The hospitality is just as genuine, but after the overnight stay at the Sitaf 's, the luxury seems overwhelming. It is difficult to forget the poverty around the corner. But one thing is clear: Islam is the common denodenominator and main focus of everyone's existence. All strive to satisfy Allah, all appear firm and unshakable in their faith. We consider ourselves fortunate to have had the opportunity to meet Moroccans from all walks of life. Rich or poor, we have never experienced such kindness, generosity and warmth anywhere else on our travels.

At the end of January, Martin receives a clean bill of health. "But you must quit this sailing of yours," Dr. Amrani declares. "Your back can't take it." A difficult period is past. We are anxious to get going.

Still, we are not looking forward to the departure. Our involuntary delay has become a positive experience. Quite a few people turn up to see us off. But it's Abdelhak who catches our attention. He looks so forlorn where he is standing dressed in Martin's old clothes. "Bon voyage! Merci pour tout!" he calls after us. "Come back soon! Chez nous you'll always have a home in Morocco." We can't help but think of the simple little dwelling. But when it comes right down to it, our friends are not so poor after all. And, of course, it is us who should say thanks. "Shukran, Abdelhak! Yes! We'll be back soon," we promise with tears in our eyes. Insh'Allah.

"Our" Moroccan family rented wedding garb and jewellery to dress Anne as a Moroccan bride.

LONESOME ON THE ATLANTIC

It is February and quiet in Las Palmas on Gran Canaria, where the popular Atlantic Rally Crossing departs for St. Lucia around November 20 every year. By Christmas, rally participants and most other sailors have reached the Caribbean. November and December are the busiest months and the best time to cross the "pond". So it is getting rather late for our own crossing. As the northeast trades settle in for the winter, the wind strength increases as well. Gales are rare, however.

Finally, on February 17, without any kind of fanfare, Nor Siglar sets out on the open ocean. The forecast is favourable: a 15-20 knot breeze from the northeast. Recovering from his back operation only seven weeks ago, Martin has to be careful and not exert himself. Thankfully, his son, Ross joins Nor Siglar for the 5-day passage from Morocco to the Canaries where our friend Pieter Jongeneel arrives for the Atlantic crossing. We are grateful to them both.

Pieter, who forwards our mail and looks after our bills in Vancouver, is an experienced singlehanded sailor. He knows the ropes. Soon, we are a good team, something that doesn't always happen with a new crew. It is important that the chemistry works, that everyone has clearly defined roles and is familiar with the workings of the ship. Otherwise, the atmosphere may become tense in the small floating community. It helps to know each other well. Therefore, we never take on strangers as crew.

Instead of following the great circle route, i. e. the shortest distance between two points, we head for the Cape Verde Islands in the southwest. This is where the trade winds kick in facilitating a course due west. This is also the classic trade wind route, which even Columbus followed more than 500 years ago. His quickest crossing was 21 days. The strategy can hardly be improved upon and is favoured to this very day.

The Canaries are under the influence of the Azores High, a high-pressure system that produces periods of calm and fluky winds. Therefore, it is important to get away from the islands as fast as possible. We are lucky. The northeaster fills in right away. Not only that. By the time the sun disappears over the horizon, it is blowing 30-35 knots. We hope it will abate during the night so we leave the main up with only one reef. We do, however, furl in the genoa. So much for that. By midnight, we have a full gale on our stern and the following waves are growing alarmingly high.

Atlantic gale.

We really should drop the mainsail. But nobody has the energy. The automatic wind vane is unable to keep the course in the rough seas, so Martin hand steers all night. Not very good for his tender back. But in these conditions, he doesn't have the nerve to leave the helm to anyone else. His corset helps. But at dawn he is utterly exhausted. And the wind is not dying down. To the contrary. Finally, through a super human effort, Pieter and I manage to get the sail down. Sick to our stomachs, we both end up hanging over the railing. Then, under reefed genoa alone, Nor Siglar continues battling the nasty seas. At least she isn't overpowered any more. Things are more or less under control and Martin can retire and leave the helm to his seasick crew.

The first four days out, winds gusting to 35 knots blast us relentlessly on our quarter. We have a fantastic start of 570 nautical miles. That is an average of almost 6 knots per hour – very respectable for Nor Siglar and her conservative crew. However, with waves crashing into the cockpit, we get soaked and have to dig out our boots and foul weather gear. We wear our harnesses and hook on whenever we are in the cockpit or venture up on deck. Alone, on watch in the darkness of night, it is scary to think what might happen if we hit a whale or a semi-submerged container at such a speed.

Cold and miserable, we long for the warm and steady trade winds when one doesn't have to adjust the sails for days. Only when we cross the Tropic of Cancer, the wind turns into a heavenly gentle breeze, while at the same time changing to a more easterly direction. Finally, we are in the tropics! The sun is warm, the crew livens up and the appetite returns. Things are looking up. Optimistic, we crawl up on deck and set sails for the trades.

Even though we have covered 33,000 nautical miles, we have not done much downwind sailing. Therefore, we have little experience using whisker poles. Unable to participate in the exercise, Martin shouts more or less welcome orders from the cockpit. It takes a while before his crew gets the hang of the manoeuvre. Stumbling about on a constantly moving surface, I am afraid of losing my balance in the swell and getting hit by the unruly pole. But we make it. The genoa is put alee and the staysail to windward. The main stays lashed on the boom for the remainder of the crossing.

Still, the wind keeps veering from northeast to southeast. So in order to keep a straight course, we have to gybe a fair amount. Just as we think we can settle down for some smooth sailing, another bout of strong wind appears out of the clear blue. And are we ever clobbered. This time, however, the crew is in good shape and ready for action. But the changing conditions are frustrating. Fortunately, the Equatorial current pushes us west at a speed of half a knot, shortening the voyage by a couple of days.

Seven days out, we change course due west towards Trinidad. We enjoy a few reasonably calm days. Finally, the conditions seem to have stabilized. But no such luck. Three days later, about half-way across, we are hit yet again by another low of 30-35 knot winds, gusting at times to 40. Few gales at this time of year? Not our experience. We are completely dejected. Where on earth are the steady trades?

As we struggle to get the whisker poles down, one of them snaps right in front of our eyes. Miraculously, the parts do not fall overboard. With a little jury-rigging, it is usable again. After this intermezzo, the steady trade winds come to stay. Flying the cruising spinnaker, we sail like proper racers for a while. But it is not easy to get a good rest in the following swells. Day in and day out, Nor Siglar rolls 20 degrees from side to side. We calculate that we will be rocking and rolling like this about 5 million times before we reach our destination. A type of exercise we can do without.

Recuperating from his operation and still wearing a corset, Martin services the wind vane on the high seas.

The best place to sleep, with the least motion, is on the floor squeezed in between the salon table and the sofa. The stern bunks are too wide in the downwind sleigh ride. We try to wedge ourselves in place with life vests and sail bags. But it is too hot. Still, Pieter sleeps like a log. The sign of a true sailor.

Galley duty is a challenge and a test in patience under such conditions. One must have good sea legs to avoid getting thrown off balance on the wobbly surface. And it is uncanny how the largest waves always strike when one is about to start cooking. So it is important to keep things simple. A one-pot meal, which can be served in a soup bowl and eaten with a spoon, works best. For it is not at all easy to handle cutlery while steadying oneself at the same time. Things tend to fly in different directions. We don't know how we would have managed without non-skid cloth everywhere. This smart invention has prevented lots of things from ending up on Nor Siglar's deck.

The galley is also the hottest place in the whole boat. It is not very comfortable, especially for someone who is prone to seasickness. It is a good idea to prepare as much as possible in the cockpit. Pieter and I have a great system going. We take turns cooking. Then, he does the dishes in a bucket in the cockpit while I rinse and put them away below.

With a fresh water supply of only 400 litres, it is necessary to ration on a longer trip. On a threeweek journey with three persons onboard, we estimate approximately 6 litres per person per day. As long as we do the dishes in salt water, we can treat ourselves to a fresh water shower every few days. If necessary, we have a water maker that makes four litres per hour. However, it consumes a lot of electricity and doesn't work too well underway.

The routine onboard consists of steering and/or monitoring the wind vane, keeping a lookout, navigating, cooking, eating, cleaning up, fishing, reading, writing, resting and socializing. A conscientious skipper takes daily rounds on deck, checking for loose screws and cotter pins, wear and tear to the standing and running rigging and effects adjustments and repairs as required.

For three weeks, we do not see any other boats or airplanes. We feel we have the ocean to ourselves. The radio is quiet except for weather forecasts and contacts with ham operators in Norway and Canada and a 74-year old solo sailor somewhere in the vicinity. There is amazingly little sea life. Faithfully trailing a fishing line, we only get one Dorado. We don't see any dolphins either, only a Right whale, which gives us a delightful performance showing off with a couple of gigantic splashes before it disappears.

Welcome to Trinidad!

On March 13 we reach Trinidad. It has taken us 23 days to sail 2,982 nautical miles. Once again, Nor Siglar has performed admirably. Her crew is still friends and the Skipper's back has withstood the challenge. Nor Siglar gets a well-deserved rest. We are also in need of a change and fly home during the hurricane season. On our return in October, we spend a relaxing time island hopping and celebrating Christmas in Bequia before resuming the journey to exotic destinations further west.

REUNION IN SAN BLAS
REALM OF THE KUNAS

But isn't that Braulio? It must be him. Never ever have we seen someone with such a broad smile. The muscular Kuna was helping passengers disembark from the cruise ship Grand Caribe at Quinquindup Cay. He looked just like the fellow we met at Chichime six years ago, when we helped a native family transport a deceased man on Nor Siglar's deck to his funeral on the main island of Carti. Was it really he? This wasn't exactly the kind of place where one would expect to run into a familiar face. For we were off the beaten track – in San Blas – an archipelago of 365 little coral islands and the realm of about 32,000 Kunas, where we had been only once before.

Surprise reunion with Braulio and the family we helped six years earlier.

The stocky Indian saw us. We could feel the instant recognition. "Haven't we met before?" he exclaimed.

"Does Nor Siglar mean anything to you?" Martin asked. "Funeral escort in 1992?" Did it ever. "But of course! That was the year old Napoleon Morris died and you helped us take him from Chichime to Carti. How could we ever forget that? Martina! Martina!" he called delighted. "Guess who are back in San Blas?" His petite wife came running down the gangway. Martina's memory was excellent. "Well, hello!" she cried. "Anne and Martin! We still talk about how kind you were to us over at Chichime."

A substantial change had taken place since our last visit. To our disappointment, the cruise ship industry had discovered the beautiful pearls. So it won't be long before tourism will have a negative affect on the unique native culture. Braulio, who originally wanted to become a missionary, had become a tour guide instead. He was American Canadian Caribbean Line's local Kuna expert. Martina demonstrated mola-stitching onboard. The design of this imaginative and colourful multilayered blouse that the indigenous women wear is very complex. Six years ago, we could get a beautiful mola for ten dollars. Now, it was at least twice that. Inflation had accompanied tourism.

The draft of Grand Caribe, which had a capacity of about 100 passengers, was barely deeper than that of Nor Siglar. The ship could tie up to palm trees on the beach and let the passengers walk ashore. The tourists were mostly old and frail. Some were in wheel chairs. Braulio was most attentive. It was odd to see how a local from such a strong native background in such an isolated place could be such a worldly gentleman. The modern Kuna was very busy and didn't have much time for us. "But at Chichime, I can take a couple of hours off," he said. "Can you meet me there?" It would be great to reminisce with him. It was a deal.

We dropped the anchor in exactly the same spot as last time. Not only did we have a reunion to celebrate, but some accomplishments as well: We had circled the Atlantic, the Mediterranean and the Caribbean since our last visit. And like then, women came paddling out to peddle their crafts. We showed them the article we had written in a Norwegian sailing magazine about our previous visit to San Blas. Visibly surprised and with a look of amazement in their eyes, they studied the pictures of the mola exhibit in front of the deceased man's home and Braulio and his family onboard Nor Siglar. They nodded in recognition. Soon, his whole family was there. But what started as a hearty reunion almost ended in a fistfight. Everyone wanted to hold the magazine. Everyone wanted to touch the photos! When Braulio arrived at the scene, there was even more commotion. "This is an occasion!" he exclaimed. "Let's celebrate!" It almost felt like we had come home.

We couldn't think of a better place to distribute eyeglasses than in San Blas where women sew molas all day long.

We couldn't think of a better place to donate some of the eyeglasses we carry onboard. So when we asked our good friend if he knew someone who needed glasses, his face lit up. Many Kunas have poor eye sight, particularly the women, who sit up all night in their dark straw huts sewing in the dim light from glowing kerosene lamps. But first, he chose a pair for himself and Martina.

We were virtually assaulted as we set up our little Gift of Eyesight booth. Kunas are clearly not used to standing in line. So it turned into a chaotic scene. Quick as a wink, little hands grabbed glasses from all directions. Giggling and joking, the small women struggled to get oversized spectacles to stay on their long noses. Was it really possible to see better with these gadgets? Full of scepticism, they scrutinized their molas. It was wonderful to see when they found a pair that fit. Delighted, with brilliant smiles and a stream of incomprehensible phrases, they took off to show what they had received from the gringos. Suddenly, everyone wanted glasses whether they needed them or not. Rumours spread quickly. Soon, we were known all over the archipelago as the yate con lensas.

Nor Siglar at anchor in San Blas.

Nor Siglar was merely a stone's throw away from a small cluster of straw huts on the tip of the islet. We were so close that we could see what they were doing ashore. It was an intriguing and educational experience. Their day started at the crack of dawn. First sign of life was smoke rising from the food hut shortly after the rooster had started to crow. Soon, the smell of smoked fish dispersed over the settlement. The sun had barely peaked over the horizon when men appeared in the door openings, taking off in all directions to attend to their respective chores..

Learning to fish in paradise.

Some armed with machetes headed in amongst the palm trees to collect firewood and coconuts. Others went fishing, either with a rod, a homemade harpoon or throwing nets from the water's edge. Chocolate brown naked little boys ran after to help, learn or play. Young strong men hoisted shabby-looking patched up sails on primitive, but amazingly seaworthy crafts, and set sail for the mainland, where they cultivated root vegetables, corn and rice and ran sugar cane, banana and coconut plantations. The older and wiser paddled quietly around in their dugout canoes, bailing water and fishing as naturally as if they had been doing it for centuries. It was an incredibly peaceful scene.

Little by little, the women appeared. One by one, they yawned out loud, had a good stretch and slowly came to life before starting to get dressed. It was quite a procedure: Beaded arm and leg bands, necklaces and gold rings, mola, sarong and head scarf – all fashioned according to ancient traditions. It became lively around the huts. An old bowlegged woman started tidying up on the beach. Another swept around the huts with a long, dry palm branch. A spry little character split coconuts, which were stacked in a pile to dry. A young girl scrubbed pots and pans with sand on the beach. Laundry was hung to dry, daughters helped and the littlest ones played harmoniously around. The women always had something in their hands and their needlework was never far away.

Traditional cayuko. The Kuna's main mode of transport.

In between the normal chores, squatting on wooden stools around the huts, they stitched their molas, chattering and laughing. Little girls were watching closely, learning how to make the traditional blouse, the very symbol of the Kuna woman's identity.

Mornings were busy in the quaint little community. Afternoons were quiet until the fishermen returned with their catch and the others from their gardens and plantations, their cayukos filled to the rim with firewood and jugs of water, root vegetables and bananas. The place was abuzz with activity until everything was fairly distributed and put away. In the evenings, the oil lamps were burning way into the night. The old man, who was the first one out at dawn, was the last to pull in his fishing line at dusk. The program repeated itself every day. Life seemed to follow the same safe pattern – the way it must have done for generations. We concluded that the Kunas are hard-working people.

We couldn't help but wonder how Braulio liked his job. Surely, it must be quite a culture shock for him? "What a change from life in a small hut to that on a large and modern cruise ship!" Martin said. "Do you like it?" Braulio became reflective. One thing was certain. He did not like sleeping in a bed. It was too warm. His hammock was much cooler, much more comfortable.

We enjoy a delightful visit from well-behaved Kuna children.

"What about the food, then?" I asked. The cuisine on Grand Caribe was supposed to be excellent. "Definitely not! Kuna food much better! Much healthier! Food onboard too fattening. Don't you see how much I have gained?" He was adamant that he would not be influenced by his new environment and lose his identity. "Island life very good", he confirmed. "Plenty of food. Conchs and fish, lobster and octopus, coconuts and bananas. True enough, our entire life is spent putting food on the table and a roof over our heads.

But island ways much better," Braulio restated as he proudly put the fashionable sunglasses we had given him on his nose.

Before Braulio left for new destinations, he introduced us to his cousin Roberto and wife Rosa. They were just as hospitable as he. We felt we had to do something in return for these nice people and asked them onboard one day.

Their children were particularly enthused. And they were amazingly polite and well behaved. They even rinsed the sand off their feet before climbing aboard. Their baby daughter had a rash on her chin so we gave them an antibiotic cream we thought might help. A cheeky little friend was taken with our dinghy. He was proud as punch when we let him take it for a run. The boy, who had never handled an outboard before, was a quick learner.

Local kids on dinghy outing with El Capitan.

In the afternoons, the fishermen came and offered their catch for next to nothing. They had all kinds of delicacies: abalone and conch, crab and lobster, barracuda and white fish. "How about a used towel and some milk powder for la niña for a couple of lobsters? Or some laundry soap, sugar and flour for the crabs?" We had to pinch ourselves. Was this real? Or was it a dream? What had we done to deserve this? Lobster in garlic butter, home made bread and wine. Balmy tropical nights under a star-studded sky. It was pure magic. Orion and the Southern Cross high in the sky, the Big Dipper barely visible in the north, lying upside down and reminding us of where we come from. Our dear, floating home, safely anchored inside a long protective reef guarding us from huge breakers crashing in from the ocean outside. And the view? The most beautiful coral island one can imagine complete with white sandy beaches, rustling palm trees and a cluster of straw huts so picturesque it is beyond belief, all framed by a sea of warm, turquoise crystal clear water teeming with colourful fish in a spectacular under water flora. And last but not least: A unique people providing unforgettable memories. What more could one want? We had found our Paradise.

We could not leave San Blas without calling on Carti. But this time we found the way ourselves. The Chief recognized us right away and invited us to a meeting in the community hall. Did we bring any glasses? "Lensas para mi, por favor," he asked with a smug expression on his face. We didn't have too many left after the onslaught at Chichime. We told him that those left were for near-sighted vision and best suited for younger people. We spoke to deaf ears. Either el cacique didn't want to hear, or he didn't understand. Like a child, he grabbed the box and chose a pair for himself first. Then he gave the rest to his buddies. Thrilled, they put them on right away. Later, during the meeting, the old Chief tripped and fell as he got up to speak!

As outsiders, it was a privilege to be admitted to casa de congreso, the very pulse of Kuna society. Here, important discussions took place and decisions were made every day. Here, all matters, both public and private were brought up; committees were appointed, i.e. social committees for organizing traditional rites and building committees for constructing homes; projects were launched, manpower allocated, responsibilities delegated, disagreements and problems solved. El congreso was also the place for reprimands and rewards. Attendance was optional for women but mandatory for married men.

That afternoon the agenda was as follows: Find a substitute for the sick cook at the dock café, hire crew for the local cargo ship, issue travel permits, mainly to Panama, effect reprimands and levy fines, plan a Puberty Ceremony, and finally, a much disputed emotional matter: should the sale of beer be allowed in the islands?

Many stood up to speak and got involved in the discussions. We were impressed. In the middle of the room, three chiefs were lying in their hammocks gently swinging from side to side, puffing their long pipes and listening. At the end of each topic, the chiefs summarized the facts and delivered their conclusion. A secretary took notes. A treasurer attended to the money matters. Before the meeting was adjourned, a long list of names was called out, announcing who had participated in last week's work on the dock, who had tidied up on the beach and who had donated fish and sugarcane to the last ceremony. Also, whose turn it was to help with the building projects next week and who were fined for having neglected their duties. They certainly don't miss much these democratic Kunas, who are most professional in their own particular way.

On Carti, another enterprising Indian, Glomildo Valles-Smith, made contact with us. "Smith?" we asked surprised. "Yes, that's right," he smiled. Young Kunas are often temporarily "adopted" by Mormon families in the States and given free room, board and education for a few years. When they return, they are expected to become missionaries and spread the faith amongst the natives. It is quite common to take the surname of the adoptive family, or "Smith" after the founder of the religion. Being fluent in English and having acquired experience from the western world, these modern Kunas command a lot of respect when they come back and usually become persons of authority in their community. Not only do they receive money from their family in USA, they also get involved in the lucrative tourist industry. According to local standards, they become prosperous – and the Mormon teachings are soon forgotten.

The day we arrived in Carti there was going to be a solar eclipse in the Caribbean. As we came ashore, we didn't see a single person in the village of 1200 people. It was dead quiet on the little island where the huts are so close that even the tiny Kunas can only walk one at a time through the narrow alleyways. Where on earth was everybody? Aha! They had sought refuge in the congreso! The natives, who are known to be superstitious, were terrified. They thought the end of the world was near. Chiefs had come from afar to perform a special song ceremony, which was supposed to scare away evil spirits and protect them from disaster.

Typical scene from San Blas

"Would you like to come in and listen?" Glomildo asked. Of course we did. "If you buy cocoa for everyone, I am sure you will be

permitted", he continued. So this is how we got to experience a traditional, four-hour melancholy song-play acted out by two old, honourable chiefs lying in their hammocks chanting in the middle of a large dark straw hut packed with their subordinates. Most of the men were half asleep. The women, on the other hand, were busy doing their needlepoint in the dark. Sitting together in a group, they looked spectacular in their magnificent dress. It was quite a sight.
In the middle of a long drawn out chant, some youngsters got up and fetched several buckets of cocoa. Solemnly, they moved down the aisles, each filling a cup, which he sent down the row for everyone to drink. People turned around and nodded at us who were seated way at the back. They obviously knew whose treat it was. I dreaded my turn. Fortunately, not everyone had a drink. So we figured it wouldn't be too impolite to decline. The teenage boys seemed awkward and self-conscious. What else is new? I thought. They react like teenagers anywhere in the world being the centre of attention.

Outside, the whole village was enveloped in smoke. Metal cans filled with dry banana and breadfruit leaves were burning outside the huts. The smoke was thought to keep evil spirits at bay. Palm branches were arranged in crosses above the doorways. Clearly, the Indians attempted to safeguard themselves. Glomildo's house was very quiet. To be on the safe side, he had locked up his dog and cat and covered the birdcage with a sheet. Even animals could be snatched away by evil spirits. The solar eclipse came and went without incident. Hesitantly, people returned to their homes. "Were you scared too, Glomildo?" we asked. He insisted that he was not. "I know better," he said. "I am not superstitious. After all, I am a Mormon, you know."

With life back to normal our new friend arranged a trip for us into the thick of the jungle. First by cayuko across an open stretch of water, then down a narrow stream and finally, an hour's hike through dense rain forest in stifling heat. Considerate, Glomildo chopped the top off a green coconut so we could quench our thirst. The fresh pipa juice and soft white flesh tasted sweet and refreshing. He cut a piece of sugar cane to chew on as well. The sugar would give us energy. The mosquitoes were bothersome. A sobering reminder. It was time for the Malaria pills.

At last we came to an opening in the virgin forest. Women came running out from their huts and stared at us. The children, who were stark naked, kept a safe distance. Hiding behind their mother's sarongs, they peaked out at us with frightened looks. Maybe they had never seen white people before? Maybe they thought we were ghosts?

The children were smeared with something black. It looked spooky. "It's the juice from the genipa plant," Glomildo explained. It protects the skin against the sun and insects." Later, we heard another theory. The children were camouflaged because of the solar eclipse. This way, evil spirits wouldn't see them. Jungle tribes believe that you are invisible when painted black.

Young Kuna mum has covered her baby in black berry juice to make him invisible to evil spirits.

"Be careful in the jungle!" a young fellow warned us. "My mother was bitten by a poisonous snake a couple of weeks ago. She died." He was on his way to her grave with food and water. "You need nourishment in your afterlife too," he said solemnly as he put a plate of rice on the new grave. There was already a pile of cups and saucers, plates and cutlery where the mother was buried with her finest molas and most treasured belongings.

Our experiences were varied and fascinating in this beautiful and isolated corner of the world where tourism is about to reach its oppressive arm and ruin an ancient civilization. A talkative old Kuna explained the impact so far:

"We're getting overrun by tourists! How much is a mola?" they ask our women. Naturally, they respond with a sky-high price: "$100.00?" "OK!" They get $100.00. "How much for your picture?" "Two dollars?" "OK!" They get two dollars. "Our people become greedy. Suddenly, they earn more in a few hours than in a whole year. They buy refrigerators and stoves, televisions and furniture. The young want T-shirts and shorts, baseball caps and sandals. Soon they can't even go barefoot in the jungle any more! Old people don't like that. We warn them against spending money on such frivolous items. For when the tourist season is over and our life back to normal, the money is gone and our stomachs are empty. Why? Because the Kunas have become lazy! They are forgetting their old skills: Fishing, hunting and gathering, growing coconuts and bananas – the very origin of subsistence living, which we have practiced since the beginning of time. A people who loses its tradition loses its soul!" the wise man declared with gusto, slamming his fist on the cockpit table. "But do you know what is worst? Our children. They have started begging. Monni! Monni! they shout, stretching out their little hands. And that is a truly sad development," concludes a very philosophical Mister Robinson, who also calls himself Yachties' Friend, and who more than willingly accepts canned goods and old clothing in exchange for his daughter's beautiful molas.

We just love San Blas. After three wonderful weeks, we virtually have to tear ourselves away from our little paradise. Once again, we have learned that it is the people we meet on this extraordinary voyage which give us the most interesting and valuable experiences.

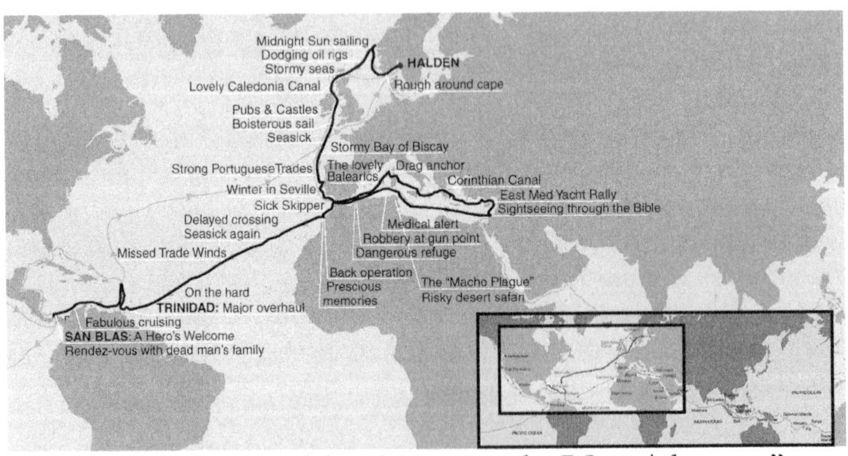

The end of Part 4 of the "9 Years on the 7 Seas Adventure", also published in print and as an eBook with the title **South to Warmer climes.**

PART 5

Opunohe Bayu Moorea. The most beautiful anchorage of the circumnavigation.

PANAMA-GALÁPAGOS

The South Seas! The paradise of dreams! Tahiti! Bora Bora! Even the names sound romantic. Beautiful alluring islands beckon with palm clad beaches, turquoise water and exotic food and drink, rhythmic music, sensuous Hula-hula-dancers and seductive tropical nights. Are we ever looking forward to it all! But when will we find the time to flake out and just relax on some of those wonderful beaches?.

Before setting out on our adventure, we thought we were going to have all sorts of time out there. But it hasn't quite turned out that way. Keeping the boat in a seaworthy condition is taking much more time and energy than we had imagined. Maintenance and logistics are surprisingly time consuming. Often, we are so busy preparing for the next leg that there is little time for much else. And we, who had looked forward to leaving all stress behind! To a life with no clocks, no deadlines, no clients, no boss. Once at sea, however, we were surprised by a whole set of new stress factors. For here, the elements reign supreme. They are in charge. They rule the agenda. All planning and execution must be done in concert with the natural forces.

El Niño is one such obstacle. The phenomenon, which appears every 4-7 years, brings about a massive warming of the ocean surface off the coast of South America disrupting the normal currents and wind patterns. We are experiencing a so-called El Niño year. Many sailors delay their Pacific crossing till next year and head for the Bay of Honduras and Guatemala instead. The alternative is tempting. We love that part of the Caribbean. As we prepare for our second Panama Canal transit in Colon, we weigh the pros and cons. The Canal fee, which has increased almost tenfold since our first transit, is supposed to double yet again by next spring. Also, we ought to complete our circumnavigation before we grow too old. We have been at sea for over six years now. And we're not even halfway yet! Age has become a frequent topic. No, we better keep moving. We definitely cannot afford any more delays.

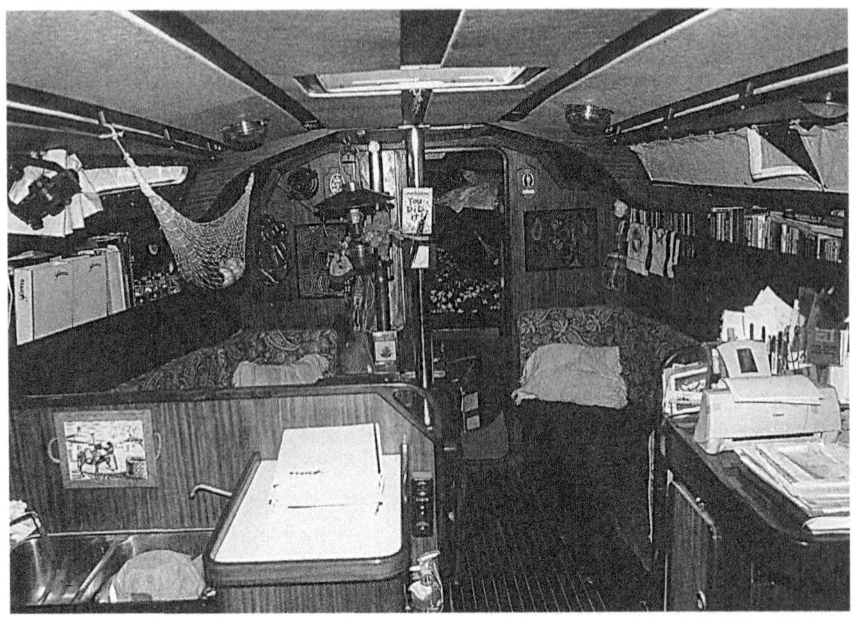

Our home for 15 years.

After several months off the beaten track it is nice to be back in civilization again. Panama Canal Yacht Club has all the facilities an offshore sailor craves. Cool indoor showers are particularly popular in the stifling heat. Washing machines are a rare luxury for someone used to washing everything from bedding to beach towels in a small bucket onboard. Hooked up to electricity, we can read till late at night without having to worry about the batteries. Ice-cold beer and delicious inexpensive food at the yacht club restaurant together with sailors from all around the world are another treat.

But all is not well. The day before we arrived, four bandits camouflaged in black balaclavas and wielding sharp knives robbed the club's bar ordering the guests face down on the floor. Fortunately, no one was hurt. Colon is an unsafe city with high unemployment, poverty and crime. The streets are dangerous. Shop windows are barred, doors locked. Supermarkets are guarded, both inside and out by armed soldiers. Taxis stationed outside the yacht club gates take us safely from door to door.

There are many things to take care of before we can head into the expansive South Pacific. Repair jobs, shopping and paper work become an exercise in frustration in this land of mañana-attitudes and petty corruption. Wild stories of unofficial fees and canal accidents abound. The atmosphere is tense. But as usual, the rumours are exaggerated and our transit proceeds just as well as the first time.

Safely anchored in Balboa on the Pacific side, our ophthalmologist friend, Anne Ziffer joins us for the 1000-mile passage to Galápagos. She comes loaded down with guidebooks, charts and a hundred pairs of eyeglasses, which we plan to donate in isolated places. The gratifying experience from our Gift of Eyesight project in San Blas is well worth repeating.

Hearing that prices in the South Pacific islands are high and the selection of groceries rather poor, we provision heaps of canned goods and staples in the local well-stocked stores. We also stock up on inexpensive first class fruits and vegetables in the bustling markets of Balboa, hoping that some will last us all the way to the Marquesas. With the boat loaded down below the water line, we're finally ready to go. There is only one problem: In all the frantic activity in Colon we forgot to check out of Panama. No big deal, we thought. We'll do it in Balboa instead. But no such luck. When we apply for the exit papers, stern officials order us to return to Colon and start the process all over again there. This would take several days and be very costly. We choose to ignore the bureaucracy and leave without the zarpe. Surely, they won't refuse to admit us in Galápagos and make us sail all the way back?

It turns out to be a typical tropical passage: Variable winds and sudden squalls accompanied by thunder, lightning and torrential downpours. We have plenty of water for a change. It is a treat to be

Equator. King Neptune rises from the ocean to christen the nymphs onboard.

able to cool off in nature's own showers on deck. Naturally, we have a period of light and fluky winds as well. All in all, the conditions in the doldrums, an area of calm near the equator between the two trade-wind belts, are exactly as expected.

And there is no shortage of entertainment: huge pods of dolphins in hot pursuit criss- cross our bows, sleepy tortoises bump into the hull, spectacular meteor flashes and shooting stars provide delightful natural fireworks. At night, we familiarize ourselves with the sky in the southern hemisphere. Midway through the crossing, miles away from land, a tired little swallow settles down onboard. It is completely exhausted and refuses both food and water. We are so preoccupied with keeping the poor bird alive that when we find it lifeless on the chart table one morning, it feels like a personal defeat. The atmosphere is rather depressed for a while.

On day seven, we reach another milestone: The equator! We are glued to the GPS. Will it change automatically from north to south? It does. The next test for our aging satellite navigator will be Y2K. Will it be able to handle that transition as well?

Closing in on our destination the visibility deteriorates. The current becomes noticeably stronger. Something dark appears on the horizon. Is it a ship? Or is it land? We are reminded of how dangerous it was for the sailors in the olden days to make landfall without reliable aids to navigation. But we know exactly where we are and realize that we have something very special in store when the ocean around us starts teaming with life. Soon, Nor Siglar is surrounded by hundreds of dolphins, sea lions and seals. Irate pelicans swoop down on us. It is a thrilling welcome with such a lively escort for the last few miles in to Santa Cruz Island where we drop anchor in Academy Bay after eight days at sea.

Yet another dream has come true: Galápagos – this fascinating archipelago whose unique fauna inspired Darwin to create his famous Theory of Evolution – and which even has a Norwegian settlement on its barren shores.

GALÁPAGOS
SLEEPLESS IN PARADISE

Galápagos, which means turtles in Spanish is also called the Colombus Archipelago. Once known as the Enchanted Isles, the volcanic islands, which belong to Ecuador, were subject to a variety of activities during the ages. Mutineers were left behind, castaways sought refuge and pirates buried their stolen treasures on the rugged and desolate shores.

For us, it was the unique fauna, which lured us there, especially the giant tortoises, which Galápagos is so famous for. But first we had to check in. Having left Panama without the proper exit documents, we were rather anxious about these formalities.

The harbour office was abuzz with soldiers in army fatigues scurrying about. They were fussing over self-important officials in white uniforms with gold stripes on their epaulettes. The Port Captain took himself very seriously. "No zarpe?" he exclaimed perplexed. "No hay," we confirmed. "No pink paper?" he continued with a growl. All we could do now was plead ignorance. Why on earth had the Panamanian authorities failed to give us the crucial zarpe? We had been to all kinds of offices and paid lots of balboas for all sorts of stamps and papers. "So sorry," I whispered.

El jefe knew to make the most of the situation. The important matter had to be discussed at a higher level. Disappearing behind closed doors, he left us waiting for what seemed like an eternity. When he finally returned, he had a dead serious expression on his face. During a rambling dissertation in a mixture of broken English and rapid Spanish, we understood that he had a brother who was in the business of selling water and diesel. So it was possible to make an exception. But on certain conditions. "Comprende?" he whispered with a smug wink. Of course we understood. We had a deal.

The tune changed instantly. "How long do you want to stay in

Galápagos?" he asked in a friendly way. The question puzzled us. Length of stay and number of visitors are restricted and carefully controlled in this archipelago where protection of the rare wildlife and environment is of paramount importance. For offshore sailors, a 3-day permit had been the norm lately. So that was all we expected. "As long as possible," we tried. "How about ten days?" he suggested. Incredible! Other sailors, who had spent lots of time and money obtaining a visa ahead of time, got ten days as well. It didn't matter whether the papers were in order or not.

Academy Bay, named after an American research vessel that called there in 1905, is a roomy but uncomfortable place to be anchored. The bay is open to the southeast and exposed to constant swells from that direction. So there were many sleepless nights onboard Nor Siglar and close to fifty other yachts, as we were rolling, heaving and swinging on our bow and stern anchors in the unprotected bay.

The elegant pink flamingos of Galapagos.

The Ecuadorian authorities take their custody of this very special wildlife sanctuary seriously. Striving to protect and keep the islands in their natural state, 90% has been declared a national park. No wonder the atmosphere is so peaceful. Private yachts are not allowed to sail around on their own unless they have an official guide onboard. Another option is to take a trip on a local excursion boat. We were worried about leaving Nor Siglar unattended in the exposed and busy harbour and settled for a few land-trips by jeep instead.

The countryside waiguanas lush and green, the gravel roads muddy and bumpy. Prickly pear cacti as big as trees and the endemic weed-tree, Scalesia dominated the highlands. In the little settlement of Bellavista we ran into the young woman, Maria Kastdalen, whose grandfather, Thorvald emigrated from Norway in 1935 when her father, Alf was ten years old. She spoke surprisingly good Norwegian. "My grandparents taught me," she said with a shy smile. Clearly proud of her heritage, she gladly talked about her ancestors and what they had done for the community so far away from home – and so different from the one they had left behind.

Marine iguana and red crab – some of Galapagos' many fascinating creatures.

How could a family from a thriving rural district in Norway end up on such a distant lava encrusted island, we wondered. "Well," Maria replied softly. "It was just before the war and times were tough in Norway." When the adventurous farmer and his neighbour saw an exciting article about Galápagos in National Geographic, they decided to try their luck there. But it was easier said than done.

To build a farm on these barren shores where trees are few and far between, the Norwegians had five tons of timber shipped there from their homeland. "My father and grandfather built the road from Puerto Ayora to Bellavista as well," she continued with pride. "It is 7 km. long. But they died far too young," she sighed. "Papa was electrocuted in a lightning storm when he was only 58 years old. Now, my brother Torbaldo runs the farm. He has 200 cows, pigs and goats. He also grows fruits and vegetables and even has a small coffee plantation. It's because of us that milk is called leche noruega on Galápagos!"

We showed Maria a picture of her brother in a book written by some sailors who had been to Galápagos a few years ago. She burst out laughing. "Torvaldo is fat now!" she exclaimed. "He doesn't get enough exercise! He is lazy!" "Doesn't he get plenty of exercise on the farm?" we asked.

"Not at all! Torvaldo is el jefe! These days farm hands do the work! Today, the farm is run Ecuadorian style," Maria explained. Her family is still known as los ultimos vikingos on Galápagos!

Rare encounter with a giant tortoise in the wild.

Hiking through the bush, we ran into our first giant tortoise in the wild. We just about tripped over the monster, which was lying in the middle of the path well camouflaged in the landscape. It was fascinating to be so close to this amazing creature, which sleeps 16 hours a day and spends the rest of its time gathering food in a 100-metre radius. Being an excellent source of food, 19th Century seafarers heavily depleted the numbers of the slow reptile which could live up to a year in the ships' holds without food and water.

At Charles Darwin's Research Station we came face to face with more tortoises. Living in captivity, they were used to an audience and willingly stretched their long and scraggly necks towards us, grabbing the leaves we ventured to feed them. With luck, one might see some of Galápagos' eleven remaining species rummaging around in the shrubs and bushes at the institute, the most famous being Lonesome George, the last of his species from Isla Pinta. A price of 10,000 dollars is promised the person who can find a Pinta female for Lonesome George so that the species may be continued. However, chances of finding him a Pinta partner are tiny. At 90 years of age, weighing 100 kilos, George is still in his prime. Yet, attempts at mating him with other sub-species have failed. He is more interested in competing for their food than bodily pleasures. So the rare Pinta tortoise is most likely heading for extinction.

The rocks and boardwalks around Academy Bay were alive with prehistoric-looking marine iguanas crawling around and chasing scarlet crabs. It was fantastic to observe these fascinating lizards in their natural element. Many were more than a metre long. Life in the sea, however, was not as abundant as it used to be. Because of El Niño, the water was ten degrees warmer than the normally cool temperature caused by the Humboldt Current, and fish and other marine life had either migrated north or died. Therefore, there were also fewer sailors and tourists in Galápagos that year. But we were not disappointed. We felt as though we were in the middle of a virtual zoological garden. Back on the boat, a friendly pelican had settled down on the pulpit. Boobies crowded the spreaders. Three curious seals had confiscated our dinghy. At first, this was just plain fun. After a while, however, they became a real nuisance. When we wanted to go ashore, it was a struggle to get rid of these heavy, lazy and foul smelling uncooperative creatures.

We were getting rather anxious about our passage ahead, the longest non-stop stretch of our circumnavigation. Not only that. We were going to do it on our own. And it didn't help matters when I suddenly threw my back out. I couldn't move. To top it off, Martin developed a nasty infection in his finger. Talk about bad timing! Fortunately, the Port Captain extended our visas without any problems. It took two weeks before Martin's finger was healed and I was back on my feet again. The unexpected extra time was well spent checking out our first aid gear, man overboard equipment and grab bag, and brushing up on our emergency drills at sea. The only bright moments during this period were the daily contacts with family and friends back home ably assisted by keen radio amateurs of the Mississauga Maritime Mobile Net and the DDD Cruisers' Net in Victoria.

While awaiting our departure, we monitored the boats that were already underway. Every morning, the skipper on Sea D, an Australian yacht with Inmarsat onboard, read the weather forecast and recorded the positions of the approx. 30 sailboats that were out there. There were frequent reports of lows in the southwest. El Niño was blamed for generating exceptionally strong squalls and unseasonable tropical storms in an area, which should not be affected at that time of year. Especially troubling was an unconfirmed report that a cyclone had clobbered a small coral island in French Polynesia. Eight people had died, 20 were lost. Not very encouraging news when you are about to head out in the same direction yourself.

CROSSING THE PACIFIC FROM GALÁPAGOS TO THE MARQUESAS

Finally, on April 20, we hoist the anchor and set out into the wide-open ocean. We program our first waypoint at 4° S and 95° W, a course that should enable us to cross the doldrums as quickly as possible. At 7° S, we'll turn due west. A pod of energetic dolphins accompany us out of the bay, setting the scene for a delightful send-off.

Little by little we fall into our offshore routine. The watches are organized according to the radio schedule. Wanting to check in to the nets back home, I take the first shift between 04:00 and 08:00. I mostly listen, as I don't want to disturb Martin who is trying to sleep on the floor near the chart table. During my afternoon watch between 16:00-19:00, I check in to the Sea D net and pass on the weather forecast and other news to Santana, a 38-foot Swedish Najad, who doesn't have a shortwave radio. We also exchange positions and discuss everything from sail combinations to what we are going to have for dinner. We are always hoping for fish, but are not having much luck even though we are trailing a line all day.

For the first time in history, I don't get seasick the first day out and can perform my galley duty right away. But my back is still tender. I have to watch that I don't sit too long or lose my balance. That is easier said than done on the constantly moving surface. The corset helps a bit. But it is extremely uncomfortable in the stifling heat.

We find that the Pacific is not pacific at all. The weather is mostly overcast and rainy and the southeast trade winds are not as steady as they are supposed to be. Apart from the squalls, which come from the west, the winds keep shifting from south south-east to south-east. The strength is anywhere from 5-10 and 30-35 knots. In the worst squall, which lasts a couple of hours, we experience storm force winds gusting to 55 knots. So the dream about leaving the sails for days on end without having to touch them does not materialize. In variable winds and a current that pushes us steadily northwest, we have to alternate between two foresails wing on wing, and a poled out genoa to port with the main to starboard. The two whisker poles are awkward to handle in the swell.

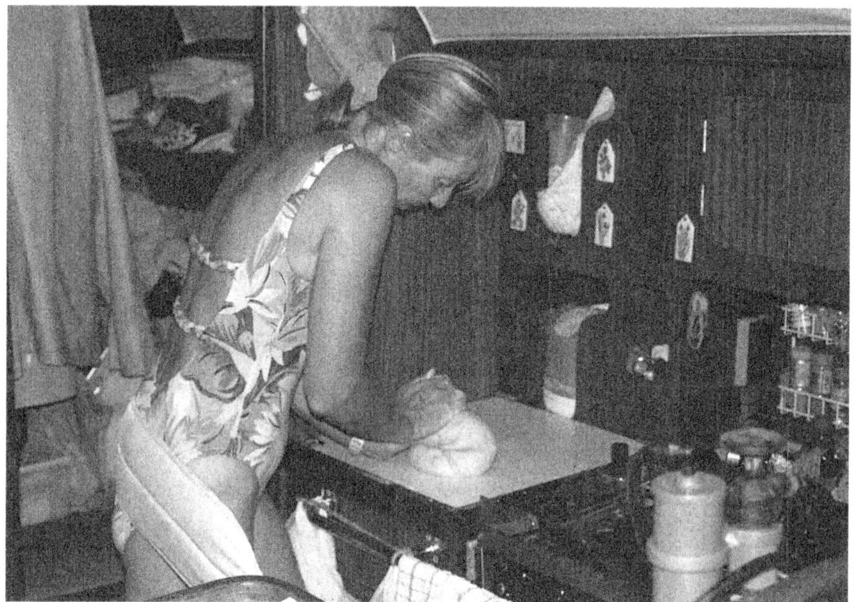

Baking bread at sea. It's important to be strapped in. Otherwise one could easily tumble in the "rock'n roll" ride.

While we are going great guns, Santana, who is only a few miles behind, doesn't have any wind at all. It is very frustrating. To enable her to keep up, we furl in the genoa and sail on the main alone. For it is comforting to have company on the open sea. At night, we tuck in behind the Swedes, who have a tricolour lantern at the top of their mast. It is so much easier to steer following a light in the dark.

Martin has trouble getting enough rest. Being a light sleeper at the best of times, he is extremely wary and spends half his time off trying to stop the constant racket from clattering cutlery and dishes trying to decide which bunk is the most comfortable before finally settling down. Actually, being a light sleeper can be beneficial at sea. That way potential problems may be detected early and corrected before they get out of hand. About half way, Martin becomes aware of an unfamiliar sound; a strange kind of squeaking noise. It is not at all normal. And sure enough, the cross beam, which supports the mast has started to slip away from the compression post. He makes a temporary reinforcement by drilling four bolts through the deck. After that, we sail even more conservatively in order to minimize the pressure on the rig.

Wing on wing. The best way to sail in the southeast trades.

One day, we pick up a scary Mayday distress call on channel 16. It is from Moon Shadow. She has hit a reef in the Tuamotus and is sinking. Fortunately, the crew is rescued. We get a serious reminder that charts are not reliable in these waters where navigational aids are either non-existent or ruined by cyclones and where land can be several miles off its charted position.Ariaka, an Australian sailboat with a singlehander onboard, has not checked in to the cruiser's net for several days. Boats comb the area where she last reported her position and call her on the VHF at regular intervals. Sea D contacts rescue centres in Australia, Peru and USA. But nobody turns up. The missing vessel is too far offshore. We hope that Ariaka is just having problems with her radio. But she is never seen again.

At 130° W, we intersect the so-called coconut route from Mexico to Polynesia. A Canadian, who has been underway for 35 days and has run out of fuel, is looking for someone who is willing to spare some diesel. An American family makes a detour in the middle of the night and transfers 100 litres in the dark. We have already used up nearly half of our 200-litre supply in the first week and have to be very frugal. At the end, we still have half a tank left.

After dinner, we prepare a couple of thermoses, some snacks and goodies for the night. Time passes faster and it is easier to stay awake when you have something to do. The routine is basically to comb the horizon at 10-minute intervals. Then, it is back to the Walkman and a book nicely lit by a miner's lamp. Safety harness and boat shoes are on, flashlight and binoculars are in their respective places. Sheets are neatly coiled. It must be tidy in the dark. Everything must be ship shape and ready for action.

At every change of watch, we brief each other on the course, wind speed and direction and make potential sail changes. If we are lucky, only small adjustments need be made. The person coming off watch updates the log and works out how many miles we have covered and how many we have left. It is exciting to monitor the progress. Every 15° of longitude, we move our clocks back one hour. At Nor Siglar's average speed of five knots, that is roughly once a week.

A birds-eye view of Nor Siglar showing her wind vane asten, four solar panels on an arch behind the cockpit, a permanent dodger and a blue awning.

We've seen no traffic for a long time. Other sailors don't bother keeping watch. It is tempting to follow suit. Being only two onboard is very tiring. But we take no chances. Besides, night watch on the open ocean is a fascinating experience.

I never tire of lying in the cockpit staring up in the star-studded sky. My thoughts tend to wander. Childhood memories, family and friends, jobs and colleagues come to mind. Philosophy, religion and all sorts of ideas swirl around in my head. Lately, we have become preoccupied with what we are going to do after we finish our circumnavigation. It suddenly occurs to me that if we change course towards Hawaii now, we can be home in B. C. in a couple of months. After a particularly nasty squall, this seems like a good idea. But not for long. We have also been toying with the idea of leaving Nor Siglar in the Caribbean somewhere and using her there during the winter months. Or we could finish our adventure in Norway. It would be pretty nice to have a floating summer home in the old country. Maybe we could even realize the dream of sailing to the North Cape. But time flies. If we take just as long on the second half of our journey as the first, the circumnavigation will end up lasting 14 years! Martin draws the line at ten. Age has suddenly become a factor.

On May 14, 24 days and 2966 nautical miles after we left Galápagos, we reach the lush and green tropical cliffs of Hiva Oa, relieved that boat and backs have withstood the challenges of the passage. "Never ever have I slept so little over such a long time!" Martin scribbles in the log. Finnish friends welcome us with fresh baguettes and huge pamplemousse. Soon, everyone is onboard for a celebratory drink. Ashore, we catch a glimpse of bronze coloured husky men and heavy-set women with flowers in their hair. Exotic music permeates the bay. Yes, we certainly have something very special to look forward to in legendary Polynesia.

FRENCH POLYNESIA
MARQUESAS
THE RUGGED ISLES OF THE SOUTH SEAS

"Kaoha! Bienvenu! Wanna lift?" A huge roly-poly size XXXL woman with a dark bronze complexion and white frangipani in her striking jet-black hair waved us aboard. "Come on!" she called with a brilliant smile. "Allez!"

It was high noon and blistering hot in the midday sun. We were dripping with sweat as we walked along the dusty gravel road leading to Atuona, the capital of Hiva Oa, to check in to French Polynesia. Even though it was only a one-kilometre walk and we needed the exercise after the long passage, we were happy to accept. Grateful, we climbed on to the back of the brand new 4x4.

The breeze felt good as we sped up through velvety green hills and villages partially camouflaged by lush vegetation. The houses were well kept and surrounded by a profusion of flowers. People obviously enjoyed keeping it nice around their homes. The air was sweet and heavily laden with the perfumed scent of flowers and herbs: Ginger, oleander and frangipani, hibiscus and philodendron. Tropical plants growing wild along the roadside looked like the ones we use in our houses and offices back home. There was an amazing variety of tropical fruit: lemons, oranges and bananas, mangoes, papayas and pamplemousse, the latter being the wonderfully juicy and large Polynesian grapefruit. Huge ferns, tall palms and giant breadfruit trees provided welcome shade.

In Atuona, sweet little charmers peaked out through dense foliage laughing and giggling. A cheeky little rascal stretched out a chocolate brown hand: "Bonbons, s'il vous plaît?" His gorgeous brown eyes were pleading. Soon we had a long tail of boisterous children behind us. "Where is the gendarmerie?" we asked. Utter pandemonium ensued. Everyone wanted to show the foreigners the way.

Bora Bora. Relaxing in paradise.

At the police station, we were ordered to make a deposit equivalent to the airfare home. The reason for this unpopular bond, which only exists in French Polynesia, is that many travellers take advantage of the local hospitality and outstay their welcome. The offenders, who often come as crew on private yachts, disembark, stay on and become a burden to the society. When their visas expire they don't have the money for the return trip home.

Next stop was the clinic where we wanted to seek advice on the local diseases. Elephantiasis, which is caused by parasitic worms transmitted by mosquitoes, is still known to exist in some of the islands. Scary-looking posters showing grotesque cases of the horrible illness were all over the place. A young doctor from France prescribed a preventative medicine, assuring us that if our legs became swollen it was not elephantiasis but a natural reaction to the immunization. We were also informed of dengue fever and urged to cover up at dawn and dusk and apply insect repellent to both skin and clothing to avoid being bitten by the disease carrying mosquito. The local sand flea, No-See- Um, although bothersome, was not dangerous. Not all is idyllic in paradise.

We were fully expecting French Polynesia to be expensive. Still, we couldn't believe it when we had to pay $25 to send a fax home. The Pacific franc sure was attractive though. Exotic beauties with flowers in their hair and macho tattooed men adorned the bank notes. Even the stamps were pretty. Like the locals, they were oversized too. Complete with colourful flowers, fruits and alluring vahines, they looked like mini-paintings. Beauty is very much in focus in Poly Nisos, which means many islands in Greek. It certainly has lured many people to its distant shores. French painter Paul Gauguin and Belgian singer Jacques Brel spent the latter part of their lives in these islands. They are both buried in Atuona's beautifully located cemetery perched on a hill overlooking the village and the azure blue sea.

After a gigantic clean up both onboard and below the waterline, we rented a jeep to visit the little village of Puamau known for its marae, an ancient ceremonial place and the location of Polynesia's biggest tikis. Following the peaks of the island, sometimes at an altitude of 1000 metres, we enjoyed the most spectacular views of the wild volcanic landscape. After three hours and 40 km on a winding, narrow and muddy road we finally stood face to face with Polynesia's revered gods. Some were several metres high. The tikis, which were carved in stone, were amazingly similar to Haida Indian carvings and totem poles, suggesting a strong connection between the Coastal Indians of the Pacific North West and the Polynesians. The theory that the Polynesians may have come south from Canada's west coast in favourable winds and currents seems reasonable considering how the two peoples also bear such a striking physical resemblance to one another.

We only visited two islands in the Marquesas. The deep and unsafe anchorages became too much for us. So after only two weeks, we set course for the peaceful lagoons of the Tuamotu Archipelago instead.

THE TUAMOTUS
THE DANGEROUS ARCHIPELAGO

The sun was high in the sky, i.e. in the north at this latitude, as we set sail for the Tuamotus about 500 miles to the southwest. Hana Moe Noe, a lovely horseshoe-shaped bay on the islet of Tahuata just south of Hiva Oa lay bathed in the glow of a magnificent double rainbow, forming a picturesque frame around the boats at anchor.

Not far from this peaceful scene, the atmosphere changed drastically. We had barely hoisted the sails when a nasty squall, which we had monitored and hoped to avoid, hit us with a vengeance. The sails came down in a flash and the flag – we have worn out eight so far – was lashed around the backstay. Then, faithful as ever, good old Nor Siglar carried on out into a sea of whitecaps and breaking waves. A relentless southeasterly gale with gusts to 50 knots kept us on our toes for a few days. We really had to struggle to keep the course in the strong headwinds and northwesterly current. This was not the Pacific we had expected. Was El Niño still to blame?

Suddenly, in a mist of cloud and foaming spray, the French Navy appeared out of nowhere. Closing in on us astern, blasting their foghorn, they scared the living daylight out of us. The encounter was not entirely unexpected, though. Because of nuclear testing at the Moruroa Atoll nearby, the Navy was actively patrolling the area. Only French boats were allowed in the southeastern end of the chain. Posing the usual questions, the officers were both courteous and friendly, concluding the interrogation with the latest weather forecast. It was not uplifting. Several lows in the west were coming straight for us.

After four incredibly long, rough and tiring days we picked up Ahe, our first atoll in the South Seas, in the binoculars. An atoll is a ring of coral reefs in the open sea formed on the crater of an underwater volcano. Remaining above the surface is a chain of islets that nearly, or entirely, encloses a lagoon. These are the so-called motus, the romantic islands with swaying palm trees and white sandy beaches, which often appear in tourist brochures and which so many of us associate with Paradise.

But it is not easy to make landfall in this paradise, popularly called the Dangerous Archipelago. The visibility is poor and the atolls low and difficult to see until you are very near. Charts are unreliable and rarely correspond with the GPS in this labyrinth of isles, which sailing ships avoided in the olden days.

Wrecks are littered on the nasty reefs. In 1947, Thor Heyerdahl's Kon Tiki ran aground on Raroia atoll. His famous balsa raft expedition proved that Peruvian Indians could have sailed to Polynesia.

There are many wrecks on the treacherous reefs – a scary reminder of how careful one must be navigating in the dangerous area that sailing ships avoid in the older days.

So no wonder we were extremely careful as we approached the atoll in the early morning hours. First, we had to find the opening in the reef. Then, the pass had to be negotiated at the exact right time, i.e. when the current was at its weakest. We arrived at the entrance in good time and waited for the tide to turn. The pass was narrow, shallow and full of coral heads. There were no markers so we had to do eyeball navigation. With the sun behind and a lookout on the boom, we made it. But we readily admit that our nerves were on edge before we were safely inside in the calm lagoon.

The Tuamotus consist of 78 islands scattered over an area 600 km wide and 1200 km long. The archipelago, which is the largest group of atolls in the world, has a population of approx. 15,000 people.

Scarcity of land and fresh water is a problem. Consequently, only 45 islands are inhabited and only a few hundred people live on some of the dry, palmtree-covered motus. The population of Ahe was only 400. A little girl offered to take us around the sleepy village. It had two small shops, a post office, a primary school, a community hall where the islanders met at night and three churches. Obviously, the islanders in these isolated communities must be quite religious.

Scouting for a safe passage through the reef.

Apart from a few bicycles, there were only pedestrians on the two narrow gravel paths of the motu. Piles of split coconuts were drying amongst the citrus, breadfruit and palm trees. It was neat and tidy in the modest settlement, which had been rebuilt after a cyclone destroyed it in 1982. Built on poles, the small houses, separated by nicely trimmed croton hedges, were bleached by the salt spray from the sea. All the homes were equipped with solar panels and a cistern. Many appeared to be abandoned. We wondered why. It also struck us that there were so few children around. It turned out that whole families migrate to the larger islands, i.e. Rangiroa and Tahiti, when their children start secondary school. The isolation of the remote atolls causes many not to return.

Originally, only two families settled on Ahe. Today's population consists of their descendants and a few other families. On our reconnoitring round, we clearly detected signs of inbreeding. We struck up a conversation with a friendly gendarme. "Everyone is related!" he explained. "It's not easy for our young to find a matc here. There is a fair amount of crime, alcohol and drug abuse too," he continued. "Yes, I know it feels like paradise to you. But looks can be deceiving. And it is all because of the pearl production", he stated. "People have too much money. They are spoiled! In the old days, people were unhappy because they didn't have enough money.

Today, they have lots. But they are still unhappy! Before, people looked after each other. Nowadays, they go to the bigger islands where they think life is better. But, as we all know, the grass is seldom greener on the other side of the fence. At the end of the day, the old folks usually return," the informative police officer concluded.

A typical atoll – a ring of coral reefs form on the crater of an underwater volcano and create a shallow lagoon.

The proud Tuamotuans have always survived on seafood, pandanus- and coconuts. Not long ago, they free-dove to depths of 30 metres for mother-of-pearl shells. Today, however, oysters are overharvested and cultured-pearl farms have sprung up instead. Every morning, modern Boston Whalers full of workers whisked by our anchorage and out into the lagoon to the international pearl farms. The black pearls of the Tuamotus have become world famous. Cultured-pearl production has become big business in paradise.

We were shocked to learn that more than 400 species of the local reef fish were contaminated and known to cause seafood poisoning. The fact that ciguatera did not exist before the nuclear testing started leads to suspicions that the program may be responsible for this development.

One can easily become weather-bound inside the lagoons. More often than not, one must wait for days on end for a weather-window. Strong winds, high waves, large swells and contrary currents make it virtually impossible for a slow sailboat to get back out through the treacherous reef opening again. Like everyone else, we were also delayed. So when the weather-change finally came, we did not hesitate. And this time we got through with ease. For now we were experienced, of course! But this time, the weather forecast bombed out. Soon, a full gale piped up from the south-southeast. Once again, we got caught in a rough ride with the wind on the nose and the railing in the water. Once again, we experienced that the Pacific, as its name implies, is not pacific at all. It must have been an exceptionally calm day at Cape Horn when Magellan named this, the biggest ocean of the world, Mare Pacifico.

THE LEGENDARY SOCIETY ISLANDS
TAHITI

Land ho! Tahiti ahead! We could clearly see the contours of the legendary South Sea Island's majestic Crown Mountain on the horizon, the very same view that greeted the European explorers when they were looking for terra australis incognita a few hundred years ago. Their welcome, however, was quite different from today's.

Tahiti. "The Island of Flowers and Love" is a beautiful, lush and mountainous island.

When the British frigate, HMS Dolphin approached Otaheiti in 1767, natives in outrigger canoes loaded with pigs, fruit and fowl surrounded the strange craft with its foul-smelling crew of pale faces. The Europeans panicked and the first meeting between the two peoples became a bloody affair. The next encounter was quite different. Iron was in high demand on the primitive island. So it didn't take long for the beautiful vahines to lure the lonely sailors, who had not been near the opposite sex for months, to exchange nails for love. Soon, the Dolphin lay dangerously low in the water. She was being ripped apart for the precious metal!

Making landfall at the tail end of the 20th century was nowhere near as exciting as it must have been in the Utopia of the 18th century. Vahines did not come out to trade. Outrigger canoes did not surround us. Instead, they were practicing for their traditional annual races as we made our way through a maze of copra ships, ferries and freighters, the Navy, mega yachts and bluewater sailors from all over the world. In fact, it was incredibly busy in historic Matavai Bay, where the old seafarers Wallis, Cook, Bugainville and Bligh bunkered, provisioned and enjoyed the warm hospitality and advances of the Otaheitans way back when. And it was crowded at the dock in Papeete, French Polynesia's cosmopolitan capital as we moored Mediterranean style in reverse, using stern anchor and bowlines to shore.

Tahiti's exotic vahines tempted the old seafarers to exchange love for nails. No wonder the mutineers of the "Bounty" returned to take Tahitians wives with them to Pitcairn Island.

Considered the eastern gateway to the South Pacific, Papeete is a popular meeting point for offshore sailors. It is a convenient place to change crew and receive visitors. Many cruisers had not seen each other since the Caribbean. We ran into some whom we had only met once or twice before. Still, we felt like old friends. It sure doesn't take long to bond out here. The close relationship formed between offshore cruisers is unique. So there were numerous celebrations in the pulsating nightlife of the exotic metropolis of the South Seas. Together we enjoyed many a night strolling along the waterfront enjoying les roulottes, gaily lit food trailers where the most amazing delicacies were produced in record time. Les Crêperies, our very favourite, served crêpes with all sorts of fillings as well as ice cream, which we always crave when we have been at sea for a while.

We were lying with the bow only metres away from busy Boulevard Pomare, which was named after the Polynesian king who gave up his idyllic kingdom to France at the end of the 19th century. Still an overseas territory, the Society Islands continue to receive generous subsidies from France. The main industries, i.e. tourism, cultured-pearl production and farming do not provide enough employment or income for the French Polynesians to maintain the living standard to which they have become accustomed. Case in point: there are an incredible 50,000 cars jamming Tahiti's 200 km of roads. On this, French Polynesia's largest island, a third of the population of 150,000 own a vehicle.

So cars were constantly roaring down the boulevard causing chaos and congesting the downtown core. The noise and pollution was bothersome for us who had been away from civilization so long. We hated all the dust and soot that settled on Nor Siglar's deck. Fortunately, we could splurge with the water and hose it down as much as we wanted. For there is plenty of water on mountainous Tahiti. Actually, it was quite a luxury to be at a dock again. So it was worth the discomfort. For the first time since Panama, we had access to electricity and fresh water. We took advantage of the situation and did a big cleanup job onboard, something that was sorely needed after so long at sea.

Papeete was the first port of call in over 5,000 nautical miles where expertise, repair facilities and boat equipment were readily available. Cruisers went wild working on their yachts from early morning till late at night. We barely had time to go ashore unless we needed something for the projects onboard. Everyone's priority was to get their boats shipshape for the next stretch of their voyage. After considerable offshore experience, most everyone had become supporters of the theory popularly called The Four P's: Prior Planning Prevents Problems!

While working flat out, we had fun monitoring the VHF, which was in constant use in the harbour. Imaginative cruisers used it to organize everything from potlucks, beach parties and outings to treasures- of-the-bilge meets, where one could buy, sell and trade a wide variety of more or less useful tools and spares clogging up the bilges. This way, books, cassettes and videos and all sorts of weird and wonderful items changed hands. The VHF provided a lot of gossip and chatter as well and was a great medium for finding out what was happening in the sailing community.

It was not difficult to exceed the budget in Papeete, one of the most expensive cities in the world. The bustling market, Le Marché was full of temptations offering everything from fresh fish, croissants and local carvings to colourful pareos, shimmering black pearls and fanciful straw hats. The market was a sight to behold enveloped in a profusion of flowers. Around the block outside, women sat all day long making floral wreaths. For in Tahiti, appropriately nicknamed The Island of Flowers, the vahines always wear flowers in their hair. It can be anything from a single Tiare Tahiti, frangipani or hibiscus to a couronne, a magnificent wreath. Apparently, a flower behind the right ear means heart available, behind the left, heart taken! Whatever the case may be, one thing is certain: The young women of Tahiti are positively gorgeous. No wonder the mutineers of the Bounty returned from Tonga for a load of Tahitian beauties before continuing their flight to Pitcairn.

We were lucky to experience the opening of the Heiva, a month-long art and culture festival with music, song and dance, plays, exhibits and competitions – and beauty pageants, of course! We were mesmerized by the vigorous dances, especially the provocative tamure, a sexy hula-hula dance, which was considered sinful by the missionaries, who banned dancing completely in the 1820s.

Polynesian warriors *Hula-hula girl*
Everything is real including the tattoos and the coconuts!

MOOREA

After three hectic but memorable weeks, we let the lines go and continued the short trip across the sound to Moorea, a lovely little heart-shaped island renowned for its two deep, long and spectacular bays. Cook's Bay is the commercial one of the two, its main

Moorea. The most beautiful bus stop in the world!

attraction being luxury hotels, restaurants and offers of "two sundowners for the price of one". Just around the corner, in Opunohu Bay, nature reigns supreme. That was the place for us.
We ended up all by ourselves anchored at the foot of the majestic shark-tooth shaped mountain, Mouaroa, spellbound by its magnificent silhouette. The romantic backdrop is eternalized in a number of films, most notably The Bounty and the musical South Pacific in which the picturesque landscape represents the mythical island, Bali Hai.

The solitude was a welcome change from the hustle and bustle we had just left behind. We thoroughly enjoyed hiking Moorea's lush and fertile hills and valleys – a virtual Garden of Eden – taking in breathtaking views from lofty lookouts. It was early July and the middle of winter at 17° S. At this latitude there are two seasons only: one cool and dry from May to October, one hot and humid from November to April. We must have become acclimatized because it felt much cooler than in the Marquesas at 10° S, not to mention Galápagos on the equator. When the temperature fell to 24°C at night, we actually had to dig out the quilt. For the first time in a long while we had to bundle up. I even caught a cold and crawled early to bed nursing a piping hot toddy several nights in a row.

RAIATEA

It was not easy to leave the beautiful surroundings of Opunohu Bay. But Raiatea, the sacred island of ancient Polynesia was calling us 110 nautical miles to the northwest. It was a nice overnight sail with plenty of opportunity to study the night sky. But that is not an easy matter in this part of the world where many constellations appear upside down or are unfamiliar to novices from the northern hemisphere.

Anchorage near the sacred marae of the ancient Polynesians.

Taputaputea Marae, the sacred headquarters of the old Polynesians is the biggest attraction of Raiatea. From the rocky shores of this stone temple, migrations to Hawaii, 2,381 km to the north and New Zealand, 2,216 km to the south began well over a thousand years ago. The impressive feats were undertaken in primitive, open outrigger canoes without charts, compass or sextant. The old Polynesians must have been incredibly skilled boat builders, not to mention seafarers, who managed to find their way solely by following the wind, current and waves, stars and clouds.

Our journey continued to Bora Bora, our last destination in French Polynesia. We had a quick and exhilarating afternoon sail of 30 nautical miles in the fresh trade winds. As it was rather overcast, we worried about how we were going to make it through the one and only opening in the barrier reef without the help of the sun. It was quite spooky sailing along the treacherous reef, looking for the entrance while watching huge rollers breaking over the corals, spray shooting high into the air. But the pass was well marked, wide and easy to see. In the 11th hour, the sun broke through and we made it safely into the lagoon where we groped our way through shallows and corals to Motu Tapu, a lovely little reef-islet. It was quite a challenge in waters where depth must be judged by its colour: blue is deep enough, turquoise questionable, light green too shallow and brown – big trouble! Brown is a sure sign of corals, or bombies as the Australians call the nasty coral heads.

BORA BORA

Imagine! Here we were in Bora Bora too, the Jewel of the South Pacific and possibly the most beautiful island in the world! Yet another dream had come true. And how fortunate we were to be able to explore this enchanting pearl on our own keel. That made a world of difference in this exorbitantly expensive paradise where we could stay free of charge only a stone's throw away from five-star hotels where "normal tourists" had to pay over US$1000 per night. The resorts were pure romance, though with their exotic reed huts on stilts over crystal clear water – a perfect hideaway for a blissful honeymoon.

The treacherous reef of Bora Bora guards one of the most beautiful atolls in the world.

We were able to pick and choose from a multitude of spectacular anchorages inside the calm lagoon where the water was smooth even in brisk winds. Wherever we went, Bora Bora's famous landmark, the jagged volcanic twin peaks of Mt. Pahia, dominated the view. We never tired of admiring the stunning profile, which changed shape according to the direction from which it was observed. While we were anchored outside Bora Bora Yacht Club, a humpback whale got disoriented somehow and ended up inside the lagoon, to the surprise and delight of tourists and locals alike. Brave enthusiasts swam so close to the huge mammal that they could touch it. For us it was more than enough to watch it at a safe distance from our dinghy.

In Bora Bora, mailboxes are used for baguette deliveries too!

Riding our bicycles around the island, we made some unique observations: Mailboxes were used for baguettes, wires were driven from the rooftops into the ground to strengthen the houses against cyclones and people buried their family in the garden! Graves were decorated with plastic flowers and enclosed with a white picket fence. How strange to have your grandparents buried outside your kitchen window! What happened when people moved? Did they take their loved ones with them?

Even though the bikes took up a lot of space, were awkward to stow, and required a fair bit of maintenance, we were glad we had them with us. They gave us much needed exercise and were a super way to make contact with the locals. On Bora Bora, everyone was all smiles, waving and calling "Bon jour!" as we peddled by. People seemed happy and radiated a certain joie de vivre. We would venture to claim

Worshippers dressed in white pack the churches of French Polynesia singing their hymens with unparalleled hoyu, gusto and harmony

that the French Polynesians have the better of both worlds: their own traditional life style and culture combined with French cuisine & comfort.

After three unforgettable months our visas expired. Reluctantly, we had to move on. On checking out, we were encouraged to follow an old tradition: When ships leave Polynesia, flowers are thrown overboard. If they float out to sea, you'll never return. If they float towards land, you will. Ours floated out to sea. Alors, au revoir Îles de la Société – et merci!

THE KINGDOM OF TONGA

It is mid July when we set sail for Tonga, watching the well-known profile of Bora Bora's spectacular twin peaks disappear astern. The forecast calls for avis de grand frais. But there are nearly always gale warnings in this area, so we don't take much notice any more. There is no sense in waiting. It may take a long time for the wind to abate.

Running before the wind, we charge ahead day after day under full genoa poled to port and the main reefed to starboard. For once, we hardly need to touch the sails. We are in the company of two Australian boats who are at the tail end of their circumnavigations. Pipe Dream and Pacific Flyer are back in home waters again. They are familiar with the local weather patterns. We learn a lot from listening to them on the radio. It is great to follow them. This way, we find out what is going on up ahead and can drop the sails in good time before the squalls reach us.

On day 6, we sight Palmerston, an intriguing atoll populated by about 60 people who are all descendants from the prolific settler, William Marsters and his three Polynesian wives. It is, of course, tempting to stop at the remote island, but we are going great guns and decide to carry on. You never know how long the weather will last. Besides, we want to spend a whole month in Tonga. So we have to skip some places. Even though we are out long-term, it is impossible to see everything. And we have experienced more than once that a quick stop turns into several days before you know it. This rings especially true in small settlements where the hospitality is usually so charming that it is hard to pick up and leave again.

Pipe Dream, who has Inmarsat onboard, had the difficult task of passing on the news to a fellow sailor that every offshore cruiser dreads: a death in the family. We have received two such messages ourselves over the ham radio: Both Martin's parents died while we were at sea; his mother when we were crossing the Irish Sea; his father when we were transiting the Panama Canal. Being in their mid 90's, the news was not unexpected. Sadly, both times it was impossible for us to leave the boat.

On day 9, we see the lights of Niue, the smallest nation in the world, to port. Again, we would love to stop. It would be fun to explore its renowned stalactite caves. But not at the expense of a shorter stay in Tonga. Later, we hear, of course, that Palmerston and Niue were the very best! Time and again, we find that places we decide to miss are everyone else's favourites.

We know we are almost there when we cross the Tonga Trench, one of the deepest ocean valleys in the world. We have 9,000 metres under the keel. It feels scary. Not a tempting place to swim. The next morning, Vava'u in The Northern Kingdom of Tonga appears in the mist. The islands are low, green and covered by dense vegetation. Playful humpback whales give us a royal welcome. Sailing back and forth at a respectable distance we enjoy the frolicking show of the big whales that have come all the way from the icy waters of the Antarctic to court, mate and calve in warmer climes.

In Vava'I, Tonga's "Northern Kingdom" one can still find bamboo docks, traditional outriggers, peace and tranquility.

When we check in to Neiafu, a sleepy little village of 4,000 people in a virtually landlocked harbour, we discover that we have lost a whole day on the passage. We have crossed the date line and must set the clocks ahead 24 hours. "The day begins in Tonga!" the port captain announces with a proud smile. "We was the first to welcome the new millennium!"

But time has stood still in this oldest and last remaining Polynesian monarchy, the only Pacific nation never to be colonized. Therefore, the small kingdom has not been influenced by the outside world. Which accounts for its charm. Consequently, it has not received much outside support either. And that shows. For Tonga is still very much a developing nation. Life is centred around the extended family that live a subsistence existence in small villages near their bush gardens. Still, people seem happy and content: "Poor pa'langi!" a Tongan exclaims with pity in his eyes. "You white people are so dependent on money! You have to work so hard to earn enough to get all the things you think you must have to be happy. Here, we have everything we need: food to eat, a roof over our heads and a warm climate. Go see your countryman at the Mermaid," he said. "He'll tell you".

We meet Ron Cherry and his Tongan wife Betty at the popular restaurant, which is known for its delicious food. "I used to be the chef at Sooke Harbour House on Vancouver Island," he explains. "That's where we met. Life is good here," the top Canadian chef confirms, who has settled down quite happily raising two children, his extended family all involved in running the business.

In Tonga it is a status symbol to be BIG. A young woman shares a coconut from her bush garden.

In Tonga, great physical size is a measure of beauty. But it's not only the big people who catch your attention. It's their dress as well. When the customs officer comes aboard, he has to lift his skirt and ta'ovala, a finely woven pandanus-leaf mat, which is fastened to the waist with a coconut-fibre cord. The dress dates back to the time when the natives used to hide their naked bodies from European intruders. Both men and women still wear the ta'ovala. Its length depends on the degree of respect to be shown: the more serious the occasion, the longer the mat, i.e. short for everyday, longer for feasts, weddings and funerals.

We yearn to experience everyday life in the real Tonga and seek out the remote village of Matamaka. Early the first morning, we are awakened by a knock on the hull. It is a good-looking fellow in his mid-thirties. He has run out of gas and would like to borrow a few litres for his outboard. He is going to an important meeting on an island nearby. The man looks respectable in his clean white shirt and ta'ovala. Martin gives him the whole jerry can. "Are you nuts?" I protest. "We'll never see him or the jerry can again!" But Martin trusts everybody. "Of course he'll be back!" he says convinced. And he is. A few hours later, David Fuapau is sitting in our cockpit. He speaks some English. We show him our picture books from Norway and Canada. His arm is not long enough. We fetch our box of eyeglasses. Delighted, he finds a pair that fits.

The following day, David, who happens to be the son of the Village Chief, gathers a group of islanders who need glasses. When we arrive at his house, everyone is already waiting, sitting cross-legged in a circle on the dirt floor, Bible and hymnbook at hand. We circulate the glasses, one pair at a time, for everyone to try. After much joy and laughter, everyone except the minister finds a pair. "You are our friends now!" David announces visibly moved as he hands us a huge tapa cloth, a type of tapestry made from the bark of the mulberry tree and a treasured gift for special occasions. We also get a basket freshly woven from green palm leaves filled with coconuts, breadfruit and bananas – and two huge crabs. "This is my gift to you!" David continues with a sincere expression on his face. "You are part of our family now." We have crossed the barrier. We are not pa'langi any more.

The next morning, there is a knock on the hull again. And sure enough: it is David. He needs more gas! Then follows a stream of canoes with locals asking for everything from glasses to mosquito repellent, medicine and clothes. In return, they offer handmade crafts, shells, polished boars teeth and jewellery carved from fish- and whalebones. Half the trade must be in pa'anga. They need cash for their children's school fees.

During the daytime, it is quiet in Matamaka. The men are out fishing or working in their bush gardens, the children are in school and the women tend their household chores. Old folks and small children sit in door openings watching life go by. We follow a loud sound and find some women sitting in a straw hut pounding tapa. It looks like a slow and boring process. When the bark is paper thin, four pieces are glued on top of each other and pounded into a runner, which is then decorated with natural colours. It takes three months to make a 50 x 1.5 metre long piece of cloth. The tapa is then cut according to need and used as clothing, bedding and room dividers, special gifts and ceremonial carpets.

In another hut nearby, we recognize some of the women who are weaving straw mats. They are wearing our glasses. Giggling and chatting away, they are having a ball. They are about to have something to eat and wave us in. Everyone has their own private bowl, which they fill with piping hot taro, cassava and bananas cooked in coconut milk. We get a taste as well. But we can only confirm that the Italian doctor we consulted in Neiafu, who is married to a local, is right: in Tonga, people don't eat for pleasure. Only to stay alive.

We wonder about some strange mounds of sand decorated with inverted beer bottles, plastic flowers and seashells and marked with flags and lace blowing in the wind. "It's our cemetery," explains an old man, who has become our self appointed guide. "We have five churches for five different denominations in our little village of 130 people!" On Sunday, everything is closed. Any kind of work, trade and even sports are strictly forbidden. Already before sunrise, the faithful are called on the traditional lali slit drum to the first prayer of the day. Tongans are great churchgoers. Most attend at least three times per week. Their singing is even more beautiful than in French Polynesia. The hymns, which were brought by the early missionaries, have been transposed into the minor key instead of the major – a harmony which suits the Tongan voice perfectly and results in the most beautiful himenes imaginable.

Before leaving Matamaka, we take the Fuapau family sailing. The children who get the afternoon off from school turn up in their smart red and white uniforms. The family is used to being on the water but have never been on a pa'langi boat before. They notice everything; especially the electronics, the gimballed stove, the fridge, the books and all the canned goods under the floorboards. Again, our picture books solve the language problem.

Our visitors admire Canada's snow covered mountains and Norway's stave churches and national holiday celebration. They are impressed with all the children dressed in national costumes waving flags as they file past the royal family greeting them from the castle balcony. "Norwegians have respect for their royal family," David states solemnly. "Just like us in Tonga".

"You are good visitors," David says as they leave. "This has been a nice experience. Especially for our children." Once again, we have proof of how important it is to seek out places off the beaten track to get the finest, most genuine experiences.

Back in Neiafu, the locals are preparing for a royal visit. HKH Taufa'ahau Tupou IV is coming to open an international conference. The red runner, which in Tonga is a 50-metre tapa cloth complete with peace doves, olive branches and the royal emblem, is artistically arranged between the audience and the royal family. The ceremony opens to the tunes of a feisty brass band followed by melodic himenes, passionately performed by young and old wearing straw skirts and flowers in their hair. The Princess Royal leads the rhythmic laka laka, a traditional song play that goes on forever.

The King of Tonga swims around Nor Siglar while anchored at his favorite beach.

We continue to Pangaimotu where it is rumoured that the king comes to swim whenever he visits Neiafu. And sure enough. Nor Siglar is well positioned at his favourite beach when the 80-year old monarch arrives in a noisy Zodiac, accompanied by six bodyguards. They dump the giant into the water right next to Nor Siglar, where he swims around in his underwear for the better part of one hour. This typical Polynesian monarch, who is 1.9 metres tall and weighed over 180 kilos in his prime, has realized that the old status symbol of his kingdom is not all that healthy. So now, he is setting a good example by exercising regularly and has lost 50 kilos.

Laka laka – a traditional song-play performed at special occasions; here during the King's visit.

We attend a traditional feast where food wrapped in banana leaves is cooked in an underground oven and a pig is roasted on the spit, a delicacy in these islands where there are more pigs than people! The food is served on leaves to guests sitting cross-legged on the ground under a straw roof. Unlike the natives, we can only sit a few minutes before having to change position. Lobster salad, mussels marinated in coconut milk, breadfruit and an assortment of root vegetables and fruit are beautifully arranged on large shells. The meal ends with an informal kava ceremony to the accompaniment of four men singing and playing guitar, banjo, base and ukulele. To the uninitiated, kava both tastes and looks like dishwater. The non-alcoholic tranquilizing drink, which actually numbs your tongue and lips, is extracted from the dried root of a pepper plant. In former times, the village virgins chewed the root and spat the juice into the kava bowl! Today, the preparation is more hygienic. Still, everyone drinks from the same coconut shell.

The dancing is the best part of the feast. One by one, charming little girls perform the dignified tau'olounga. Acting out the story sung by adults in the background, the girls use graceful arm and hand motions, while keeping their knees closely together – not swinging their hips like the erotic French Polynesian hula hula.

We crave solitude and a break from the social activities of the yachting community and sail south to Ha'apai, a group of coral islands in The Middle Kingdom, which are even harder to tackle than the Tuamotus. Most sailors avoid the area and the locals are not used to visitors from outside. They are just as curious about us as we are about them. The children are even afraid of us! We are taken aback when a little boy reaches out his hand yelling: "Gimmi monni! Gimmi monni!" The begging ends abruptly when we counter: "Gimmi bananas!"

We are near the location where Captain Cook received such a warm welcome in 1773 that he named the archipelago The Friendly Islands. Little did he know that the natives had intended to roast and eat him and his men. Cook's gratitude and generosity made them change their minds. Among other things, he presented the Chief, Tu'i- Tonga with a tortoise from Gálápagos, which actually rummaged around in the Royal Gardens until 1966 when it died at a ripe old age of over 200!

Walking through the bush inspecting the local agriculture, we run into three lively girls sitting on a palm picking lice from each other's hair. They are delighted to have their picture taken. "How many children do you have?" the oldest asks. "Two sons," Martin replies. "Oh!" she cries. "Are they married?" "Not yet," he says. "Really! We'd love to marry a pa'langi and move abroad! My sister is married to a man from Tumbler Ridge, B.C. He is 69 years old. She is very happy. Would you like a daughter-in- law or two from Tonga?"

The girls were not joking. Tonga, which consists of 170 islands stretching across an area of 350 km. is becoming over-populated and running out of land to feed its people. Therefore, nearly half the population has emigrated to New Zealand, Australia and North America. Most Tongans have relatives abroad who send money home.

We did not see Palmerston. Nor did we experience Niue. But when our month in Tonga is over, we have had both time and opportunity to feel the pulse of the unique kingdom. Enriched by so many meaningful encounters, we drift slowly out to sea, past the volcanic island of Tofua, where the mutiny of the Bounty took place in 1789. It was here that William Bligh was put to sea with 18 loyal seamen in a small 24-foot tender. The famous incident resulted in the longest, most epic voyage ever undertaken in an open boat: 5,800 km in 44 days to Timor in Indonesia. We follow in Captain Bligh's wake. But we intend to make many stops on our way.

FASCINATING FIJI

I am sitting au naturel in the shade of the cockpit awning on my afternoon watch. We have just cleaned up after lunch. Martin has gone below to rest. It is peaceful onboard. Nor Siglar is barely moving, her sails fluttering in the gentle breeze. The sound of water trickling against the hull is soothing. A slight swell forms tiny ripples on the shimmering azure blue ocean. There is no sign of life on the horizon. We are underway from Tonga to Fiji 450 nautical miles to the west. We are in no particular hurry. It's just nice to be in the here and now.

The sun shines brightly into the salon where Martin is trying to sleep. He puts a newspaper over the hatch. We really ought to hoist the cruising spinnaker. But today we feel lazy and prefer peace and comfort to the exhilaration of speed. A day like today is a precious gift, a wonderful opportunity for reflection and relaxation. Today, the goal is not important. Just being underway.

It is September 1, exactly seven years since we left Vancouver and almost thirteen since we moved onboard. It is hard to believe that Nor Siglar has been our home, our one and only home for so long. We have grown really fond of our floating nest, our faithful vessel, which has brought us safely from port to port, slowly but surely across the big oceans of the world. And even though Nor Siglar is only a modern lightweight fibreglass yacht, we would venture to claim that also she has soul. Surely, not only wooden boats can lay claim to that? Piles of charts, books and pictures, trinkets and treasures from afar, flags from close to 40 countries and a guest book with an international register must be evidence enough that there is

both life and soul onboard? Don't people, events and experience contribute to give a boat character? Of course, Nor Siglar has soul!
At the halfway point, we cross the 180th meridian and are back in the eastern hemisphere again. On day 4, Viti Levu, the main island of Fiji emerges on the horizon. As always while underway, we have prepared ourselves for the next destination. Studying the Lonely Planet, we have familiarized ourselves with Fiji's history, culture and sights. Viti Levu is the largest in a group of 322 gorgeous islands.

Carefully, we poke our way past an old shipwreck on the reef at the entrance of the capital, Suva, and locate the quarantine buoy. A few hours later, we have filled out a huge pile of forms and received our cruising permit and passports duly stamped.

We move across the harbour to Royal Suva Yacht Club, an old relic from British colonial days, and anchor among roughly 30 other boats. Most cruisers are continuing to New Zealand, an often rough and demanding crossing of about 1,200 nautical miles. The rest, including us, are heading west to Australia to seek shelter during the cyclone season, which lasts from November to May. There is full activity in the harbour. Boats come and go. We hear Stillehavskrysseren call Suva Port Control on the VHF. The Norwegians are told to spell the name. "Sierra-Tango-India-Lima-Lima…." It takes a long time to spell 19 letters in the nautical alphabet. There is a long pause. Then it comes: "I'll just call you Stilla!"

It is obvious that we have arrived in Melanesia, meaning black islands in Greek. The indigenous population has tight curly hair and a darker complexion than their neighbours in Polynesia. One should almost think they originate from Africa. However, like the Polynesians, the Melanesians come from Southeast Asia too. About 120 years ago, British colonials started bringing indentured workers from India to the sugar plantations on the islands. Today, the population consists of two ethnic groups: one half indigenous Fijian, one half East Indian. The contrast between the two peoples' culture, traditions and cuisine is striking, not to mention their dress; the Indian women in sparkling colourful saris, their native sisters in the more practical wraparound sulu.

While at RSYC, we get a serious reminder of the many dangers of life at sea. First, we hear that Ariaka, the boat that disappeared between Galápagos and Marquesas, has been found 600 nautical miles southwest of Acapulco. There was no one onboard. The boat had been robbed; her sails were in shreds. Had the single-hander been attacked by pirates? No one will ever know. Then, an English ketch runs hard aground on the approach to Suva. Attempting to make landfall in the dark, the Skipper fell asleep at the wheel. After a long and hard struggle, fellow cruisers manage to rescue the boat in the 11th hour. The wife has had it and wants to go home. The husband persuades her to continue to New Zealand. Closing in on the coast, they run into problems again. But this time, they are shipwrecked. The husband survives but his wife drowns.

Fortunately, there are pleasant happenings too. While we were wintering in Halden, another Canadian, Tony Jarrett and his Norwegian wife, Ruth, hailed us from the dock: "from Vancouver, eh?" Tony was dreaming of going offshore. "Just go home, quit your job, buy a boat and take off!" Martin recommended. Five years later, Dandelion Days from Vancouver sails into Suva harbour. A happy skipper calls us on the VHF: "I did what you told me, Martin!"

In an acute case of Alzheimer's Light, we leave our passports in the back seat of a taxi. It takes forever to get new ones. So when we hear of a new marina at Vuda Point where boats can be laid up safely during the cyclone season, we decide to leave Nor Siglar there. We are not the only ones to end the sailing season in Fiji, tired after months of battling unstable El Niño conditions and happy to escape the challenging 10-day passage to New Zealand.

Our philosophical friend Mundo, who helped us get Nor Siglar ready for our 5-month absence.

We calculate that we have covered 8,600 nautical miles – more than a third of a circumnavigation – since we left Trinidad ten months ago.

It has been a busy year: three months at sea, seven in ports. We are beginning to feel that the crossings are far too long and the layovers way too short!

We are dying to take a break from the boat. The timing is perfect for a visit to Vancouver, our sixth and final trip home during our adventure. But before we can leave Nor Siglar, we have to haul her out for some much needed maintenance and rapair. We hire a husky Fijian at $10.00 per day. Mundo lives from hand to mouth. He is very poor. At least according to our standards. He is strong as a bull and looks just like a Neanderthal. When he is serious, he looks almost dangerous. But not for long. For he has an impressive row of bright white teeth and a brilliant smile. We like Mundo and learn a lot from this fellow who is surprisingly philosophical, constantly impressing us with words of wisdom.

Mundo is critical of his own people and their capabilities to govern. He would like to see the Indian candidate win the upcoming election. "Our Chiefs are lazy," he states. "They drink too much kava!" And if the Europeans had not come to Fiji, the natives would still be cannibals! He urges me to show respect for men and to call Martin Mister Martin. Martin, on the other hand, can call me anything he wants. Mundo's view on the Clinton- Lewinsky affair? "Men do those things! Right, Mr. Martin?

You and I do those things. Leave Mr. Clinton alone and let him get on with being the President!" We receive a lot of pleasure from our short acquaintance with Mundo, another proof that it is the people we meet on our travels who make this sea gipsy life of ours so thought provoking and meaningful.

After four busy weeks in unbearable heat, Nor Siglar is literally moved from the "cradle to the grave." Her keel is carefully lowered into a hole in the ground while the hull is placed on a layer of old tyres, a simple and safe storage method during the cyclone season. Everything on deck is removed: outboard engine, dinghy and sails, sheets, lee cloths and tarps. Dodger, wind instruments and solar panels are dismantled, the engine overhauled, batteries and electrical components disconnected.

Nor Siglar safely stored in a hole in the ground during the cyclone season.

To avoid mould and mildew in the hot and wet tropical climate, it is important that everything is dry and sparkling clean below. Equally important is good ventilation, a dilemma during the rainy season when leaks must be avoided at any cost. We tape shut all seacocks and hatches, thereby also preventing ants and cockroaches from making an invasion. Finally, we sprinkle insect killer and mothballs throughout, open drawers and cupboards, spread sheets over the

settees and pull the curtains so the sun won't bleach the upholstery. Now, all we can do is hope for the best. The marina is only three years old. Still, it has survived three cyclones
without any disasters. We feel reasonably confident that Nor Siglar will be fine as we leave her in her hole in the ground.

Five months later, we find Nor Siglar in the same condition as we left her, thanks to kind cruiser friends who kept an eye on her in our absence, but also because there were no cyclones that year. Yet, we hardly recognize her! Her name, homeport and boot stripe have been removed. She is chalk white all over. We had forgotten that we had instructed the marina to sand down the gel coat while we were away to prepare her for a paint job on our return. To our relief, everything below is in order as well. No leaks, no ants, no cockroaches, no mildew. But it sure smells of mothballs!

Bright and early the next morning, Mundo reports back to work. He has been waiting and waiting for his Mister Martin. Grinning from ear to ear, he waves a crumpled bill in the air. Now there is money to be had again! Everything that was dismantled before must be reinstalled and hooked up again. It takes a while before everything is back to normal: the radar and short-wave radio, GPS and solar panels, fridge and stove, fans and navigational lights. We take advantage of the cheap labour and embark on some major projects.

British ketch aground at the entrance of Suva. She is rescued but sinks later off the coast of New Zealand. The skipper makes it, but his wife drowns.

After 13 years of living aboard, there is a fair amount of wear and tear. It is time for a face-lift. In Trinidad, we reupholstered the salon. Now, the carpets need to be replaced. And the foam backing on the vinyl is disintegrating causing the wall coverings to come off the bulkheads in the forepeak and stern cabins. We replace it with local straw mats, a pleasant Fijian touch. The renewals are purely cosmetic, not crucial for the seaworthiness of the boat. But they contribute in a big way to make our home nice and cozy and to create a pleasant atmosphere onboard, something that is most important when being so confined all the time.

A shipment from Vancouver containing spray paint, boot stripes and the name, a new fridge and 200 pairs of glasses is three weeks delayed. It takes another nine days to get it cleared through customs. This despite the fact that it is imported duty free to ship in transit! We are beginning to get fed up with the infamous Fiji Factor. Everything takes time. Nobody can be trusted. How late will the workers be today? Maybe they won't even turn up? Even Mundo sloughs off. That hurts. We feel we have been extra good to him, giving him a bit extra from time to time. Nothing seems to matter. Obviously, one cannot expect much for two dollars an hour. Island Time is a standard excuse for the poor productivity. In the final analysis, labour costs and services are nowhere near as reasonable as we had been lead to believe.

After two frustrating weeks in the "grave" and four in the "crib", Nor Siglar is finally ready to be launched. We are completely exhausted. Work, stress and excessive heat have worn us down. Martin swears he'll never do such a big refit again. All around us boats are catching mice onboard. We become so preoccupied with getting on our way that we forget the old superstition and leave on a Friday. But we are only taking a short trip across the sound to Malololailai where cruiser friends from the old country are waiting to celebrate May 17, Norway's Constitution Day.

My girlfriend, Marit Endresen has just arrived from Oslo and we have lots to talk about. In a moment's distraction, the nightmare every boater dreads happens: We run aground! And it is a dreadful feeling indeed. Fortunately, it doesn't take long before a local dive boat sees us and comes to our aid. The crew grab the mainsail halyard, winch us over onto our side and pull us sideways out in deep water again. Nor Siglar has escaped unscathed. Only the Skipper's pride is hurt. Never on a Friday….

On May 17, patriotic boats are decorated with signal flags, balloons and ribbons. Maria Two hosts a luncheon, and as nostalgic countrymen climb aboard, their national anthem sounds over the ship's loudspeakers enveloping the deck in a festive atmosphere. In the afternoon, a little dinghy-flotilla makes its way to the shore where a small but enthusiastic May 17 parade takes place in uncharacteristic tropical surroundings. People must wonder what is going on in Musket Cove on this normal working day. But for us it is a very special occasion, which culminates by the pool of a romantic restaurant where we savour a splendid curry buffet, sip kava and are entertained by exotic Bula music in the background. High in the tropical sky, the Southern Cross reminds us that we are very far from home on this last May 17 of the Millennium.

On June 1, we up the anchor, certain that the cyclone season is over for this time. Nor Siglar looks elegant in her new and shiny white coat as she floats out to sea leaving Fiji's beautiful coastline behind, ready for the second half of her circumnavigation.

VANUATU
THE MOST TRADITIONAL ISLAND OF THE SOUTH SEAS

Help! A mouse! We've got miiiiiice onboard! We were underway from Fiji to Vanuatu when the stowaway suddenly appeared in the dead of night. On my watch, of course. It was raining and miserable. I had tried to read a bit but was feeling rather unwell and had to put my book down. When I attempted to pick it up again, a soaking wet mouse sat on top of it shaking like a leaf. We hadn't escaped the plague at Vuda Point Marina after all.

How on earth could I get rid of the poor little thing? I would have to kill it. Oh no! I couldn't possibly do that. But I didn't have a choice. Having mice onboard is no joke. They can cause great damage. Electrical systems have been ruined by mice gnawing the wiring to shreds. Martin was sound asleep so I didn't want to disturb him. I had to get hold of myself. Before I knew it, I had grabbed "Captain Cook's Voyages" and thrown the unsuspecting intruder overboard. "How cruel!" Martin teased when I told him what had happened at the change of watch. But guess who was relieved, when he realized that the strange squeaking we had heard lately didn't come from the steering cable after all!

During the rest of the passage, we hunted high and low for mice. But it must have been the only one that managed to get onboard. We had another souvenir from Fiji as well. Stitches! The day before we left, Martin had a mole removed from his back. There was no way he would postpone our departure just to have some stitches removed. So now it became my job. There is no end to what one must be prepared to do out here.

Otherwise, the 600 nautical mile crossing was relatively uneventful. With one exception. A container was reported lost in the vicinity. Not a very nice warning. A partially submerged container is one of the biggest hazards confronting a sailboat on the high seas. We took the situation very seriously and tried to calculate where it would drift according to current, wind-speed and direction and made a big detour to be sure to avoid it. Even though chances of seeing a container in the dark are minuscule, we were careful to keep a close lookout. So while we were "racing" along at a speed of 5-6 knots, there is no denying that our thoughts were preoccupied with what would happen if we collided with such an object so far from land.

After five days of running before the wind constantly surfing and rolling in the fresh southeast trades, it was heavenly to put the anchor down and relax again. We found a perfect spot in a roomy bay near Port Vila, the cosmopolitan capital of Vanuatu, considered one of the most beautiful natural harbours in the world. The first person aboard was a young quarantine officer. Speaking fluent English and French, he impressed us with his language skills. In fact, he knew seven languages! And that was not unusual, he said, in Vanuatu where about 115 indigenous languages are spoken. Although English and French are the official languages, Bislama is the national language. The local variation of Pidgin developed as a traders' tongue during the sandalwood period (1825-1865) when contact between the Europeans and the Melanesians was established. Then followed the era of the hated Blackbirders who recruited and/or kidnapped 50,000 ni-Vanuatu to work the sugarcane plantations in Australia and Fiji. Few returned. Those who did often brought with them disease and alcohol, as did the white man himself, reducing the indigenous population from half a million in the early 1800's to 40,000 by 1920.

It is relatively easy to learn Bislama. Verbs are not declined so the grammar is quite simple. Using the present tense only, the past and future are expressed by using the words before and after or finish and tomorrow. So Bislama is an uncomplicated tongue while at the same time being most descriptive. The spelling is based on how the English word sounds to the natives. For example, beer is called bia and school: skul. The word blong indicates possession, i.e. Vanuatu becomes Ripablik blong Vanuatu, history: taem blong bifoa and helicopter simply: mixmaster blong Jesus.

Even though people spoke good English, misunderstandings still occurred. But most were due to cultural differences. Saying "no" is taboo for many native peoples. So it is for the Melanesians. They would rather lie than use the bad word. Therefore, questions are always answered in the affirmative. So to get a correct reply, the query must be formulated in such a way that the response requires an explanation rather than a "yes" or a "no". For example, one must not ask: "Is the bank open on Sunday?" Then the answer will definitely be "yes". Instead, one must ask: "What are the banking hours on Sunday?" Then the answer will be: "The bank is closed on Sundays." This way, you avoid the "no" dilemma! We received a lot of conflicting information before we finally learned this trick!

Most ni-Vanuatu live in straw huts in small villages, make a living from subsistence agriculture and fishing and survive on a diet which, according to our standards, satisfies the bare minimum. On the coast, outrigger canoes are their only mode of transport. In Havannah Bay on the main island of Efate, we got the feeling of being transported into a bygone era. We had barely put the anchor down when a couple came paddling out to us with fresh fruits and vegetables from their bush garden. We got some taros, citrus fruits and bananas for a pencil and a few coins. Judging from their smiles, they were pleased with their trade. We certainly could not complain about ours.

Our first contact in Vanuatu. A couple stops on their way home from their bush garden to trade.

Soon after, two soft-spoken fellows came by. One held up a bloody hand. He had cut himself with his machete collecting coconuts in the jungle. They had managed to stop the bleeding with a leaf bandage. While Martin helped them tie up alongside, I got out the first aid kit. It impressed the natives who rely on natural remedies alone. But even with our modern gadgets, it was not easy to treat the nasty wound. His hand was caked with mud and dirt. We cleansed the deep cut and bandaged it as best we could. Then we gave him a couple of aspirins and told him to come back the following day so we could inspect the injury and change the dressing.

The fellows were all smiles when they returned the next morning. Fortunately, there was no sign of infection. Everyone was happy. "Can we do something for you?" they asked. "Not at all!" we replied. "We're happy we could help. Although, a little run in your outrigger would be fun! And we'd love to see what you are growing on your jungle plots." The men seemed almost childishly proud to show us their crops. And they sure were bountiful! Bananas, papaya and mango and to us unfamiliar root vegetables like taro, yam and manioc thrive in the tropical climate. It was at least 35°C, even in the shade. So it was lovely with a brisk sail in the outrigger. They took us over an open stretch to their island where a group of men were putting the finishing touches to a brand new outrigger. They were just about to launch it, a big event in the remote settlement. The whole village was present. I was overwhelmed when they asked me to come along on the maiden voyage. And not only that. They named the outrigger Anna after the kind nurse from the frozen north!

Maiden voyage of the outrigger, "Anna" named after the kind nurse from the frozen north

The village used to be located in Havannah Bay. But the mangroves were full of mosquitoes, so when it was destroyed by a cyclone in 1993, it was rebuilt on the island further out. This story was a serious reminder that we were in the midst of the malaria belt. It was time to protect ourselves and to put mosquito nets on all the openings and hatches. We also burned citronella coils in the cockpit and below. It became unbearably hot inside and we had trouble sleeping at night.

Considering the significant malaria danger, we assumed they would have local expertise on the matter and decided to seek advice at the nearest clinic. We were taken past a long line-up straight to the doctor's office. Although it was nice not having to wait, it didn't feel right to receive such preference. "Nonsense, Madame!" the jovial Polynesian doctor laughed. "Natives in ex colonies are used to white people enjoying certain privileges." "What should we do about malaria?" we wondered. "How long are you staying?" he asked. "A couple of months including the Solomon Islands," we replied. On that note, the doctor put his hand on the bible and tapping me on my shoulder, stared deep into my eyes and said: "Don't worry, dear. God will look after you."

Needless to say, one must know a bit about injuries and disease and be prepared to deal with just about anything when travelling alone far away from professional help. Despite the local expertise, we seriously considered taking malaria pills. However, being worried about potential side effects, we decided to hold off. Instead, we tried as best we could to stay inside at dusk and dawn when the mosquitoes are the most active, used insect repellent and wore socks and light clothing that was tight around the ankles, wrists and neck. It was not very comfortable in the oppressive heat.

Since we only had time to stay for three weeks, we could only see some of the 83 islands in the 1300 km long Y-shaped archipelago. Together with our friend Mike Sauze, his son Marc and daughterin-law Helen, who joined us for a two-week visit, we chose to concentrate on a few select places and spend more time there rather than rushing through a whole lot, ending up with nothing but superficial impressions. We moved along at a comfortable speed from one picturesque anchorage to another where we snorkelled among turtles and manatees and were entertained at all hours of the day and night by church bells and drums from land. Further north in the island chain, the landscape turned volcanic with high and jagged mountain peaks and black lava beaches. Here, there were poisonous snakes and sharks in the water. So that was the end of our swimming for a while, hard to resist in the incredibly tempting water which was so clear that you could see a clothespin at seven metres depth!

On the island of Epi, a father and son came paddling out to us with a weird selection of homemade crafts. The workmanship was rather coarse. But we didn't have the heart to say no, where they were sitting in their rough dugout canoe looking at us with expectation in their eyes. We chose a bow and an arrow, a flute and a shell necklace. In return, we offered them some lightly used Tommy Hilfiger shirts. But they were not at all happy. "Do you have some sugar, rice and soap instead? Or cigarettes?" the man asked softly. Brand name t-shirts meant nothing to them. The explanation is obvious: food and articles for everyday use are more important than fashion so far from civilization. The men used mostly Adidas shorts and t-shirts while the women wore their colourful floral Mother Hubbard island dresses complete with ruffles, ribbons and lace. Most were barefoot or used flip-flops.

Ceremonial area for ancient rituals and coming-of-age rites. The spirits of the ancestors live inside the beautifully carved ating-atins.

Ambrym Island, known for its majestic scenery, active volcanoes and strong traditions became the highlight of our Vanuatu experience. Here, we spent considerable time ashore attempting to learn how people live in this isolated island nation. In the main village of Ramon, we were introduced to the Chief who appointed his assistant to look after us. Ronny took us to their ceremonial grounds where ancient rituals and traditional coming of age rites took place. "The spirits of our ancestors live in these ating-ating," Ronny said with reverence pointing to a collection of 3-4 metre high beautifully carved tree-trunks. "The size and number of carvings signify how far the boy has come in his graduation rites to become an adult," he explained. Nearby, a group of young boys were playing their "innocent" war games. It struck us how blissfully ignorant they were of what lies ahead. One of the many requirements to attain adulthood is to kill a pig with nothing but a wooden club.

We followed the sound of tam-tam drums to an opening in the jungle where a wild war dance was in full swing. The men, who wore hibiscus flowers in their bushy hair had nothing on except the traditional namba, a penis wrapper attached to a broad leather belt decorated with leaves and ferns. Their strong and glistening bodies dripping with sweat, the men were stamping their feet in a circle singing at the top of their voices, their shrill chants echoing in the hills. Off to one side, an elder was beating an ating-ating. The genuine kastom dance was quite a sight. But poor Martin was rather disappointed that there were no similarly clad women to be seen.

We are lucky to stumble upon a wild kastom war dance in the jungle.

Vanuatu's ancient traditions reflect a society of powerful and influential clans, arranged marriages, grandiose gift ceremonies and festivals complete with ritual killings and spiritual rites. Contrary to Fiji, where the position of Chief is inherited, strength, power and wealth have to be proven and earned to become a big man in Vanuatu's complex graded society. Amassing wealth in pigs is a way to accomplish this. Pigs are highly valued, especially if they have tusks. Therefore, it has long been the practice to breed pigs, mostly for their tusks. The male's upper canine teeth are knocked out so his lower tusks have nothing to grind against. Some times they even penetrate the cheek. In six or seven years the tusks have grown into a full circle. Both tusks and meat are prized items at initiation rites and funeral feasts. Thus, tusks play a central role in Vanuatu's culture and are even pictured on the flag and the money. And the local beer is Tusker, of course!

The payment of bride price is still common throughout this macho male dominated society where a wife is considered part of her husband's wealth. The price consists of money, pigs, cows and a selection of traditional gifts. The amount of cash depends on how large and well-to-do the bride's family is, how good the suitor is at negotiating and how keen he is to get his girl. In order to keep inflation under control, a ceiling of Vt 300,000 has been placed on the bride price. Currently, the market value of a wife is about a quarter of the cost of a car. Consequently, young females are called Toyotas! "How much did you pay for Anne?" Ronny asked in dead earnest. "Nothing!" Martin teased. And that was hard to believe for a man who admitted he had not been able to pay for his wife yet. He had bought her on credit.

"Tell us more!" we begged as we were sitting in the shade of a huge banyan tree sipping mango juice. "Tell us about marriage!" "Sure! If the boy gets the father's permission to marry his daughter, the date for the wedding is set. It is usually within a year. In the meantime, his relatives help him clear a plot of land where he can grow fruit and vegetables for his future family. By the way, it is just as valuable to have many daughters as sons," he interjected. "Not only can they be sold. Girls take care of aging parents as well." "Do you like this system?" we asked. "Does it work well?" "There is no question whether we like it or not. It's our culture. Old traditions cannot be changed just like that." We understood that the whole structure of their society was based on the principle of the extended family. "We have a duty to take care of one another," he continued. "Here, that is the responsibility of the family, not the government. Here, no one ends up in an institution like in your part of the world," Ronny concluded with a touch of contempt in his voice.

After three fascinating weeks, we reached our last goal, Luganville on Espíritu Santo. To our surprise, we found an Internet café there. It was run by a modern ni-Vanuatu educated in Australia. So we were quite shocked when he introduced himself as Me monkey Roy! He laughed out loud when he saw our reaction. "You monkey Martin and you monkey Anne!" he explained. "This is how we introduce ourselves in Bislama!" The sympathetic man was just as interested in us and our culture as we were in him and his. "Would you like to come sailing one day?" we asked. The following day, the computer expert and his wife, Raylene, a teacher also educated in Australia, joined us. They had never been on a modern sailboat before. So it was a successful outing. In fact, we had so much to talk about that they invited us home the next day. We can count on one hand how many times that has happened during our offshore adventure.

Rattling along in Roy's rickety old Datsun on a road built by the Americans during WWII from crushed shells and corals, we had a wonderful opportunity to see some of Vanuatu's beautiful interior. Safely arrived at their college compound, Roy and Raylene treated us to lap lap, Vanuatu's national dish. Yams were grated and kneaded to a paste to which coconut cream, garlic and aromatic leaves were added. Chicken was included for the occasion. The mixture was then poured onto a bed of banana leaves, folded into a compact package and placed on glowing hot rocks in an umu umu. After an hour in the underground oven the dish was ready and carried inside where it was served on a mat on the floor. The lap lap was to be eaten with the fingers, but not until an emotional grace had been said. For they are very religious, these people, whose ancestors cooked the missionaries in the cannibal pot. As a matter of fact, cannibalism was practiced till well into the 20th century in some of the more remote islands.

The ni-Vanuatus were slow to accept Christianity. Tribal religions are still practiced. To this day, the natives even believe in ghosts and evil spirits. Rites and superstitions are very much alive. Many things are taboo. Many practise black magic. A girl had just been murdered in the vicinity. The Hill people were blamed for the crime. The bush tribe believe that if they can get hold of someone's inner organs or body parts, they capture the individual's spirit, strength and knowledge as well. Our friends were clearly spooked. They were afraid to talk about it. "The Hill people are like the Pygmies," they whispered. "They are shy and live hidden away deep in the jungle. When they occasionally come out in public, they are easy to recognize. They only wear the namba. Thank God for our strong faith," they sighed. "It helps us overcome our fright."

Unfortunately, we were too late to see the famous land divers of Pentecost where men tie liana vines to their ankles, then jump head first from atop 30-metre high man-made towers, jerking to a halt just centimetres from the ground. Slack in the lifeline vine eases the shock as it stretches to its limit and the platforms are designed to sway so the jumpers are rarely injured. Today the daring feat forms part of the yam festival.

It was time to provision and continue to our next destination. The shops, which were mainly run by French-speaking Vietnamese, were literally crawling with cockroaches and weevils. Fortunately, we didn't need very much. But this time, everything was thoroughly scrutinized and washed before it was brought onboard. We had been free from cockroaches for quite some time, thanks to a sweet little gecko, which had settled down on Nor Siglar.

The beautiful and serene Marova Lagoon.

SOLOMON ISLANDS
THE BEST KEPT SECRET IN THE SOUTH PACIFIC

We were anchored in Pelekula Bay, a remote cove on the east side of Espíritu Santo waiting for customs to clear us out of Vanuatu. We had just settled down in the cockpit after a frightening experience. Before taking Nor Siglar in through the maze of corals and sandbanks, we had been out in the dinghy taking soundings to find a safe passage. Suddenly, Martin leapt to his feet. "There!" he shouted. "Look there, Anne!" A fin was piercing through the water in our direction. It was a shark! I just caught sight of it before it disappeared. "Oh my God!" I gasped. "What if it tips us over? Or even worse…" I whispered. Knees trembling, we remained calm as could be waiting for the next move. It seemed like an eternity. But that was the end of it.

Closer to shore, two men were standing in a small outrigger throwing a circular fishnet – much the same way their forefathers must have done it for centuries. They were at it all day. "Are they ever patient," I thought. In the evening, the fishermen grilled their catch on the beach. It looked like tiny sardines. They offered us a taste. It was delicious. The scene was magic, the atmosphere peaceful. Well, not quite. Early the next morning, a couple of noisy Hercules aircraft came roaring in across the bay to land at the airport nearby. They were from New Zealand and on their way to the Solomon Islands with troops and equipment. We tuned in to BBC who announced that a state of emergency had been declared in the capital, Honiara on the main island of Guadalcanal. Australia was calling its citizens home. Clearly, it was not a good time to go north. Cruiser friends changed their plans and headed for New Caledonia instead. We were devastated. We had been looking forward to these remote islands for so long. We definitely did not want to miss them.

Most ni-Vanuatu lives in straw huts and make a living from subsistence farming, fishing and hunting.

So we were overjoyed when we happened to make contact with a Canadian sailboat in the New Georgia Group who reported that conditions were calm in the entire Western Province. Repose had sailed in the area for 15 years. The couple loved it there. "Just come!" they urged. "As long as you stay away from Guadalcanal and Malaita, the islands at the centre of the crisis, you'll be fine." The problem was that we had to check in to Honiara first, the official port of clearance in the Solomons. "No worries! Just carry on to Gizo and do it there! Nobody can force you to stop in Honiara under these circumstances."

Tom and Jean offered to keep in touch while we were underway on the daily Comedy Net, a maritime mobile net where sailors in the area reported their positions, discussed weather and exchanged information. This way, they could keep us posted on the developments. It gave us a comforting feeling. The decision was made. Solomon Islands next!

But what was this? Murphy must be lurking onboard. After having sorted through a pile of charts, we discovered that we were missing the most important ones: The New Georgia Group! While planning, we must have decided to bypass them. "No problem!" Tom declared. "Take Blanchard Channel to Rendova Bay. We'll meet you at the entrance and escort you in. You can have our charts while you are here." Unbelievable! How could total strangers be so nice and trusting? We were reminded of another time when an American cruiser gave us a hundred charts in Sicily. We had never met him before either. He was done with sailing and didn't need them any more. So the moral of the story is: it's not necessary to spend a fortune on charts before leaving home.

The 725 nautical mile passage was one of the quickest we have experienced. Running before the wind in strong south-easterlies, Nor Siglar was surfing along at record speeds. Still, our agile lady rarely took any water into the cockpit. It was a challenging crossing dominated by tropical squalls, which left us little time for relaxation. "Maybe we should put another reef in the main?" we thought when the first black cloud appeared on the horizon. But we let it be. And as we know only too well by now, we should have done it the minute we thought of it. For when the first raindrops hit the deck, it is too late. And so it was. In a matter of seconds, the wind piped up to 50 knots accompanied by a torrential downpour, thunder and lightning. There was only one thing to do: get the main sail down. By now, the

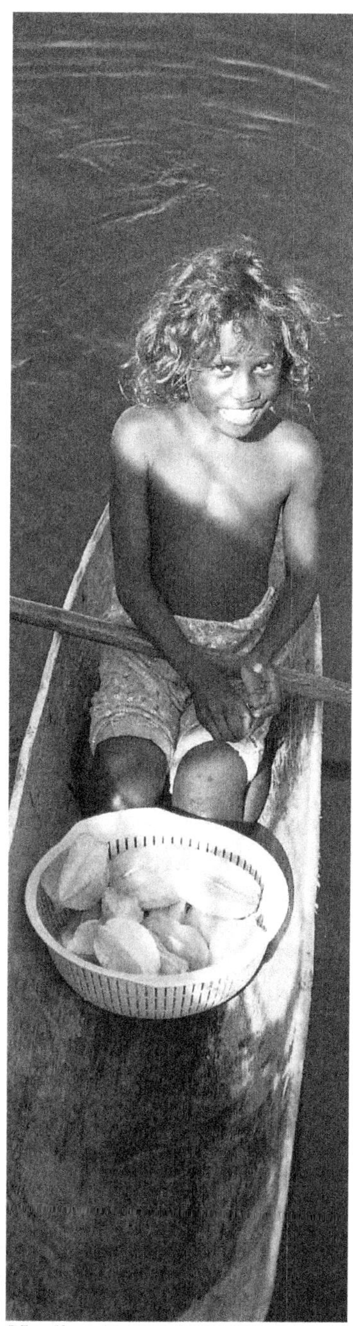

Hardly a day went by without a visit from the charming children of the Salomon Islands.

routine is automatic: Martin in the cockpit at the helm handling the mainsheet and halyard; me on deck working the preventer, topping lift and reefing lines. Normally, the operation is done in a couple of minutes. But not this time.

"Easy does it," I thought as I fastened my safety harness to the jack line and crawled up on deck on all fours, positioning myself within the safety of the granny bars at the mast. "What a wonderful support," I

thought as the boat took a sudden lurch and I was thrown off balance backwards against the solid bars. Martin was having trouble keeping the boat into the wind. It was truly the mother of all squalls. The sail was flogging so wildly that the battens got caught in the lazy jacks and my sunglasses were swept right off my face into the foaming sea. "I bet we'll tear it," I thought as I struggled away, yanking and pulling at it like mad while holding on to the swinging boom for dear life. Miraculously, I got it down without a tear and securely lashed around the boom. After that incident, we changed to two poled out foresails, which are much easier to handle than the main.

When it was all over, we breathed a sigh of relief. For the first time ever Martin admitted that he was getting tired of sailing. "Time to go home!" he exclaimed. "Tough luck," I countered. "We're not even halfway yet!" But from that moment on, we started the countdown of the longer passages. We also began talking about what we were going to do when we come home. "I am dying to get back to my woodlot," Martin said, his eyes glazing over. "Just think how quiet and peaceful it is there."

Slowly but surely, we were closing in on the equator again, latitudes decreasing from 15° S to 8° S. The temperature kept rising. It became terribly hot and humid. About halfway, we crossed an active underwater volcano. The last eruption was 45 years ago. "Hold off a little longer for the next one," we prayed keeping our fingers crossed.

Three days later, Repose met us at the head of the bay as promised and escorted us in through the reefs and shallows. After all the radio contacts we felt like old friends. We hit it off right away, something that is not at all unusual among fellow hams. Not only did we get the charts we needed but lots of useful information too about the area where they had been so long. The next day we continued to

Gizo where the authorities were both understanding and forthcoming and checked us into the country without any hassle. "What's the reason for the unrest?" we asked. "Ethnic squabbles," the immigration officer replied. "The Melanesians on Guadalcanal want the Malaitans, who are of Polynesian origin, and who are settling down on Guadalcanal, to go back to Malaita where they belong. But you don't need to worry. This is our problem. Nothing will happen to you."

The first European to "discover" the Solomon Islands was the Spanish explorer, Alvaro de Mendaña de Neyra. He came from Peru in 1568 in search of an elusive El Dorado, which, according to Inca legend, was located 600 leagues west of Peru. But his expedition did not find any gold. Still, the conquistador gave the islands their exotic name, implying that they might be the source of King Solomon's legendary gold mines, which supplied the gold for the temple in Jerusalem.

The Solomon Islands and Vanuatu have much in common. Like Vanuatu, the Solomons were "rediscovered" by French and British explorers and subsequently colonized. They also had similar periods involving sandalwood and slave traders, whalers and missionaries. Like the ni-Vanuatu, the Solomon islanders were exploited and almost exterminated by the white man. No wonder the natives were not particularly friendly towards these intruders, which earned them a reputation of being extremely dangerous. Unlike Vanuatu, several islands in the Solomons were occupied by Japanese troops during WWII. The archipelago was in the midst of the battlefield and played a central role in the war between Japan and USA. Today, diver enthusiasts from afar come to explore the many aircrafts and shipwrecks scattered on the bottom of the sea from this tragic era. We had barely settled down in Gizo Harbour when a fellow, black as the

A carver reveal a red betel smile. Betel is a popular substitute for alcohol and cigarettes in this strictly religious society.

ace of spades came paddling out to us with his bare hands in his tiny dugout canoe. "Hello!" he called. "My name is Bill! Do you know JFK?" Without waiting for a reply, he continued: "My grandfather rescued President Kennedy when his torpedo boat was cut in half and sunk by a Japanese destroyer during the war!" Then the man held up a magnificent mask. It became our first acquisition in the Solomon Islands. Imagine owning a carving made by the grandson of the man who rescued JFK!

We didn't really know what to believe. But one thing was sure: Bill was a fabulous carver. So this encounter became the first of many, many trading sessions in these islands where people were obviously much more vain than their neighbours to the south. Carefully, Bill chose some of Martin's old Nike shorts, a pair of runners, a couple of t-shirts and a baseball cap. "Do you have a mirror?" he asked as he was dickering over a pair of sunglasses. He wanted to make sure he looked good before making his choice. All I could find was a cracked pocket mirror. Bill studied himself thoroughly. "Me very happy!" he exclaimed visibly pleased. "You happy?" "Yes, we happy too," we smiled. "Good! Everybody happy!" Bill chuckled with delight as he gathered his things. "May I have the mirror too?" he asked with a sheepish grin. "Yes, of course! But it's broken," I said. "No problem! My wife will be very happy! It's better than nothing!" He offered us a miniature dolphin for the lousy mirror. "No," we laughed. "That's a gift." Bill was ecstatic when he loaded his canoe and paddled away to show off the loot he had traded with the newly arrived gringos. We had obviously been far too generous.

We did not feel entirely happy with the malaria expertise we had received in Vanuatu and decided to seek advice in Gizo as well, the second largest town in the islands with a population of 5,000. "Vegemite!" the native doctor recommended, laughing out loud. "Two teaspoons a day! Mosquitoes don't like the smell. My family takes vegemite every day. When you live in the malaria belt, you cannot keep taking malaria pills all the time. Extended use may produce severe side effects, even death.

Whatever you do, don't take doxicycline, which so many offshore sailors do. Used over a long period of time they can make you immune to antibiotics. Chloroquin is still the best prevention." Church bells sounded in the distance. "No, there is no service today," the affable doctor declared. "Here, we use church bells for all sorts of things: to announce meetings, deaths and the arrival of important visitors – even as an alarm clock to get people up in the morning and the children off to school on time!"

Since we had set a date to join a group of boats in Gove for our onwards sail to Indonesia, we could only spend three weeks in the Happy Isles. Again, we had to make a choice. We decided on Marovo Lagoon, a jewel of its kind nominated for Unesco World Heritage Site status. Scattered inside an enormous semicircular reef we found a multitude of densely forested lush green islands and uninhabited palm clad islets nestled in a pristine landscape of unparalleled beauty.

The dazzling water was teeming with tropical fish and a spectacular underwater flora, a truly unique marine ecosystem that attracts divers and underwater photographers from afar. And best of all: No tourists apart from the occasional offshore sailor and super keen diver! Marovo Lagoon is known for its excellent carvers. In fact, the carvers from the little village of Telima are reputed to be the best in the whole South Pacific. Here, we received the most touching welcome. No sooner was the anchor down before two sweet little girls approached us in their tiny dugout canoe with a lovely bouquet of flowers. Hovering at a safe distance studying us for a while, they were clearly summoning courage for the encounter. Ever so slowly, they closed in on us. Then, handing us the flowers over the railing, they

Welcome to Telima! The sweetest reception we have ever received.

whispered barely audibly: "Welcome to Telima!" This was our first meeting with the adorable children of the Solomon Islands who were going to give us so much pleasure and become the highlight of our stay. They were all smiles, shrieking with delight as they raced their small canoes splashing each other with water or diving in their birthday suits from rickety bamboo docks and impressing us with their water skills. Not one day passed without a visit from the wonderful youngsters who always brought us a handful of something or other. When we reciprocated throwing candy in the water, they went wild with delight. And we went equally wild with the camera. They were soooo charming!

It did not take long for the carvers of Telima to discover that they had a new visitor in the anchorage. Soon, we were surrounded by half a dozen canoes packed with trinkets and treasures. The typical outrigger of the South Seas was nowhere to be seen. Here, a much sturdier long and narrow canoe was the norm. Waiting their turn in an orderly fashion, they approached us one by one asking permission to come aboard to show us their creations.

The carvings were of exceptional workmanship, quality and design. The material was black ebony and a brown-streaked kerosene wood inlaid with mother-of-pearl from the beautiful nautilus shell. We went berserk trading everything from distinctive Nguzu-nguzu canoe figureheads, traditional masks and model canoes to turtles, sharks and dolphins and intricate sculptures inspired by motives from the sea. Living far off the beaten track, people were keen to trade. That was fine with us. At this point, we had lived onboard for 14 years and had lots of things we wanted to get rid of. Although they had seen better days, they were still of use to the locals. The most popular items were laundry soap, shampoo and towels, bed sheets, clothing and tennis shoes, flashlights, batteries and tools, glue, sandpaper and toys, crayons, paper and pens, fish hooks, fishing line and foodstuffs. There was never any question about alcohol or cigarettes. Most people in the lagoon were Seventh-day Adventists and did not drink or smoke.

We put the items we wanted to trade in a big basket, which we placed in the cockpit for the natives to pick and chose. It was interesting to watch them sort the things into piles. They were quite excited. After a while they stopped and announced that that was enough. Then it was up to us to start the negotiations and to determine whether they had taken too much. But first an amount of money had to be agreed upon. For half the trade had to be in cash. The trading sessions, which could last for hours on end were tiring but entertaining. Going on from early morning till late at night, we hardly had time to break for lunch before the next lot arrived.

After a few days of this we were so worn out that we fled to Chea, a peaceful little village where the population was exclusively Seventh-day Adventists. It was Saturday and their day of rest, so we knew we would be left alone. For they were neither allowed to work nor trade on their Sabbath. The following day, fairly recuperated, we went ashore to explore. As usual, a bunch of excited kids came running to greet us. Some had fair, almost blondish hair, a common feature in these isles where complexions differ from the almost blue-black Papuans to chocolate coloured Melanesians, bronze skinned Micronesians and relatively fair Polynesians.

The main road, which was nothing but a path of crushed shells and corals, was lined with rows of straw huts on stilts. In the shade beneath, men were carving and chipping away at their artefacts. Young boys in charge of the finishing were polishing the items with fine sandpaper. All day long. It was incredible to observe the technique of the carvers at close range and to see how they could create such beautiful things with such simple tools. The women attended to their household chores, washing clothes or sitting on the ground weaving pandanus mats, palm strands for thatched roofs and Bukaware from long, stiff vines. No wonder their hands were rough. The women seemed to avoid us looking the other way when we approached. They did not want to talk to us. At first, we thought they were shy. However, they were subject to a myriad of taboos, one being not to talk to strangers. They could only communicate through a man. That was kastom.

During our stay in Chea, we were taken care of by a spokesman with a bright red smile. Oxley was chewing betel, a widespread practice in the western part of the Pacific. Betel chewing produces bright red saliva, the unpleasant evidence of which can be seen on the ground all over the place in this paradise. In the olden days, red lips and black teeth were considered a sign of beauty, especially in females. Today, young and old, men and women chew the mixture, which consists of three ingredients: the nut of the areca palm, leaves of the fruit of the betel pepper and lime. Betel, which has a calming effect, is a popular substitute for cigarettes and alcohol. So there were many red lips and ugly teeth to be seen in this archipelago, whose feared ancestors were the vicious head-hunters. Oxley took us to a sacred cave in the jungle where evidence of their bygone activities was kept and guarded: a big pile of human sculls.

Descendants of the feared head-hunters reveal relics from the past.

Today's descendants have a much calmer disposition. In fact, it was easy to become close to these friendly people. So we decided to donate some eye glasses in the well-organized village. The Chief posted a note at the community hall. Soon half the village was gathered around a long rectangular table where we put the glasses for everyone to try. The likelihood of obtaining glasses in these remote islands is small. Besides, people couldn't afford them anyway. There is not much cash in a society where people live in harmony with nature tending their family plots basically surviving on subsistence agriculture and fishing alone. The likelihood of obtaining glasses in these remote islands is small. Besides, people couldn't afford them.. There is not much cash in a society where people live in harmony with nature tending their family plots basically surviving on subsistence agriculture and fishing alone.

It was not easy to leave such an idyllic spot where we had had so many wonderful people experiences. But our time was up. While preparing for our departure, we noticed a suspicious sound. Could it be the transmission? Martin was not keen to take it apart. But we couldn't count on local expertise either. Could it be something else? The noise reminded us of a previous incident when the zinc ring had come loose and was rattling on the propeller shaft. "Hopefully, that's

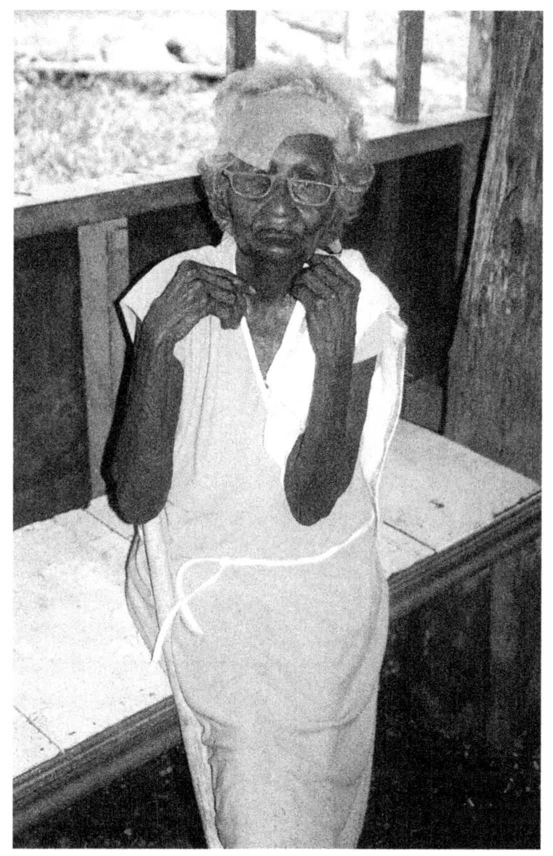
An old woman finds a pair to match her outfit.

what's happening now too," Martin said. "You're not going down in these waters!" I cried. "What about sharks and crocodiles?" "If kids swim here, so can I," he said and jumped over the side. Sure enough: the anode was loose. But while trying to tighten it, the ring slipped off the shaft and disappeared into the deep blue sea. We did not have a spare onboard.

Back in Gizo to check out, we met a sailor who was an engineer. He assured us that the permanent zinc at the end of the propeller shaft would prevent electrolysis. We were not convinced. Yet, we hoped the replacement could wait till Gove.

While sailing or at anchor, usually all by ourselves in the New Georgia Group, we never noticed any of the problems that had been reported before we left Vanuatu. To the contrary. The visit turned out to be a wonderful experience. We were glad we took the chance and didn't allow ourselves to be discouraged by either malaria or unrest. In fact, we would have loved to stay much longer. However, Australia was calling. It was time to make another move on the chessboard of the ocean.

IN THE WAKE OF CAPTAIN BLIGH FROM THE SOLOMON ISLANDS TO AUSTRALIA

"Nor Siglar! Just one more, please!" We recognized the fellow who was waving a carving after us. He was wearing Martin's old t-shirt. "Very good price!" he called. We couldn't help but laugh. We already had 50 carvings stowed away in the bilges. "Sorry! No more," we called back as we left the Happy Isles behind us for good.

It was late July when we set out into the Coral Sea. Being in the middle of the inter tropical convergence zone, the area is plagued by frequent lows. Normally, the southeasterly trades blow steady in this corner of the Pacific. However, on our first leg to the Louisiades, a group of sparsely populated islets in southern Papua New Guinea, the wind blew up from the southwest – completely unheard of at this time of year. So we had to brace ourselves for relentless banging and bashing into rough seas and strong gale force winds smack on the nose while tackling one nasty squall after another. It was quite a trip. And cold too. Despite being at 10ºS, we had to haul out our foul weather gear in the miserable conditions.

Four incredibly uncomfortable days later, we reached Jomard Passage, a busy shipping channel to and from the Far East. We were unlucky with the timing and didn't make it to the entrance before dark. But it was full moon and good visibility, so even though huge waves were breaking across the reef on both sides of the narrow pass, we decided to continue. That was easier said than done. We knew the current would be strong in the strait, but that it was going to be that bad, we had never imagined. It was dead calm, so we had to fire up the engine. Running at full throttle, we hardly moved in the 6-knot current. In the end, our good old Mr. Perkins had to capitulate. Besides, Martin had discovered a tear in the generator belt. If it broke, the engine would cut out in the middle of the pass. We would lose control in the strong current and surely go aground on the reef. There was not enough wind for the sails alone to give us enough steering speed to get us through. So we turned back and anchored near the opening to wait for the tide to turn.

Riding the rough waves of the Coral Sea.

At daybreak, we virtually flew through the strait swift as an arrow. Once on the west side of the Louisiades, the wind turned to the southeast and we could ease the sails. It was lovely. But not for long. Further out to sea, the wind speed increased rapidly to 30-35-40 knots. The waves built up accordingly. Soon, they were the highest we have ever seen. We even took water across the stern and into the cockpit. Not only that. We had other challenges to deal with as well. Water pollution! The debris came from the many deltas and estuaries along the coast of Papua New Guinea. Staying 40-50 nautical miles from land, we kept a careful lookout. Still, we kept bumping into coconuts, tree branches and deadheads floating in the water. Some impacts were so powerful that we thought the hull would crack. So we kept checking the bilges for possible leakage. We lucked out, but another sailor in the vicinity was less fortunate. A heavy waterlogged tree trunk ruined his wind vane in the middle of the night.

Thus, the crossing to the Torres Strait became a test of endurance. By the time we reached Bligh Entrance in the northern part of the Great Barrier Reef, it felt as though the entire Pacific Ocean was trying to get rid of us with all its might. At a speed of 8-10 knots, we were literally catapulted in through the narrow opening in the huge swells and following winds. Depending heavily on our invaluable GPS, we made it safely through the nasty reefs and shallows. How Captain Bligh managed to find his way in a small tender packed with 18 men through these very same coral strewn waters all the way from

Tonga, solely by memory and a chronometer is beyond us. About 200 years later, our achievement of getting through the passage so aptly named after the legendary seafarer, was nothing by comparison. The two of us had only been underway for nine days in a 40-foot sailboat using both GPS and charts as aids to navigation. Still, the challenge was more than enough for us.

No stopping was allowed before the nearest point of clearance, i.e. Thursday Island in the western part of the 120 nautical mile strait. Therefore, a substantial part of the transit had to be undertaken at night. Not an easy task in the treacherous waters. We chickened out and stopped at night anyway enabling us to sail in daylight only. So when an Australian coastguard plane discovered us at anchor, we became really worried. But they only instructed us to refrain from going ashore or have contact with anybody until we were officially checked into the country.

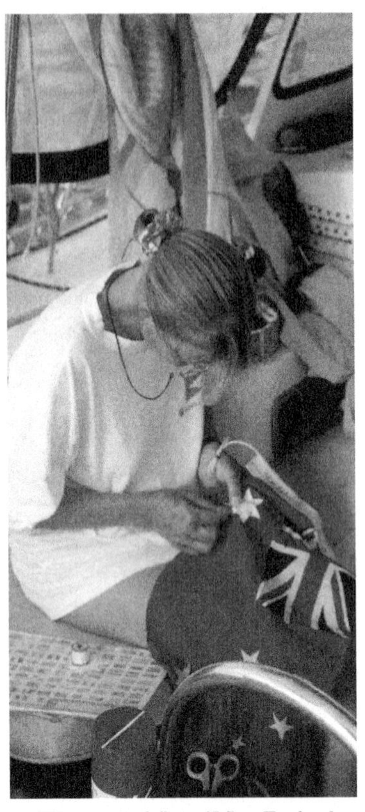

The nautical flag of New Zealand becomes Australian by adding two more stars!

In Prince of Wales Channel at the western exit of the heavily trafficked strait, we met a huge tanker at the narrowest point in the middle of a dogleg. The encounter was rather unnerving in the strong following current. But we made it and rounded Cape York Peninsula in one piece. Ahead lay the Gulf of Carpentaria, another frequently rough stretch. However, at this point we felt we could take just about anything. We had long since found our sea legs and could sense the end of the passage.

After 1,400 nautical miles and 14 long days at sea, it was wonderful to reach our destination: Gove in the Northern Territory, Australia's least populated area. After a thorough inspection by two pleasant Customs and Immigration officers who confiscated a couple of onions and a bag of trash – and even scanned the whole interior with some sort of electronic tape in search of narcotics – we were free to go ashore Down Under.

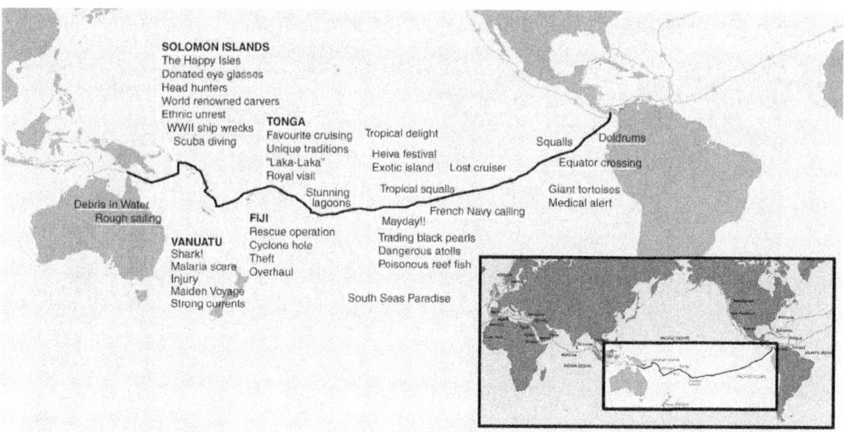

The end of Part 5 of the "9 Years on the 7 Seas Adventure", also published in print and as an eBook with the title The South Pacific - the Sea of Dreams.

PART 6

After 14days at sea it was wonderful to reach Gove, where we met other cruisers who also wanted to sail to Indonesia.

SOUTH-EAST ASIA
AUSTRALIA – MALDIVES

AUSTRALIA

The beach at Gove Yacht Club was adorned with big warning signs about saltwater crocodiles and deadly box jellyfish. There were poisonous snakes in the water as well. So we did not swim here either, something which was going to have serious consequences. For we really should have inspected the propeller to see if there was any evidence of corrosion since the zinc ring fell off in the Solomons. But what is worse? Crocodiles or electrolysis? Martin was adamant that he should go down and have a quick look. "It will only take a minute," he insisted. "Are you nuts?" I cried. "Don't you remember the sailor who was attacked by a crocodile recently while he was snorkelling to check his anchor? No, this dive will have to wait for safer waters."

During our short stay on Australian soil we were mainly preoccupied with provisioning and getting ready for our 2-month Indonesian adventure. Still, we managed to squeeze in a trip to Yirrkala, an aboriginal village known for its small but excellent museum of ancient art forms and traditions. So far, we had only witnessed the sad part of their existence, as aboriginals from a bordering reserve keenly frequented the yacht club bar. So it was good to see the positive aspect of their unique culture, which has been so suppressed after the Europeans arrived on their continent.

The newspapers were full of articles on violence and unrest leading up to the referendum on the independence of East Timor. There were also reports of tension between the Christians and the Muslims in certain islands. And with the economic crisis in South East Asia, crime and theft had escalated, not to mention piracy attacks, which were rumoured to have doubled in the past year. Australia warned its citizens not to travel to the region. The annual Darwin-Ambon and Gove- Saumlaki regattas were cancelled.

Needless to say we did not swim in these waters.

Discussion raged within our little Indonesia-bound flotilla, with whom we had agreed to sail for safety reasons. Eventually, we all decided to carry on with our plan and instructed the yacht club to go ahead and obtain our cruising permits. They obliged. But we were told in no uncertain terms that we were going at our own risk. Other sailors chose to bypass the archipelago by taking a southern route non-stop from Darwin to Bali. But with our positive experiences in the Solomon Islands fresh in mind, as well as other successful visits to so-called unsafe countries like Algeria and certain parts of Panama and Honduras our decision was made: Indonesia – here we come!

INDONESIA

Feeling there is safety in numbers, our little international flotilla set out for the famed Spice Islands in Indonesia's troubled eastern corner. Our group consisted of six adventurous sailboats: two from Australia, two from New Zealand, one from Sweden and us. We had decided to keep in touch on an SSB-frequency twice a day and to monitor Robby's Net, a ham net run by a Dutch-Indonesian radio amateur. Apart from weather forecasts, he could give us valuable information on local conditions, places and sights, customs and events. Robby could also send and receive e-mail for us. That way we could maintain regular contact with our families back home. They were obviously concerned while we were in such an unsafe area that was making headlines in the news around the world every day.

A typical Indonesian outrigger with a patched sail.

Halfway across the Arafura Sea, we were startled by a call from the Australian Coast Guard. But they only wanted to know if we had seen anything unusual on the way - something that could be of interest to them. They were obviously referring to boat people – to the illegal influx of refugees to Ashmore Reef, which Australia was trying to curtail. Fortunately, we had nothing but ideal conditions to report. So after four lovely days under poled out foresails on a comfortable downwind run, we made landfall in Saumlaki on the island of Tanimbar in the Moluccas. We had reached the legendary Spice Islands, an alluring goal for colonials and traders half a century ago. There is no denying that we were pretty worried when a strange-looking craft closed in on us in the early morning mist. But it turned out to be nothing but a local fishing boat going about its normal business of hauling in fishnets in the early hours of the day.

The atmosphere was rather tense in our little group, so we anchored close together to keep an eye out for each other. And when BBC reported that 30 people had been killed in a bombing raid on a church in Ambon not far from Tanimbar, we wondered if we had made a reckless decision after all. Things did not feel any better when an overloaded wreck of an old freighter with a considerable list to port came in and docked at the town quay. It was carrying 2000 Christian evacuees from Ambon. 300 were destined for Saumlaki. These poor people had lost everything they owned in a recent attack when hundreds of homes were looted and burned.

Unbeknownst to us, the chairman of last year's Gove-Saumlaki regatta had been alerted of our arrival. So we were not only surprised, but also relieved to receive a warm welcome. She brought with her a representative from the Department of Tourism who advised us on where we could travel safely in Indonesia. We chose our route accordingly: bypass Timor and continue west along the Nusa Tenggara chain to Bali. From there we could turn north to Kalimantan on southern Borneo and onwards across the South China Sea to Singapore. "But be very careful on 9/9/99 at 9 o'clock!" he warned. "Why is that?" we asked. "Judgement Day!" he whispered, visibly frightened. "What will the Indonesians do then?" we wondered. "We'll stay home and pray," he answered in dead earnest.

We sailors, however, had another form of judgement day to worry about: 22/8/99 at 00:00:00 UTC. That was the precise date for the Global Positioning System time rollover. Virtually hypnotized, we monitored our 9-year old Magellan as the crucial moment approached. But while its calendar did in fact disappear, our lat/long-position stayed exactly the same. In fact, all else remained functional. Now the next test will be whether it will survive Y2K as well. To be on the safe side, we have a small handheld Garmin as backup. We might us well admit it: the sextant has only been used once on our voyage! And we are not alone. Most sailors out here have several GPS-receivers. Sensible or not: celestial navigation is a tool of the past.

In order to pass East Timor as quickly as possible, while at the same time putting some miles under the keel in this archipelago, which has the longest coastline in the world, the group decided to sail 500 nautical miles without stop to the islands of Solor. The news on BBC was dramatic. With the referendum only days away, the conditions were chaotic with demonstrations and revolts. Scores of people were killed. We were nervous. What if the militia had bases on the islands? What if people escaped to sea? It was highly possible that we could become involved in a rescue operation. Under the circumstances, that was something we wished to avoid at any cost. We certainly did not treasure ending up with refugees from East-Timor onboard. However, if we came across people who were in trouble and needed our help, we were obliged, according to maritime law, to render assistance. On that thought, we hoisted full sails to get by the troubled area as fast as we could.

Refugees, pirates or fishermen?

So we did not feel very happy when we noticed that we were being followed one night. Were they pirates? Or refugees? At this point, we were only 40 nautical miles from the capital of Dili. The boat did not show any red or green lights. Only a weak oil lamp astern. It moved around in all directions. We had no idea what its intentions were. It certainly did not follow any navigational rules. However, once again, we realized that it was a fishing boat tending its nets in the dark.

In the daytime, we found the local traffic to be both aggressive and unpredictable. It was unnerving. Every once in a while, an overloaded rust bucket with 20-30 persons onboard would come right up alongside, nearly swiping our topsides. "Oh no! Now we're going to be attacked," I thought the first time it happened. We'd better keep our cool. "Selamat pagi! Good morning!" I called as cheerfully as I could. Some of the men looked like criminals in their black balaclavas. So we were really surprised when they started waving and shouting: "Hey Mister! Cigarettes? Water?" They were obviously just curious and wanted to see if they could get something from the rich yachties. Camouflaged in their scary-looking balaclavas it was easy to mistake the innocent maniacs for pirates. But the fact is that many fishermen in this part of the world use this kind of headgear simply as a protection against the wind and the sun.

Superstitious fishermen cum pirates frighten us "rich yachties" by skirting our bows in an attempt to get rid of evil spirits.

Robby told us that Indonesians tend to be superstitious. Especially the fishermen. If they have poor fishing luck, they think there are evil spirits onboard. In order to get rid of them, they try to transfer the spirits to another boat by crossing its bows dead close at full speed while making a sharp 90-degree turn and circling it a few times. This way the evil spirits were forced across to the other boat! Also, the fishermen clearly enjoyed frightening the "white monkeys", as they called us foreigners. It took a while before we became used to this behaviour, which the cruisers dubbed: "The scare the Yachties Game."

The non-stop voyage past Timor turned out to be a great passage, a true balm for body and soul. We had five wonderful days on a lovely broad reach in a gentle to fresh southeasterly breeze on calm seas enjoying fiery sunsets, a full moon and shooting stars, volcanoes glowing in the dark and those velvet nights so soft and warm that can only be experienced in the tropics. By day, nature revealed a landscape of rugged mountains, isolated fishing villages with eye-catching minarets and mosques with golden domes, clusters of homes scattered along steep hillsides clinging to streams of petrified lava, brown sunburned slopes and fertile valleys abundant with succulent crops.

The quaint fishing village, Leba Leba at dawn.

Safely arrived in Leba Leba, an incredibly picturesque fishing village, we anchored in amongst all sorts of weird and wonderful craft: spindly bamboo outriggers, sampan ferries with tattered sunroofs, tiny one-man canoes and dugout logs with scruffy patchwork sails. The scenery was stunning. Two spectacular conical volcanoes spewing steam formed a dramatic backdrop in the distance. The atmosphere was misty. A combination of smoke from active volcanoes and natives' slash burning fires produced the softest hues of pink dawns one can imagine. So when little old women in coolie hats came paddling out at daybreak to fish, it felt as though time was standing still. The scene was so peaceful and authentic that it gave us the feeling of being in the middle of a motif worthy of the cover of National Geographic.

The children in this isolated corner of Indonesia were all smiles, but rather aggressive. They clambered right into the cockpit without asking permission and proceeded to beg for everything in sight. After a while, we learned that the best way to get rid of them was to fold our hands and pretend that we were going to pray. This was something the young Muslims understood and respected. They were gone in a flash.

Market day in the quaint village was a noisy and vibrant affair. There was lots of commotion with people shopping, trading and bargaining with shrill intensity. The lack of cleanliness was appalling. Although the products were both fresh and inexpensive, we were not tempted to buy much except fruit and vegetables that could be peeled. As a matter of fact, we were very careful with what we ate in this tropical climate where food and water may often be contaminated and cause the outbreak of infectious disease. Normally though, we ate the foods available along the way and almost considered ourselves vegetarians as we seldom ate the local meat. But if the locals drank the water, so did we.

We never bought bottled water. It took too much room. Nor did we boil the water. It took too much propane. If we were uncertain of its quality, we added chlorine. Contrary to most of our sailor friends, who were much more careful than us, we never got sick from the local food or water. Our theory is that when one is moving as slowly as one does in a sailboat, there is ample time to become acclimatized and immune to the local bacteria. For tourists who fly from one side of the globe to the other in a matter of hours, the situation is, of course, quite different.

In Indonesia though, we had to use the watermaker for the first time in a long while. Here, it was not safe to drink the water, nor was there enough rainwater to collect. The dry season was coming to an end. The northwest monsoons were upon us, a period characterized by torrential rainfalls, terrific thunderstorms and lightning. No, there is never a dull moment out here.

AGROUND AGAIN!

On September 1, it was exactly eight years since we set out on our offshore adventure. We celebrated the anniversary with our flotilla friends toasting in local Bintang beer and Norwegian Linje aquavit, a rarity for our new friends from Down Under. The mood was upbeat. Little did we know that it would change drastically very soon.

The following day, we were going to tackle the narrow Strait of Solor. We set sail at the crack of dawn in order to get through before the tide turned. But the current was already against us by the time we were halfway through. We had to use the engine to make it. "Let's go closer to shore," Martin said. "The current is weaker in the back eddy there." The other boats did not follow suit and were lagging further and further behind. Little by little, one after the other had to capitulate and wait for the next change of tide. We made it. But just barely. Had we been only minutes later, we would not have succeeded. I went below to bake bread. Suddenly, there was a big jolt. We came to an abrupt halt. I lost my balance and hit my head on the chart table. "Oh no! Not again!" Martin called in despair. He was up on deck hoisting the mainsail. "We're hard aground!" Boy, did that news ever hurt. It felt like a thunderbolt had struck the very core of my soul. It was our second grounding in three months! And we didn't have a good excuse this time either. There was virtually no wind, the visibility was excellent and the water crystal clear. And we knew where we were. Or so we thought! The reason for the blunder was our chart. It was a poor photocopy. We had to use a magnifying glass to find the reef. And sure enough: there it was marked with some tiny dots. Right on the fold, of course.

Oh No! Nor Siglar is hard aground.

This grounding was much more serious than the one in Fiji. Hitting the reef at a speed of 4 knots, we were completely stuck. On a high tide, no less. After checking that we were not taking in any water, we tried to back off the reef. But however hard we tried Nor Siglar did not budge. She was not going anywhere.

We called up the other sailboats on Channel 16 and conveyed the bad news. But they were unable to come to our assistance until the current reversed. Only Santana managed to make it against the strong current. Some local fishermen stopped by to help. We handed them the spinnaker halyard so they could pull us over on our side while our Swedish friends tried to pull us off. We held our breath. The halyard snapped. The locals did not know how to tie a proper knot. We showed them how. But despite all the goodwill in the world, the language problems lead to confusion. So after a few attempts, we just had to give up.

Now, all we could do was wait for the next high tide. The six hours that followed were the longest and worst in our history of cruising. In the meantime, we put out a stern anchor to prevent the boat from swinging sideways, a motion that could smash the rudder, which was embedded in some nasty corals. In a way, this was a stroke of luck in our misfortune and a factor that probably saved the rudder. On the other hand, it became even more difficult to get loose, since the keel had become thoroughly stuck in another crevice in the coral bed. As the tide was ebbing, Thomas and Martin were standing on the reef trying to protect the hull against the sharp coral with sheets of plywood, which we had onboard for use in an emergency.

Language problems prevent rescue efforts by helpful locals.

It was terribly unnerving to feel the boat heeling over more and more. Nor Siglar was bumping up and down in the swell rubbing alarmingly hard against the coral. It was a dreadful sound that gave us a sinking feeling we'll never forget. Each minute felt like an hour. It was nerve-racking having to wait to see if we would get enough water under the keel to float off the reef.

Five hours later, Minaret and Chantecleer made it through the strait. Grahame and David put out another anchor fastened to the end of the spinnaker halyard about a hundred metres abeam. We did not have any tide tables so when we thought it was maximum high tide, John and Ingrid on Beyond, a 52-foot American ketch who had heard us on Channel 16 and come to our rescue, tried to pull us forward, while Grahame winched us over on our side with the spinnaker halyard. The pressure on mast and rig was enormous. Yet, Nor Siglar did not move.

We had to think of something else. Maybe we could use our dinghy for something. But it only had a 5 HP engine. Richard from Papagayo turned up with his powerful dinghy and tried to push us sideways. No luck. Then he, Thomas and Ingrid took it out to the anchor abeam and started to yank on the spinnaker halyard while David shoved the main boom way out to the side and started jumping up and down on it to get a pendulum motion going. Martin was in the water snorkelling to see what was going on below the surface. I gave full throttle ahead. The water turned muddy. But we were still in the same spot. We tried again and again. Beyond's engine was overheating. The situation looked gloomy. It was depressing. Especially when Grahame suggested that I should collect our valuables. Just in case. No, it did not look very good for our dear old Nor Siglar. What if we couldn't get her off the reef? The incident was not lifethreatening, though. For we could wade ashore.

The tide was starting to turn. It was now or never. Suddenly Martin started waving his arms, splashing and yelling. He saw the keel smash through the coral like a battering ram. Nor Siglar started jerking and moving ever so slowly forward. And lo and behold: all of a sudden she slid several metres ahead, righted herself beautifully and floated gracefully out on deep water as though nothing had happened. What a relief!

As far as we could determine, Nor Siglar had only sustained superficial damage. We could not see any cracks or structural damage to the keel or hull. Only a small corner of the rudder was chewed off. It was impressive to see how much beating a fibreglass hull can take.

How could we possibly go aground twice in such a short time? Had we become complacent? No doubt, we had been much too careless. First of all, we were going too close to shore. Secondly, the quality of the chart was poor and the scale too small. Finally, there was nobody at the helm when the mishap occurred. Regardless of how many miles one has sailed, one must never let one's guard down. It was a frightening, albeit valuable lesson.

During the rescue operation it was heart-warming to experience the close friendship and camaraderie that had developed in our team in such a short time. We discovered that we are not alone out here. In fact, we are like a big family. We actually feel a certain responsibility for each other. We need each other and sort of depend on one another. So termima kasih dear friends – thank you from the bottom of our hearts. Oh, yes. What happened to the bread you might ask? Well, apart from being somewhat lopsided, it turned out well!

RITUALS, RITES AND REALITY

Judgement Day came and went without incident. We couldn't help but think of all the frightened people who stayed at home praying. To be on the safe side, we spent the day at sea. We did wonder, though when we saw some violent explosions nearby. Waterspouts spurted into the air. A couple of fishing boats were alarmingly close. Suddenly, we realized what was going on. The fishermen were using dynamite!

We were working our way west along Nusa Tenggara, a volcanic string of islands where some of Indonesia's most spectacular attractions can be found. On the island of Flores, we anchored off and took a tour to a 3,000-metre high volcano, which is famous for its crater with three lakes in different colours; light turquoise, olive green and black. This unusual phenomenon was the highlight of an unforgettable panoramic drive through mountain villages known for their traditional dancers, ikat-weavers and colourful markets. Later on, on the nature reserve at Rinca Island, we came face to face with the deadly Komodo dragon, the largest lizard in the world. The endangered species can reach a length of 3 metres and weigh up to 130 kg.

The currents run strong through all the straits in the Nusa Tenggara chain, previously called the Lesser Sunda Islands. In the Strait of Lombok a 6- knot southwest-flowing current shot us across to Bali in record time: 50 nautical miles in only seven hours. After a month on Indonesia's remote southeastern shores, we were looking forward to some luxury at Bali International Yacht Club. Here, we could safely leave the boat and take a trip inland to explore the real

Bali. We could also check the propeller. Fortunately, it did not show any signs of corrosion.

Most tourists don't venture far beyond Bali's biggest resort, Kuta Beach with its international hotel chains, fashionable shops and bazaars overflowing with cheap souvenirs and mass-produced clothing. And that is a real shame. For Bali is a rare pearl with picturesque terraced rice fields dominating brilliant green landscape where farming is still done the traditional way. The complex, but highly functional irrigation system is ancient too. Although the scenery is Bali's biggest attraction, the island has much more to offer as well: an interesting mix of religions, a rich culture and authentic theatre and music, Balinese dancing, intricate silver and batik-work and last but not least, amiable people. After giving us a tour of his rice-fields, a friendly farmer took us home for a drink of arak, a potent homebrew treasured throughout Southeast Asia.

Nominally a Muslim nation, there is an amazing diversity of religions in Indonesia. Bali is predominantly Hindu, but Buddhism is present as well. We were taken by the ornate Hindu temples and decorative family shrines where flowers, food and drink were offered to revered gods at dusk and dawn. The Buddhist temples were also a sight complete with golden Buddhas, life-like dragons and glittering designs.

"How does it work to have people of three major religions living so close together?" we asked our chauffeur. "I'll tell you," he said. "Muslims live on the coast in fishing villages. Hindus are mostly farmers. Buddhists, who are mainly Chinese, run their various businesses in the cities while the Indians, who are either Hindu or Muslim, work on plantations inland or as merchants and moneychangers in town. This way we don't interfere with each other's lifestyle and culture," the Balinese driver explained. He only charged a hundred dollars for a two-day trip of 700 km with many stops.

"There is a Hindu funeral in my village today," he said. Would you like to attend?" It was an opportunity not to be missed. A long procession was already underway when we arrived. Men in black balloon trousers, red shirts and Malayan headbands were beating drums and chanting a monotonous hymn at the head of the cortege. Behind them, men in black shirts and colourful sarongs carried the coffin high on an intricately decorated platform adorned with flowers and colours that sparkled in the sun. A large photo of the deceased was displayed at the back. At the end of the procession women dressed in batik sarongs and black lace blouses carried baskets with offerings on their heads. Every once in a while, the men carrying the coffin ran around in a circle. They were getting rid of evil spirits. Just like the boats we had encountered! The air was filled with the scent of incense and perfumed flowers. A veil of mystique enveloped the ancient ritual.

Funeral procession in Bali

Hindu cremation

At the cremation site, the coffin was transferred to the ground and broken apart. Then the corpse, clothed in a white shroud was placed on the pyre where offerings and items of personal importance had been placed. This was the moment for the family to say their good-byes. Then the cremator arrived with matches and propane. Before we knew it, the pyre was ablaze. As the smoke spread over the crowd, people started to leave. The ashes were to be scattered on the river at dawn.

It was both odd and dramatic to be present at such a personal ceremony. We were struck by the absence of grief. There were no tears. Could it be because Hindus believe in reincarnation? That all beings have an immortal soul that is reborn. Death is not the end of life. It is, in fact, a new beginning.

After a 10-day break packed with fascinating encounters with new cultures, we set out into the strait again. This time, we were not going to cross it but rather follow the coast north to the Java Sea. This time, we didn't manage to get through before the tide turned. So the last few hours became a struggle against current and short steep seas. In the middle of it all we witnessed a show without equal: hundreds of "spider-boats" flying triangular sails appeared out of nowhere and started scooting back and forth fishing in the afternoon rip tide.

Local "spider boats" fishing in the riptide create havoc for sailors by scooting back and forth across our bow with only metres to spare.

We had our hands full making our way safely through the unruly fleet, which created havoc for us sailors by crossing our bows with metres to spare. We had several close calls and were both exhausted and relieved when we finally made it through unscathed and could carry on to Kalimantan. During this crossing, our short-wave radio went on the blink. "What now?" Martin sighed disillusioned. "This is our 4th mishap in 3 months!" It felt terribly lonely without our dependable contact to the outside world. Little did we know that this was the first sign that something much more serious was in the offing.

Five uneventful days later, we entered the big river of Kumai abuzz with prahus characteristic of the region. Despite torn and shabby sails, they looked rather elegant with their sloping decks and prominent bows. All sorts of craft were plying the wide and muddy river. Even an islet came floating downstream in the strong current!

We were nearing 2° S, it was October and the monsoons were generating terrific downpours that caused all sorts of debris in the water.

Our main reason for coming to Kalimantan was to take a 3-day river safari to Tanjung Puting National Park, a rehabilitation centre for young orang-utans. Considered a status symbol pet, poachers captivate the babies illegally and sell them around the world. Therefore, orang-utans are in danger of becoming extinct. If discovered, the tame animals are taken to a rehabilitation centre where they are integrated back into their original environment. It was delightful to watch them in their natural habitat.

At a rehabilitation centre in Kalimantan we meet the mighty orangutan, man's closest relative.

We did not have time to see more than a dozen or so of Indonesia's 13 667 islands. We did, however, sample a representative selection. Again, we were glad we decided to come despite the many warnings. Nicer people and a lovelier cruising area are hard to find. And since Indonesia is not on the regular around-the-world cruising route, we could enjoy the jewel virtually alone, in the company of a few likeminded sailors. We never had any problems with the authorities. Nor with people in general. We did get a bit tired, though of the constant calls of: "Hey Mister!" Still, that was a pretty innocent annoyance. What about violence? No, we never felt threatened. Theft? Only a minor incident. And pirates? No, but we haven't crossed the infamous South China Sea yet.

TROUBLES ON THE SOUTH CHINA SEA

The transition between the southeast and the northwest monsoons is characterized by a period of little or no wind. Never before have we had to use the engine so much. And for the first time, we ran out of diesel. Nor Siglar has a fuel capacity of only 250 litres. That was more than enough for the Atlantic and Pacific crossings. But the South China Sea was calm as a mirror. We had to resort to the iron horse for most of the 600 nautical mile passage from Kalimantan to Batam Island, our last port of call in Indonesia. We also had to hand steer, as we don't have an electric autopilot. The wind-vane only works when we are under sail or motor-sailing. So our "Mr. Perkins" had to work extra hard. Especially as the current was against us most of the time. Our group had split up, but luckily we were still in the company of Maria Two. So when we only had a few litres left, she came to our rescue and gave us a couple of cans.

About halfway, a familiar-looking freighter passed us within half a mile. It was a Gearbulk vessel! The Raven Arrow! I had organized a string of receptions on the B.C. coast on the occasion of her maiden voyage from Japan in 1982. Excited, I called her up. The Captain couldn't believe his eyes when he realized that the woman hailing him from the sailboat was the same one who was in the picture on the wall in front of him!

Then, on October 17, we crossed the equator back into the northern hemisphere again. With all the bad luck we had had lately, we thought our old GPS might conk out on us. But no, it switched automatically from S to N and King Neptune received his ceremonial drops of aquavit. Otherwise, the event passed without fanfare. We made much more of our first crossing. Are we getting blasé, or what?

There is a lot of pollution in the waters of Indonesia. So when the engine started to vibrate one morning and the speed decreased, we figured something was stuck in the propeller. Martin went down to have a look. Seconds later, he popped up like a cork and yelled: "the propeller looks like a saw blade!" We were shocked. Only two weeks ago, it had been just fine. How could it possibly have corroded so fast? It was very strange. Could the defective radio have anything to do with the corrosion?

Nor Siglar in tow across Singapore Strait. *Electrolysis!*

We only had a few hundred miles to go. All we could do was continue at slow speed. But during the night, the vibration escalated. The revolutions dropped. Regardless of how much we accelerated, the boat kept slowing down. Maybe we had lost a piece of the propeller? As soon as the sun was up, Martin dove down to check. I expected the worst. But this time, the prop was full of debris. Our relief was short-lived. For when he came up the ladder and grabbed the railing, he got an electric shock! That could mean only one thing: electrolysis!

When we shut the engine off, the railing was no longer "alive". Clearly, we had to stop motoring. Otherwise, the engine might corrode as well. Again, Maria Two came to our assistance and took us in tow. Now that we didn't have to steer any more, there was lots of time to ponder. It had not been a good year. "Two groundings – and now this! It's definitely time to go home," Martin sighed. "I am getting too old for this."

Maria Two towed us slowly but surely for 24 hours to Nongsa Point Marina where we checked out of Indonesia. Only 30 miles away, Singapore's modern skyline was beckoning with its expertise and conveniences of the western world. But it was not easy to get across the busy strait with its continuous traffic moving to and from the Far East. It was tricky to find a gap between the ships, which moved in both directions at a speed of 15-20 knots. But Maria Two rose to the challenge. After eight nerve-racking hours, we were all safe and sound in Singapore harbour.

SQUABBLES IN SINGAPORE

It did not take long for the experts in Raffles Marina to diagnose the problem: a short in the alternator. This caused a chain reaction. When the alternator cut out, the short-wave radio, which is grounded to the engine block cut out as well. The permanent sacrificial anode at the end of the propeller shaft had not been able to prevent the electrolysis due to a stainless steel plate separating it from the propeller.

As expected, the damages from the grounding were mostly superficial. In fact, they were almost negligible compared to those caused by the electrolysis. It was quick to fix the scratched up keel, repair the rudder and apply a coat of bottom paint to the areas in question. Likewise, it was easy to replace the propeller as we had a spare with us from home. While preparing for our adventure, we had been discussing at length whether we should spend a thousand dollars on something we hoped we would never use. As far as the radio was concerned, we rectified the problem by grounding it to a new dynaplate under the hull instead of the engine block.

We were working flat out from early morning till late at night. Still, we found the time to see a good portion of Singa Puru, also called the "City of Lions", where Sir Thomas Stanford Raffles established a British trading post at the beginning of the 19th century. Since then, the island state, which originally was an uninhabited jungle, has turned into a melting pot of over 4 million people from different cultures.

Located near the equator, Singapore is hot and humid year-round. It is hard to say what was worst: the heat or the mess. With all the projects going on plus a gigantic job stowing provisions, which we hoped would last all the way to Israel, I felt I was spending all my time tidying up. So in the evenings, it was nice to enjoy some luxury: a cold drink on a bar stool in the swimming pool of the marina and great Chinese food at its air-conditioned restaurant.

One day a sailboat came in and docked right next to us. It had sailed non-stop from Bali. The skipper and his one-man crew were not on speaking terms. They had seen a dead man floating in the water just off the south coast of Java. The crew wanted to take the decomposed body to Singapore. The owner did not want anything to do with it. They started arguing and had not been talking since.

That evening, the sailing community met in the bar to discuss the case. Some felt it would be far too risky to come in to port with a dead body onboard. Who knows? One could end up being accused of the person's death oneself. Others felt that the discovery should have been reported on sight. But to whom? In this part of the world, there is neither a Coast Guard nor a Navy to rely on. The body could at least have been towed to the nearest harbour, someone suggested. What would we have done? If the man had been alive, we would, of course, have taken him onboard. Or would we? It could be a trap. One could risk becoming involved in something or other. Worst-case scenario: we could be blamed for something we had nothing to do with. Our boat could be confiscated. We could even be put in jail. Best-case scenario: A delay. And who knows how long that could be - entangled in the justice apparatus of the Far East. Had we been in familiar waters, the situation would have been different. We hoped we would never get into a situation where we would have to make such a decision. The matter was not solved that evening. The skipper and his crew parted ways.

The stopover in Singapore became much longer than anticipated. And since we had a deadline to meet friends in Malaysia, we were time pressed and had to carry on alone. Ahead of us lay the most pirate infested waters in the world: the infamous Strait of Malacca. The local papers were full of reports on recent attacks. The only consolation was that pleasure boats had not been targeted for a long time. Our intention had been to take short daytrips up the strait together with our flotilla. However, now we didn't have time for that. We had to do the 4-day non-stop transit on our own.

MALAYSIA
THE INFAMOUS STRAIT OF MALACCA

I had butterflies in my stomach and Martin did too, when we set out into the notorious Strait. So when we noticed some dark shadows approaching us in the moonlight, we wondered if we had made a foolish decision to leave the safety of our group and attempt the transit alone.

In the Strait of Malacca the question surfaced again!
Are these characters innocent fishermen, dangerous pirates or both?

We changed course and increased our speed. The little craft, which were unlit, did the same. We changed course again. So did they. My heart started pounding. Martin hailed them on Channel 16. No reply. We turned 180 degrees. They followed suit. My imagination went wild. I envisioned the headlines: "Canadian couple attacked in the

Strait of Malacca." The boats kept closing in on us. We thought we could see some scary-looking characters on the bow. They were wearing balaclavas. But what on earth were they doing? Aha! They were hauling in an enormous fish net! Once again, we experienced that the perceived pirates were merely innocent fishermen.

We never encountered any of the dreaded pirates of the Strait of Malacca. Still, the transit was not without problems. A steady stream of freighters and super tankers plied the waters at approximately 15-minute intervals. But the international traffic, which stayed within the shipping channel, didn't worry us too much. Our strategy was to follow the 25-metre contour line which separates the main shipping lane from the fishing banks, an area too far from shore for the fishing fleet and too close for the big freighters. But it was also an area used by local commercial vessels. And most were unlit. We got quite a shock when a 15,000 tonner without navigation lights steamed right by us at full speed. It was very scary. So the night watches were extremely stressful.

In fact, there was no shortage of drama and excitement. A single-hander we knew fell asleep at the helm and ran into a huge tanker only a few metres aft of its bow. He woke up with a jolt when his boat smashed over on the side, its mast and railing scraping the entire length of the big vessel. Had he been only seconds earlier, he would have been hit square on and sunk. The sailor escaped with a fright. But he learned a serious lesson. And we were reminded of how sensible our policy is of always keeping watch - not only near the coast but on the open ocean as well - regardless of how tempting it is to take a short nap once in a while. And in this particular area, you certainly could not relax. Further north in the strait, a sailboat lying at anchor was rammed by a fishing boat in the middle of the night.

After a nerve-racking 4-day transit motor sailing in fluky winds and contrary currents, we sailed into Langkawi, a lovely group of verdant limestone islands in the northern part of the Malay Peninsula. We docked at Rebak Marina where we enjoyed a few days of luxury with its laundry facilities, showers, swimming pool and wonderful restaurant. Our friends from Norway came loaded down with brown goat cheese and aquavit, Christmas presents and mail from home. We took a week's "holiday" and cruised around the peaceful archipelago, which due to its strategic location near the north entrance of Malacca Strait was a perfect hideout for pirates in the old days.

Rebak Marina was a safe and popular place to leave the boat while travelling inland. Some sailors even lived there year round! Exotic lands like Laos, Vietnam and Cambodia were within reach. So was China, not to forget Nepal, a favourite destination for keen hikers and mountaineers. Being short of time, we settled for a two-week tour of Thailand, a welcome change after having sailed over 6,000 nautical miles since leaving Fiji only five months earlier.

Fortunately, the marina restaurant was willing to store the perishable food we had onboard while we were gone. But when the cook saw us putting a package of bacon in his freezer, he turned pale. "Oh no!" he exclaimed shocked. "Pork? We are not allowed to eat pork. We can't even touch it! Now we have to empty and disinfect the whole freezer! And the Imam has to come and bless it again!" We were obviously in for a new learning experience in Malaysia's mostly Muslim society.

THAILAND
CHRISTMAS IN SPLENDID ISOLATION

Glittering temples, golden Buddhas and monks in saffron coloured robes, sparkling steeples and colourful mosaics, the splendour of the ancient cities of Siam and, of course, its gentle people – those were only some of the images we brought back to Nor Siglar mid December.

It was time to continue our adventure in the Land of Smiles on our own keel. A stunning picture on the cover of the "Sail-Thailand" guide lured us to Phi Phi Don, one of Asia's most beautiful islands.

Nor Siglar in isolated phan Nga Bay on the last Christmas of the Millennium.

Hiking to the peak to get the same photo, we also got to see hundreds of swifts busily making their precious nests that are used in the coveted bird's-nest soup.

We had long dreamt of spending Christmas in remote Phang Nga Bay, a unique region of rugged beauty renowned for its amazing limestone monoliths soaring hundreds of feet out of the sea. But it was not an easy place to reach. Bordered on the west by the island of Phuket the bay is dozens of miles wide and often subject to strong winds. So it was a dream we had to fight for. Our cruiser friends chose to stay in southern Phuket where there were lots of fine anchorages. But there were lots of tourists too. So we decided to pursue our goal and challenge the elements. For two full days, we had to beat hard on the wind in a full gale from the northeast generated by a hurricane in Vietnam and storm in the Gulf of Thailand. But the struggle was worth it. We received our reward in spectacular Koh Raya Ring. Exhausted, but relieved we dropped the anchor in the middle of an extraordinary landscape of steep, jungle clad limestone pinnacles towering over pristine deserted beaches and jade green waters. The only sign of life was an occasional longtail-boat bringing locals to a Muslim village perched on stilts at the end of the bay.

That evening, a fisherman came by with fresh prawns, which he gave us for next to nothing. Soon, they were simmering in garlic butter. Sipping wine and feeling snug and mellow, we dug out Nor Siglar's motley decorations and adorned her cabins with trinkets and treasures from afar. We were ready for Christmas in splendid isolation.

On Christmas Eve, it was so windy that we had to retreat down below. But that was just as well, for here the atmosphere was cozy with gifts and decorations, candles and the scent of incense and festive food. We reminisced a bit, nursed our nostalgic souls with a shot of aquavit and took our time unwrapping the presents. They were few, this year, but all the more exciting. Familiar carols filled the cabin with the spirit of Christmas and warmth. It certainly didn't feel like we were on the other side of the globe on this, the last Yuletide of the Millennium. Except when we savoured our traditional rice pudding on deck surrounded by exotic scenery. A brilliant full moon completed the magic setting of the tropical night where Nor Siglar lay all by herself in the midst of nature's own cathedral of pillars and columns.

We explore James Bond Island with its unique limestone pillars covered with tropical vegetation.

We were boat-bound for three days. But that was fine with us. We enjoy life onboard. On Boxing Day, the wind abated enough that we could get the dinghy launched. Somewhat unwillingly, we crawled out of our safe cocoon to begin our re-entry into civilization again. First, we went on an outing to the local mangroves and lagoons and James Bond Island where "The Man with the Golden Gun" was filmed and where "the Saint", Roger Moore, has even left his autograph on a smooth rock shelf. Then we wanted to explore one of Phang Nga's many unique hongs. Meaning "room" in Thai, hongs are in fact lagoons hidden inside the limestone "sea mounts" surrounded by vertical walls open to the sky. The hong on Paradise Island was especially intriguing. Here, one could only enter by dinghy at low tide through a long and dark tunnel.

At the entrance to the cave, two young men were relaxing in their longtail-boat. They waved cheerfully as we paddled by. The hong was breathtaking. We took lots of pictures. Normally, we take both prints and slides. Suddenly, we realized we had forgotten our print camera. We turned back to get it. Exiting the cave, we captured another photo opportunity of Nor Siglar framed by picturesque stalactites. But what in the world was that? As soon as the men in the longtail-boat saw us, they started whistling and waving like mad. They were signalling to someone. There was a longtail-boat alongside Nor Siglar! Someone was onboard!

We rushed out and caught two men in the middle of breaking in.

Burglary in Paradise!

Touring one off Phang Nga's hongs. A natural wonder hidden inside limestone islets.

One leaped into his longtailboat and started up the engine while the other came flying out from the companionway and jumped overboard. "What the !@#$% is going on?" Martin yelled. He was furious. We grabbed the railing and tried to stop them. But then the bandits threatened us with an iron bar. We shoved them away. They gave full throttle and took off.

At first, it didn't look like anything was stolen. Binoculars, GPS and computer equipment were exactly where we had left them. We obviously had surprised them by returning so soon. Tourists probably spend at least an hour in a hong. So we were incredibly lucky. No destruction, no loss or damage. Only some marks in the gel coat from the dramatic escape of the longtail-boat. Later on, however, we discovered that they had made it to the forepeak and taken a bag of souvenir money. It was the first time we had had uninvited guests onboard. Not a very good feeling.

"Didn't you see the break-in on Nor Siglar?" we asked the captain of a sightseeing boat nearby. "Me no speak English. Me no see nothing!" he answered shrugging his shoulders embarrassed. "But it's broad daylight! Nor Siglar is right next to you!" Either he didn't want to understand, or he didn't care. We wouldn't be surprised if the local sightseeing boats were in cahoots with the crooks.

It was not the first time there had been a burglary at Koh Hong. Other sailors had been less fortunate and robbed of both money and passports. We had been warned and had locked the boat. However, because of the heat, we always left a small cockpit hatch ajar. These hatches are so small that only a child can squeeze through. Or so we thought. Thereafter, rain or shine, we closed absolutely everything and coordinated our outings with other yachties so that someone always stayed behind watching the boats while the others went exploring.

We continued south to Phuket to celebrate the Millennium with our cruising friends. According to tradition, hundreds of long-distance yachts had congregated at Patong Beach to ring in the New Year. In multi-cultural Thailand, 2000 AD was just a normal year. For the Buddhist Era started 2543 years ago and the Islamic 1421 years ago. So the Buddhists have already entered their second millennium while the Muslims have yet to welcome theirs. The Jews, on the other hand, began their reckoning from the time of "Creation". They are in their 5760th year and have already celebrated five millennia. It sure is an interesting world!

THAILAND – THE MALDIVES
THE FIRST PASSAGE OF THE MILLENNIUM

Our adventure was nearing its end and we resumed the countdown of miles and longer passages. Ahead lay the Bay of Bengal, Indian Ocean and the Red Sea. Once in Israel, our circumnavigation would be complete. The voyage itself, however, would not be over until we reached Norway. It seemed odd to be thinking of the end already now when we still had more than 8,000 nautical miles to go. But that is nothing when you have been out for more than eight years and sailed at least six times that far! All is relative - obviously.

Having such a long ocean crossing ahead of us with only one anticipated stop, we had to provision really well. Martin always worried about running out of potatoes and hoarded 20 kilos. I stocked up on other fruits and vegetables. Nobody was going to contract scurvy on Nor Siglar! On January 8, we were ready to continue our journey west. The route was planned and waypoints entered for our first passage of the millennium: 1,070 nautical miles to Sri Lanka, 1,250 to the Maldives and 2,790 to Oman. It was the last day of Ramadan, the holy month of fasting for the Muslims, so we were glad we had done our shopping and filled up our water and diesel in advance. For even in the Land of Smiles, where most of the population is Buddhist, it was impossible to get anything done that day.

We had a lovely start across the Andaman Sea in a light breeze from the southeast. The northeast monsoons are supposed to be prevalent at this time of year! Were we going to have unusual conditions again? Strange weather patterns have been with us throughout our voyage. Not again!

Little by little, Thailand's active fishing fleet and beautiful coastline disappeared in the distance. As darkness fell, a thunderstorm was threatening to come our way. Automatically, we started up the engine, put the GPS in the oven and offered the lightning rod at the top of the mast a friendly prayer. We prepared for the worst but hoped for the best. Now, all we could do was cross our fingers. Soon, the sky was ablaze with fireworks. We felt incredibly exposed and vulnerable all alone on the high seas. Nor Siglar's solitary mast was a definite target. With all the bad luck we had had lately, we would not be surprised if it were our turn now. Other sailboats had been struck by lightning in the same area. They had lost everything from rig to electronics. But we were spared this time as well.

Three days later, as we passed the Nicobar Islands, the northeast monsoon settled in. We were able to continue under poled out foresails in a pleasant following breeze. But Adam was not long in Paradise. That afternoon, a squall line began to form on the horizon.

We had just started to talk about furling the sails when the wind hit us with a vengeance. In no time at all, it piped up to 30 knots. Soon it blew 40 - gusting to 50. Furling became a real struggle in the rolling seas. The blast was over just as quickly as it struck. It became dead calm. We were still in the intertropical convergence zone.

Struggling to secure the furling jib in rough seas without falling overboard.

Why on earth didn't we reduce sails the minute we thought of it? We never seem to learn. Despite the number of miles we have covered. We saw the squall coming. And it is such a quick job. We must have reefed and furled the sails a thousand times by now.

Still, there is always the chance that one could save oneself the effort. Dare we admit that we have become a bit lazy after all these years?

"I'm getting too old for this," Martin sighed when the panic was over. "I can't take these long passages any more. They are so tiring. I don't seem to have the energy any more." "Maybe it's the malaria pills," I suggested. "Could be. But I am getting so fed up with all the stress and bother. Whisker poles up. Whisker poles down. Hoist, reef and drop the sails - time and again. Tack, gybe and move the preventer and running backstays. Check the rig and engine. And on it goes. There is no end to it all! We never have time to relax." "It wasn't long ago that you thought all this was fun," I tried gently. "And now it is too much?" "Yes, I never thought the day would come when I would admit it: I really don't enjoy it any more. It's no fun. I guess it's high time to go home." But then a pod of lively dolphins appeared out of nowhere and delighted us with a fabulous show. The stress was soon forgotten and we enjoyed living for the moment again.

Some slow and easy days followed in gentle variable winds. We barely made a hundred miles a day. But we didn't want to use the engine. We were not sure whether we would be able to bunker on the way. Besides, it was wonderful to just relax. The tropical nights were mild and pleasant; the new moon a sliver in a glorious star-studded sky. A steady stream of red and green blinking lights in the sky above reminded us that we were below the flight path to the Far East, where tourists from the frozen north were transported comfortably to exotic destinations. It was strange to think that we would need half a year to sail the same distance they covered in 24 hours.

Somehow, both of us started dreaming during our night watches of what we were going to do when we arrived home. We were beginning to feel the need for a change - for a stable lifestyle ashore. But first, we had to find a place to live. Nor Siglar had been our only home for close to 14 years. One minute, the dream was a whitewashed cabana with blue doors and shutters; the next a rustic log house. Whatever the decision, it would have to be suitable for all the precious mementos we were bringing home from our odyssey!

I got all excited and tried to talk Martin into taking a year's break. I suggested we leave Nor Siglar in Turkey so we could go home in the spring and start building right away. Not a chance. "I can't stand the thought of having to put her "on the hard" one more time! And I am fed up with all the maintenance! No, let's take the quickest way home. I thought we had agreed to sail to Norway and leave her there? Nine years offshore has to be enough."

Nine days out of Thailand, we ran into a fleet of shrimp trawlers in the dead of night. Surrounding us like pearls on a string, they lit up the sky like cruise ships. As we closed in on the shipping channel, the traffic increased. Local boats started to come up to us. But as usual, they only wanted cigarettes or something to drink. The next morning, Sri Lanka emerged on the horizon. The water became noticeably more polluted and Martin had to go down and clean the propeller for the nth time.

The historic port of Galle is a popular stop for circumnavigators. This year, however, the inner harbour was closed for expansion. It was possible, though to anchor in the outer basin. However, it was exposed to the open ocean and very rolly. Also, 40 boats from the Millennium Yacht Rally crowded the anchorage. Although Sri Lanka was a real temptation beckoning us with its beautiful nature, rolling tea plantations, famous elephant orphanage and ancient temples, we simply didn't dare to stop there and leave Nor Siglar in the busy and unprotected harbour. So as the sun set on the velvet green island, we decided to carry on to the Maldives where we could treat ourselves to a longer stay instead.

That night, a full gale blew up. It became very rough. At dawn, a big bang had us scrambling up on deck. The intermediate forestay had come loose! It was flogging wildly in mid air! The deck fitting had broken off. Fortunately, the sail was not unfurled. By some miracle, we managed to get hold of it without getting hurt or falling overboard, and lashed it to the pulpit. When the crisis was over, we wondered what our next challenge would be.

But all's well that ends well. The current had been with us most of the way and towards the end, we recorded 150-160 mile days in the log. But when we drew near the Maldives, it turned against us. We had to struggle to stay on course the last few miles. It was not easy to see the small islands, which only rise a metre or so above sea level. And if the threat of global warming becomes a reality, they may even disappear altogether by year 2020.

Early in the morning, 13 days out of Thailand, we made landfall in tiny Uligamu in the northern part of the island chain. For the first time in seven years, I did not get seasick on a longer passage.

THE MALDIVES
THE LAST PARADISE ON EARTH

"You are the fourth yacht to call on Uligamu this year," the Customs officer announced as he came aboard to check us in. "Last year, 146 sailboats stopped here." Then he proceeded to outline the rules and regulations imposed on yachts visiting the northern part of the Maldives, which is off limits to "regular tourists". No locals were allowed onboard; gifts had to be approved before taken ashore; alcohol was not allowed on land; a special permit had to be obtained to visit other atolls. Tourism was strictly regulated in the Muslim archipelago where the Maldivians were striving to minimize the adverse effects of foreign influence on local traditions and culture. Offshore sailors were among the privileged few that had the opportunity to experience the isolated paradise and the genuine Maldivian way of life.

One of the most interesting aspects of circumnavigating the globe is to be able to observe at close range how people's racial origins gradually change as one moves slowly around the world. Uligamu was a perfect example. Here, Indian features were predominant. The dress was elegant. Females wore tunics and slacks and lots of gold chains, rings and bracelets. Males wore mostly sarongs and shirts. The children looked like little adults with their painted eyebrows and gold jewellery. The women were shy and turned away when asked to have their picture taken. They did not like to be photographed. Their religion frowned upon it. The men, however, were more than happy to pose for the camera.

The agent's 14-year-old son, Niyaaz walked us around the island

and the village of Fahivaa, which had a population of 400 people. The settlement was laid out in a square grid pattern, its pink coral houses perfectly spaced along neatly swept white sand paths lined with coral fences, beautiful shells, coconut palms and shady breadfruit trees. There was no traffic, not even bicycles. We commented on the complete absence of animals. "Dogs and pigs are considered unclean according to our Muslim faith," Niyaaz explained. We also noticed that there were only old people, women and small children in the village. "Teenagers attend boarding school on another island," he continued. "Most men work in the capital of Malé and the tourist resorts in the south. They come home only once a year. The rest of the men are out fishing."

Peaceful Uligamu in the northern Maldives where influences from the outside world are not welcome.

It felt as though time had stood still in the peaceful little village. Girls were scrubbing pots and pans with sand on the beach; women were sitting on the ground cleaning rice or twirling hemp from coconut fibre. Older men were playing cards or rolling dice in the shade of a huge banyan tree. In the afternoon, youngsters got together to play volleyball and soccer and at dusk, the fishermen came in with their catch. Their Viking-ship inspired longboats were fully laden with tuna. The beach came alive. This was where Fahivaa's population congregated when something was happening. To see the catch brought ashore, cleaned and distributed in orderly fashion was definitely the highlight of the day. People appeared content, seemingly living a simple life in peace and harmony.

But changes were on the way. A generator had just been delivered to the atoll. It was to be used for streetlights and TV. Such a modernization will undoubtedly affect their outlook and way of life. So it is only a question of time before the isolated community will be influenced by the outside world. Regardless of sensible rules and regulations.

The Port Captain got a group of islanders together who needed eye-glasses and we spent a couple of entertaining hours distributing them. After this interesting session, we could not go anywhere in Fahivaa without being recognized. Children came running from all directions and showered us with cowrie shells. We reciprocated with our pre-approved trinkets. Afterwards, Niyaaz invited us to his father's house. His mother lived on the other side of the street. "My father has four wives," he explained. "They live in different houses. He takes weekly rounds!" Then he introduced us to his "direct" brother. Did that mean that they both have the same mother and father? Or do all

Muslims consider themselves brothers and sisters?

To us, Uligamu was the ultimate paradise. In the absence of tourism, there were no aggressive hawkers or anybody yelling Hey Mister or begging monni-monni. There were no crocodiles or sharks, no mosquitoes and no malaria. But we did not find the underwater paradise we had expected. The reefs were largely destroyed. The corals had been utilized for building material. The rest had been damaged and bleached by the effects of a recent El Niño in which the water temperature had risen to more than 30 degrees. Still, we had some fantastic under-water experiences. Every morning at 07:00 sharp, a school of manta rays swam into the anchorage to feed on microscopic plankton. It was thrilling to snorkel amongst these graceful mammals whose enormous mouth span is well over a metre wide. But it was rather frightening when they came straight at us, swirled around on their backs and slid underneath us showing off their white bellies and glaring up at us with piercing eyes. Although they are supposed to be harmless, I had my doubts.

Our two-week stopover was coming to an end. As we were scrubbing the bottom for the next leg, we discovered a crab stuck in the impeller. The hull was also covered with sticky polyps. We had been idle too long. It was time to move on. But we didn't want to go. The disadvantage of this wonderful lifestyle is that when you really start enjoying yourself, it is time to leave for the next destination.

We stocked up on the local delicacies: papaya, bananas and a pile of rotis, a sort of crêpe filled with potato salad, tuna, curry and the like. To everyone's surprise both water and diesel were available. Niyaaz and his friends came out with a few jerry cans in their dhoni. We were both having trouble with our backs and asked them to help us fill the tanks. But they refused to come aboard. "Don't worry," we pleaded. "It'll only take a minute." But the boys were adamant. They were not allowed, under any circumstances, to go onboard a foreign sailboat.

We had long been looking for a special place to leave our Bluewater Cruising burgee. Uligamu was a perfect spot. The agent was delighted and hung it up in his office, a popular meeting point for circumnavigators. Then we weighed anchor and set course for Oman, our last long ocean passage. Or so we thought.

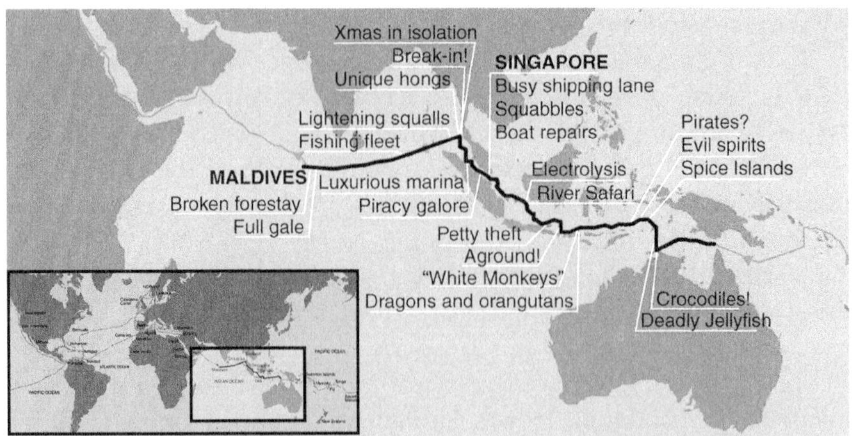

The end of Part 6 of the "9 Years on the 7 Seas Adventure", also published in print and as an eBook with the title

Our South-East Asia Adventures

PART 7

THE INDIAN OCEAN - RED SEA AND THE MEDITERRANEAN

THE MALDIVES – THE ARABIAN PENINSULA

Headwinds on the Indian Ocean? At this time of year? Impossible! But that's exactly what we got the first three nights out: wind from the north-northwest. Gale force, no less. And a current that pushed us west. We had to sail hard on the wind. Even so, it didn't take long before we were way off course. We had to tack. Back and forth. Disappointing when you expect a pleasant passage with the wind on the beam. Between January and March, the northeast monsoon blows steadily on the Indian Ocean. It is the best time for the crossing to the Red Sea. The old seafarers knew to take advantage of the monsoons, which alter direction according to season. But that was not to be for us. Thankfully we have a fast boat that sails well into the wind.

Gradually, the wind veered towards the northeast and moderated enough that we could shake out the reefs and keep a reasonable course. Life became comfortable onboard. There was no shortage of diversion. In the mornings, the deck was littered with flying fish. But they were so small and smelled so foul that we were not tempted to fry them for breakfast like the "old salts" did. In the daytime, we enjoyed watching schools of dolphins frolicking around the bow and thousands of tuna performing spectacular leaps into midair. At night, we were guided by the Big Dipper in the north, the Southern Cross in the south and Orion directly above. Never before had we seen so much phosphorescence in the sea. It was chock full of plankton that sparkled, glittered and shone, turning the whole ocean into one big fireworks.

We were moving into unsafe waters: Somalia, Yemen and Oman to the west-northwest, Iran and Pakistan to the north and India to the east. The further north we went, the more anxious we felt. And it didn't help matters when we heard that a sailboat had been attacked in the Gulf of Aden. The cruisers became jittery. We established the "Red Sea-Indian Ocean Cruisers' Net" to keep track of each other. About 30 sailboats participated in the net. It was reassuring to be close to the cruising family in such troubled waters. The net was also a good way to exchange weather information in an area where no other forecasting service was available.

Indian Ocean sunset.

One morning, an Englishman reported that he had been followed during the night. Half a dozen 20-25 metre long wooden dhows had come after him from different directions. Kotic changed course and increased his speed to 8.5 knots. The powered dhows chased him for a couple of miles before giving up. They had been close enough that he could see some men on the bow. It looked like they were planning to board him. But he did not think they were armed. So it was impossible to know what their intentions were. The episode frightened everyone in the sailing community. Few could motor as fast as Kotic and have the ability to outrun a large powered vessel.

After this incident, similar reports kept coming in from the same waters. But nobody was attacked. It would appear that there was a fishing fleet in a 10-12 mile radius around 13° N and 60° E. Most likely, they were only fishermen who wanted to see if they could scare or get something from the "rich yachties". But you never know. Besides, we were getting closer to Socotra, an island off the coast of Somalia notorious for piracy attacks on boats that came too near. So we were startled by a call on the emergency channel: "Tourist boat! Tourist Boat!" Was someone calling us? We didn't see anybody around. Should we answer? I didn't think so. "Why not?" Martin asked. I was afraid it could be a trap. Better to avoid questions that could lead to a possible confrontation. If we were asked for help, we were, according to maritime law, obliged to comply. But why in the world were they calling a "tourist boat"? Martin felt they might have a warning of some sort. In that case, wouldn't a professional mariner make a standard "securité" call?

Before we could reach a conclusion, Cormoran, a British ketch about 20 nautical miles behind us answered. That triggered a well of questions: "Where you from?" Cormoran: "Ireland." Caller: "England?" Cormoran: "No. Ireland. Where are you from?" Caller: "Iran. How many people on your boat?" Cormoran did not reply. After some unintelligible chatter in the background, the Iranian returned: "You speak Arabic?" Cormoran: "No. Never been to an Arabic country. What language do you speak?" "Arabic, Iranian and Somali. Me English no good." Cormoran: "Better than my Arabic. Are you a fishing boat?" More mumbling. "What your position?" Cormoran declined to answer. Long pause. Then the Iranian announced: "Me position: 13°46´ N, 60°10´ E." End of conversation.

His position was in the exact same area where Kotic and several other sailboats had been chased. It was only 12 nautical miles ahead. We did not like that the Iranian wanted to know how many people Cormoran had onboard. So we dropped the cruising spinnaker and rolled out the genoa to sail harder on the wind in order to get by the troubled waters as quickly as possible. As darkness fell, we refrained from using our navigation lights to avoid being seen. But we neither heard, nor saw anybody. So that was the end of the intermezzo. Again, they were probably only curious fishermen. Maybe they just wanted to practice their English? Were all the rumours making us so nervous that we made a big number of nothing?

Five days out of Uligamu, we reached the halfway point. That night, it blew up from the northwest again. We put two reefs in the mainsail and furled in half the genoa. At midnight, just before change of watch, I noticed a strange vibration in the boat. Suddenly, the sails started fluttering and slamming like mad and the speed dropped from 6 to 1.5 knots. I didn't understand a thing. The compass turned 180 degrees and the waves came crashing across the transom. Martin was up in a flash. "What's going on?" he cried confused, rubbing the sleep from his eyes. Then we both saw it at the same time: a gigantic "V" sparkling in the phosphorescence behind us. We were caught in an enormous fishnet!

Automatically, Martin grabbed the paddle of the wind vane to save it from getting torn off by the net. Hitting his head, he just about lost his glasses in the process. Blood was streaming down his face. Nor Siglar was bucking and heaving like mad. She was virtually at a standstill in the steep seas, waves washing into the cockpit soaking us to the bones. The strong commercial fishnet must have been several kilometres long. It was pulling and tugging so hard at the boat that we thought it was going to tear both rudder and propeller right off. And the enormous stress on the rudderpost could easily break the hull open. It was not hard to imagine what would happen to us then in the middle of the Indian Ocean.

We were in serious trouble. It was decidedly the most dangerous situation we had experienced. For the first time ever, we were truly scared. We needed help. At any cost. Ignoring the piracy danger, we sent out an emergency call. But there was no reply. We had to manage on our own. First, we had to get the sails down. And that was not an easy matter in 30-knot following winds on a surface that was in constant motion. But miracles happen. We made it. The next step was to get untangled from the fishnet. It was impossible to reach it from the deck. And there was no way Martin could dive into the pitch-black turbulent waters to cut us loose under those circumstances. We had to do it from the deck. "I can't hold it with the boat hook," Martin called in despair. "It's too heavy. We've got to get it closer to the hull somehow."

We attached some big fishhooks to a rope, caught the net and tried to winch it closer that way. But the hooks were not strong enough. They ripped right out. We never thought of using the little dinghy anchor. That would have worked. But we didn't think clearly in the panic. Finally, we spliced two broom handles together and lashed a long sharp knife to the end. With a superhuman effort, Martin managed to hold the net long enough with the boat hook for me to reach it with the knife by lying flat on my stomach and leaning out over the gunwales and the roaring sea. The edge of the fishnet was tight as a violin string and snapped the minute the knife touched it. What a relief! As the net gave way, it felt as though all of Nor Siglar relaxed. Our first crisis was almost resolved. But what now? What if the rudder and propeller were damaged?

Half the night was gone before we managed to get ourselves free. We had been totally absorbed in what we were doing and had not noticed that several fishing boats had arrived in the meantime. We were surrounded by lights! How were we going to get ourselves out of this maze unscathed? We were terrified of getting caught in another unlit fishnet. So we sailed short distances back and forth on the same course until daylight.

Once more we got caught in something but lost it again after a few 360-degree turns. Our nerves were clearly fraught and our imaginations working overtime. For when we heard a strange rattling sound, we thought the propeller was falling off. But it only turned out to be some empty bottles that had fallen over and were rolling around in the lazarette.

As dawn was breaking, we got away as quickly as we could, worried that the fishermen would discover that we had cut their net, and then, perhaps come after us. Fortunately, the wind had changed to a more easterly direction so we could hoist the cruising spinnaker again. Later that day, we discovered a tear in the mainsail. Where was this going to end? We seemed to be caught in a vicious circle. Martin, dejected and sporting a big bandage around his head, exclaimed: "There's got to be a limit to what we have to go through before this is all over! I am getting sick and tired of it!"

We knew we didn't have far to go when the offshore wind Belat blew up and filled the air with sand and dust from the Arabian Peninsula and terns and frigates settled down on the spreaders. Finally, after eleven stressful days, it was a huge relief to reach Oman and the safety of the ultra modern port of Mina Raysut just west of Salalah. The anchor was barely down before we dove in to inspect the damage. Only a few bits of fishnet remained tangled around the shaft. Apart from a small nick in the rudder, nothing was damaged. Nor Siglar had done it again!

The Indian Ocean did not live up to our expectations. But now, that crossing was behind us as well. And it is strange how quickly one forgets. Once in calm waters, the challenges at sea are soon forgotten and you are ready to start all over again. What is really interesting is that when something so dramatic happens, you discover new qualities about yourself. Qualities you are unaware of. Being alone, far away from civilization, you only have yourself to trust. You have to be able to tackle whatever comes along. In this case, we both discovered a strength we never knew we had.

PROSPEROUS OMAN AND IMPOVERISHED YEMEN

"Allah Akbar! Allah Akbar!" Dawn was just breaking as the muezzin on the Navy ship in the harbour started summoning the faithful to prayer. The call, often dubbed the "Muslim alarm clock", woke us up setting the tone for our first day in Oman.

We received a one-week visa to explore this nouveau-riche oil country where the camel, the "Bedouin's Best Friend," still reigns supreme. Camel breeding is a lucrative business and racing extremely popular. Apparently, a first class camel can be as valuable as a Rolls Royce. Consequently, it is quite a status symbol and a popular trading item. You can even get a woman for a couple of camels in this world where you not only receive a substantial fine, but a jail term as well, if you hit a camel crossing the road. Should you happen to do the same to a woman, you would only get a small fine! Or so we were told. No wonder cars slowed down when camels were near.

Oman is truly a land of contrasts where macho men in kummar caps, muzzar turbans and bright white dishdasha robes race around in modern 4x4's on dusty roads crowded with goats, camels and "Ship of the Desert" warning signs. During the daytime, there were almost only men to be seen. Women did not appear until dark. Moving around in groups, completely covered in flowing black cloaks with only a narrow slit revealing mysterious eyes, they looked like ghosts to us. Having finished their chores of the day, they gathered in the women's souq. It was overflowing with exotic products like dates, herbs and spices, fragrant perfumes, gold, frankincense and myrrh. During Biblical times, Saudi Arabia became wealthy from the trade of the valuable frankincense - the dried sap of the endemic Boswellia tree. On our way to the local gardens, we relived a bit of history, visiting the Prophet Job's Tomb and the ruins of one of the Queen of Sheba's many palaces.

Omanis in dazzling white dishdashas. How can they stay so neat and clean in the perpetual desert dust?

Since the U.K. educated Sultan Qaboos bin Said Al Said deposed his father in 1970, Oman has gone through extensive reforms. So it is a modern country. At least by local standards. Salalah's first Internet café opened while we were there. In fact, I was the first client. I must admit that it was rather odd to be served by data specialists in Biblical attire.

We had long been fretting about the Gulf of Aden and the Strait of Bab el Mandeb on the Horn of Africa. This was where a sailboat had been attacked recently. The couple were sailing by themselves when five armed pirates from Somalia boarded and robbed their catamaran, wounding the wife with a gunshot to her leg. The year before, a Finnish couple was attacked in the same area. That time, the pirates were not satisfied with money and equipment only. They took the boat and the couple hostage as well. Several months later, after considerable suffering and despair, the Finns were released. They got their boat back in return for a large sum of money. By that time, however, their boat was in shreds.

So rumours flourished. The cruisers discussed at length how we could get by these dangerous waters safely. The conclusion was to sail in convoy, 5-6 nautical miles off the coast of Yemen. The local police were known to be involved in piracy activities, regularly scanning the radio frequencies for cruisers' locations. So we were afraid to reveal our exact latitude and longitude to each other on the net. We created waypoints with code names like "Henry Morgan" (Aden) and "Blackbird" (Bal el Mandeb). This way, we could report our position as "x" nautical miles from the coastline and "y" nautical miles from the waypoint in question. The transmissions had to be short. Women were not allowed on the air. A female voice would be a dead give-away of an offshore cruiser.

The ocean was calm as a mirror when we left Salalah. Just as well. It was easier to stay together when everyone was using the engine. A few boats approached us on the way. But no one bothered us, probably because we were part of a group. Our strategy worked. Three tense days later, we arrived safely in Al Mukalla, a few hundred miles east of Aden. The Friday prayer was in full swing with muezzins calling from half a dozen minarets, the echoes competing in the hills.

Captivated by a spectacular sunset on ochre coloured cliffs, and swinging peacefully at anchor, we were startled by a knock on the hull. It was the officials who wanted to check us in. Due to recent kidnappings of tourists, a curfew was in effect: we had to be back on the boat by 9 o'clock at night. We also had to relinquish our passports in exchange for a three-day visitor's permit; barely enough to get a taste of the realm of the legendary Queen of Sheba, who was so powerful about 3000 years ago.

A young Yemenite poses with is keffiya.

On an outing to the countryside, we were accompanied by soldiers armed with machine guns. They were protecting us from kidnappers, they said. Time and again, we were stopped at military checkpoints and interrogated. Not understanding a word, we were rather intimidated. We did not at all feel safe in this country, which had been ravaged by civil war for two decades. Although Yemen is unified now, the political situation is still unstable. Watchtowers of sun-dried clay, half finished mud and brick houses and military compounds partially camouflaged by cement walls dominate the dry and desolate landscape. Unlike Oman, there were no camels to be seen, for Yemen is an impoverished land. Most people live from subsistence farming and fishing. And when shepherds crossed the road right in front of our car with their herds, then wandered off into the hostile desert amidst thorny shrubs, we felt as though we were a thousand years back in time.

It feels like history is turned back 1000 years at this main road near Al ukhalla.

Like their sisters in Oman, the women in Yemen were dressed in black from head to toe. However, they were out and about during daylight hours and seemed much more open and liberal.

Muslim girls in sewing class.

They certainly did not avoid us when we tried to make contact. "Our dress is not a sign of oppression like you think in the west," an animated young woman explained. She was keen to practise her English. "It is a sign of modesty. Every woman with respect for herself and Allah wears the abaya, hijab and burqa. Mine are the latest fashion from Paris!" she joked as she made a coquettish pirouette on high-heeled shoes swinging an elegant Gucci handbag on her arm.

Later, I just had to try the Islamic dress. It made me feel like I had lost my identity. I couldn't help but think that that was exactly the intention in this male-dominated society. From the anchorage, Al Mukalla looked like a scenic town with its picturesque façade of cream coloured Moorish buildings, mosques and minarets. On closer inspection, however, the "white city" was far from it. Paper, junk and plastic were scattered all over the place.

The smell of sewage penetrated the air. Sheep, goats, cats and chickens were rummaging around narrow alleys and steep lanes. But the place had an infectious atmosphere. In the evening, the men flocked to the mosques. Afterwards, they spilled out on the sidewalk where they sat till late at night, sipping piping hot sweet tea in small glasses, their cheeks bulging from chewing qat, a mildly stimulating fresh leaf, as they were playing their games of domino and cards.

Nor Siglar's crew in local garb.

The restaurants were for men only. However, an exception was made for tourists. So the last evening in Yemen, we went out to dinner. It was quite an experience. At the entrance, there was a tap of running water for rinsing hands before and after the meal. Bread was used in lieu of cutlery. We watched as flat disks of the unleavened bread were baked plastered against the side of a glowing hot clay cylinder. Copying the locals, we broke the flatbread into pieces and scooped up different kinds of dips and the fish, which was fried whole and served on a newspaper. It was delicious. In the absence of "Ladies", I had to use the "Men's". That was a mixed pleasure. The adjoining room was full of prayer mats readily available to patrons and staff.

It was nearly two months since the end of Ramadan, and Eid-al-Adha, the "Feast of Sacrifice", was near. Next to us in the anchorage, a big dhow was lying dangerously low in the water. It was full of goats! They had been shipped from Somalia to be slaughtered for the three-day celebration, which marks the end of the Muslims' annual Pilgrimage to Mecca. We could probably expect to meet many such craft on our way to the Red Sea. No doubt, we would mistake them for pirates.

THE DREADED RED SEA

It was time to tackle the infamous Red Sea, every sailor's nightmare. The long and narrow inland sea is known for its notoriously strong northerly winds. Usually blowing days on end, the persistent headwinds can make the voyage north a real test of endurance. Especially if one is in a hurry. However, if one is prepared to wait for weather windows, the Red Sea can be a great experience. The distance from Bab el Mandeb on the Horn of Africa in the south to Suez in the north is about 1,200 nautical miles. Under normal circumstances, a sailboat can cover such a stretch in a couple of weeks. But not in the Red Sea. Unless willing to face a lot of discomfort, one should allow 6-8 weeks for the transit.

The best time to sail north is from February to May, a period when the unforgiving northerlies are at their weakest. We were right on schedule. On February 29, we left Al Mukalla for the 600 nautical mile passage to Massawa halfway up the Eritrean coast. We were still in pirate-infested waters, so our little flotilla stayed together along the rugged coast. Two uneventful days later, outside the port of Aden, the other boats wanted to go in and top up their fuel and water supplies. We had plenty to reach Eritrea, so since the weather was benign, we decided to continue on our own. We stayed parallel to the shipping lane where we should be able to get help if necessary. At one point, someone started cursing, swearing and calling obscenities on the emergency channel. What kind of people would do that? Was the foul language intended for us? It was rather scary and not very pleasant to listen too. We did not see anybody to whom the profanities could be traced.

Fortunately, nothing came of the incident. A day later, we left the Gulf of Aden behind for good and sailed in through Bab el Mandeb, also called the Gate of Tears. Large military installations in both Yemen and Djibouti guard both sides of the 27 km wide strait separating eastern Africa and the Arabian Peninsula. The pass, as well as the southern part of the Red Sea, is reputed for its strong southerly winds that can blow up to gale force strength without much notice and cause dangerous waves. However, our transit became a real anti climax. Not a breath of wind - and glassy calm seas!

Sawakin mosque.

Despite busy freighter traffic, we chose to sail up the centre of the Red Sea rather than risking unfriendly encounters with the hostile military closer to shore. In fact, we did not want to stop until we reached Massawa. The ports on the way were reputed to be unsafe due to border conflicts and local strife. We also kept a safe distance from the Hanish Islands, which were disputed by Yemen and Eritrea. Sailboats anchored in the lee of the islands had been shot at recently. The Eritrean port of Asad was also to be avoided. For here, innocent sailors accused of being spies have been taken hostage from time to time.

Before long, the Red Sea lived up to its reputation. Despite a peaceful introduction, we were soon clobbered by fierce southerly winds and the highest waves we have ever seen. After a few days of exhilarating surfing, the wind abruptly veered to the north. We put two reefs in the main - and didn't shake them out until we reached Suez two months later.

WAR-TORN ERITREA

After a stressful six-day passage from Al Mukalla, we were relieved to arrive safely in the war-torn port of Massawa where the ruins and destruction from bombing were clearly visible. Despite this the port was well-organized and the check-in formalities went surprisingly well, considering the devastated condition of the country. We even received permission to stay for a whole month. For the first time, we had to sign a document that we did not have any stowaways onboard.

As usual after a longer trip, we were exhausted and retired early. We were just about to doze off when we heard a gentle knock on the hull. "Hello! Need some help?" A kind-looking man of slight build was standing alongside in his small makeshift pram. "My name is Solomon," the soft-spoken man said, reaching his hand over the railing in greeting. "I have a donkey and a cart and can get you diesel and water." This was how a pleasant relationship started with a proud representative of Eritrea's friendly population. Solomon was not only an enterprising and hardworking man. He was knowledgeable as well, and more than willing to share his wisdom.

"I am named after our famed ancestor," he declared in reasonable English. "Eritreans are descendents from the legendary union between King Solomon and the Queen of Sheba." Giving us a short summary of the nation's history, he recalled with a sigh: "I was only 12 years old when Massawa fell to Ethiopia during a Soviet-supported air raid in 1977. My family lost everything. Then came the drought followed by poor harvests, hunger and starvation in the 80's." The mild-mannered man was very thin. "I am not used to eating very much," he said. "We are very poor. But we are not starving any more. Life has not been easy. But now we are anticipating a better future," he concluded. "By the way, we'll never give Ethiopia access to the Red Sea!" he added as an afterthought. That was a comment we heard often during our short stay.

Haile Selassie's summer palace in Massawa.

We remained at anchor for almost two weeks in the large well protected lagoon-type harbour, which commanded a dramatic view of the ruins of past Emperor Haile Selassie's bombed out summer palace. We were shocked at the terrible destruction and all the men hobbling around on crutches. Many had amputated arms and legs. So our first impression was not very uplifting. The Eritreans, however, were the nicest, most positive people imaginable. It was easy to make contact, and one day, we invited a young couple back to Nor Siglar. We did not think they had been on a foreign sailboat before. But they had. Five years ago. It was even from Norway! And believe it or not: Martin knew the skipper's family who was from Sagesund where he grew up!

Akberet and Ermias were engaged to be married as soon as the peace treaty with Ethiopia was signed. Both had fought in the war. We will never forget Akberet, who, at only 15 years of age, was sent out to defend her border. "Did you have to kill anybody?" we asked. "Offff courrrrse!" she exclaimed, her lovely hazel eyes flashing with indignation. "Otherwise they would have killed me!" Now, Akberet was 25 years old. It was hard to imagine this stunning woman in army fatigues and wielding a gun. In 1993, the small patriotic population of Eritrea succeeded in defeating and gaining independence from the much bigger Ethiopia. No doubt, it seemed to us, that the feat was due to its exceptionally strong and proud people - especially the women, who must be the most liberated in all of Africa.

We couldn't think of a better place to donate the things we didn't need any more now that our voyage is almost over, than in this poor war-torn country. Akberet volunteered to distribute the rest of our eyeglasses. We also gave her some first aid supplies and clothing. Grateful, she invited us home for an Eritrean Coffee Ceremony, an hour-long ritual during which guests converse and watch the traditional preparation. Skillfully, Akberet roasted the green beans in a metal pan with a long handle over a small charcoal burner. Then, she ground the beans by hand, boiled the coffee in a small clay urn and served it piping hot and sweet in tiny cups in three separate servings. A wooden crate nicely decorated with bougainvillea and greens served as a table.

We stayed for dinner as well. It was a hot and spicy meat and vegetable stew served on several layers of injera, a spongy slightly sour pancake made from sorghum. Eating from the same platter, we felt as if we were part of the family. Everyone broke into the section of injera in front of them, tearing off a piece and dipping it into the stew in the centre. Before and after the meal, the youngest girl in the family came around with a washbasin for everyone to rinse their hands.

The family of ten lived in a brick house of two small rooms and a kitchen. At night, some of them slept outside under a mosquito netting. "That's no problem in this climate," the mother said. She didn't know how old she was. Maybe 55, she thought. She looked much older. Still, she was very beautiful. The family was doing better than average. The father had a good salary. A supervisor at the Department of Fisheries, he earned US$100 a month. Akberet was a secretary at a local shrimp farm. She made US$60 per month. Like Solomon and his family, they had lost everything during the war. But now, they were optimistic about the future. Their first priority was a bathroom. "I am afraid our toilet isn't working," Akberet said, embarrassed as she led me behind a big rock on the beach.

During a two-day outing to Asmara, the capital city, Solomon looked after Nor Siglar for us. When we returned our faithful helper, who wanted only US$10 a day for his services, invited us home to meet his wife and son. "Our home is modest," he warned us. "But we are grateful for what we have."

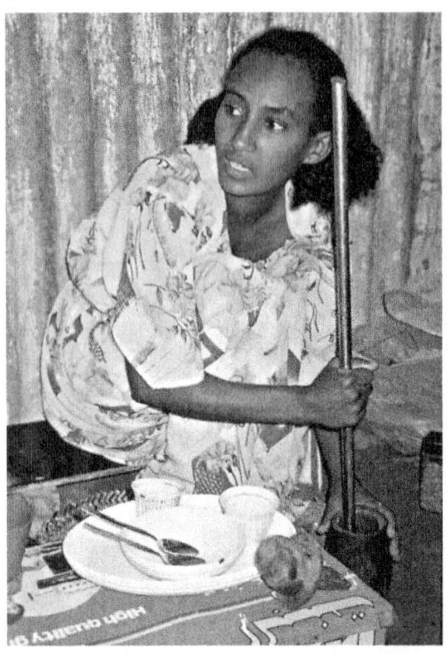

A beautiful Tigrinya woman grinds beans for a traditional coffee ceremony. She gives us the only decoration she owns right off the wall of her one-room hut.

His home was nothing but a shack with a tin roof, corrugated walls and a dirt floor. It was situated on a hill above a cluster of similar dwellings. "There is more breeze up here," Solomon explained. "Not so many mosquitoes. And we even have a view of the harbour! So we are really quite fortunate," he said. "Brick houses are too warm in this climate," he continued. "Besides," he joked, "you can make your own air conditioning by poking holes in metal walls!"

It was clean and tidy in the one-room hut where the family had all their worldly belongings: a wooden table stacked full of kitchen utensils; sacks of sugar and flour, with cans of cooking oil and kerosene neatly organized below. The walls were decorated with magazine clippings of soccer stars and sailboats, a handmade wall hanging, a blackboard for home schooling and a picture of a black Christ. Clothes hung neatly spaced on nails on the walls. "I have made our bed myself," Solomon said. He had used iron bars for the frame. The mattress was tightly braided from a strong nylon twine. "I have made this basin for drinking water too. It is fibreglass. An American sailor helped me." They had no electricity, no running water and no toilet. Their sanitation facilities were an outdoor communal affair located on the outskirts of the settlement.

Despite such incredible poverty, they treated us to a coffee ceremony. And it was a true delight to see Solomon's 19-year old wife perform the whole ritual, sitting erect as could be on a tiny stool while at the same time breastfeeding their 2-year old son, Alexander. Winny was from the Tigrinya tribe. She was exceptionally beautiful, her hair tightly braided from forehead to crown where it cascaded out over her shoulders like a fan. Her bright white teeth sparkled when she smiled. And that was often.

As we were ready to leave, Winny took down the wall hanging, dusted it off and handed it to us. "For you," she said with a shy smile. "She has made it herself," Solomon explained. "We wish to thank you for everything you have done for us. I wish we had something nicer to give you. But this is all we have to offer." It blew us away. These people had nothing. Still, they had something to share.

Eritrea is the poorest country we have seen. It couldn't possibly be worse. Or so we thought.

DESTITUTE SUDAN

We took our time along Sudan's desolate coast exploring its many khors and marsas – calm, safe anchorages that are accessed via narrow gaps in the coral reefs that run parallel with the shoreline. Some khors are at the end of inlets that wind their way for miles into the desert. About a daysail apart, they offer perfect shelter to exhausted sailors.

In Marsa Sheikh Ibrahim, our very first marsa, we also had our very first encounter with the Sudanese people. We hesitated to go ashore in a land reputed to be a haven for Muslim fundamentalists, and for harbouring and training terrorists. So we were not at all certain how we would be received. But as we have experienced before in places of unsafe reputation, we were met with only kindness.

"Salam' alaykum!" we called to two men on the beach as we were rowing ashore. They looked up, dropped what they were doing and came running down to meet us. "Wa alaykum as-salam!" they greeted, helping us with the dinghy. Their body language indicated that we were welcome. Our few words in Arabic appeared sufficient to create a feeling of goodwill. With the help of finger language and a bit of English, we actually managed to communicate a little.

The men, who were boiling tar in a rusty oil barrel, had three horizontal scars on their cheeks. In Sudan, tribal origin is still identified by facial marks. They were about to put a coat of tar on the bottom of their wooden boats. Pointing to a truck nearby, they seemed to imply that the boats were going to be transported overland. The fishermen were nomads! They were moving from fishing ground to fishing ground by truck! In an attempt to combat espionage and smuggling caused by border conflicts and strife, nearly all inshore traffic has been eliminated in the Red Sea. Consequently, there is hardly any local traffic along the sparsely populated coast. The result is an exceptionally diverse and colourful underwater flora and fauna. And we were among the privileged few to be able to enjoy it.

"Salam' alaykum!" Nomade fishermen greet us warmly in a land where we hesitated to go ashore unsure whether we were safe or even welcome.

We thought Eritrea was poor. But Sudan was even poorer. The fishermen lived in tiny hovels put together with whatever they could find: bits of cardboard, burlap and wooden crates, plastic tarps, twigs and twine. Still, they were unbelievably generous, offering us coffee and giving us the largest, most beautiful shells in their pile. The men seemed pleased with the cigarettes, matches and engine oil that we gave them.

Entering the port of Sawakin, the last slave trading post in the world, was a most dramatic experience. Winding our way for two miles through a narrow channel that brought us within a hundred feet of the crumbling ruins of the once important trading centre, we ended up in a large landlocked basin overlooking the spooky ghost town, where slaves were traded until the end of WWII. A new town had sprung up a little further inland. The atmosphere reminded us of scenes from the film, "Lawrence of Arabia"; the most dominant feature being tall and dashing macho men in turbans and flowing jalabiyyas sporting long silver coated swords or intricately decorated curved daggers. Less visible were the women; tall and lean, enveloped in colourful tobes, a 9-metre piece of cloth, which they also used as camouflage and protection against the desert dust. The market was a virtual Wild West and likely just as lively today as it was way back when. Most chaotic was the noisy and smelly animal market where men were bartering and trading dromedaries and donkeys, chickens and goats.

What a life! For once, we had the opportunity to taste both camel meat and milk. But as the meat market was not very appetizing, we played it safe and stuck with familiar fruits, vegetables and pita bread. Watching the commotion, we felt a thousand eyes upon us. Clearly, people were not used to seeing Caucasians.

At night, the decaying coral buildings of Old Sawakin were bathed in a shroud of darkness. It was eerily quiet too. No music, no noise, not even the monotonous chant of the muezzin. There was no electricity in that part of town. In the daytime, it was busy in the harbour. Busloads of people from all over Sudan came to take the ferry across the Red Sea to Saudi Arabia to participate in the annual pilgrimage to Mecca, not far from Jeddah. Incidentally, our agent, who checked us in and looked after the formalities, was very helpful. Forgetting for a moment that Islam forbids alcohol, we offered him a beer. His face lit up. But we had to go down below where no one could see him drink it.

We needed propane and had to go to Port Sudan to get the container refilled. At the bus station, three little boys were running around selling biscuits, chewing gum and Kleenex. They were real charmers and we bought something from them all. Delighted, they gestured that we should take their picture. We thought it was a trick to make more money. Not at all. Considering how poor they were, we were surprised that they didn't beg.

The bus was packed so we had an excellent opportunity to get close to the passengers. Literally! A man behind us spoke some English. He had "only" two wives and six children. His father had four wives and 26 children. "I am too poor for that," he said. "Besides," he added with a twinkle in his eye: "many wives - many problems!"

On the bus to Port Sudan. "Many wives – many problems," a man explains on the topic of Muslim men having four wives.

The bus trip allowed us a glimpse into the real Africa. The images are imprinted on our minds forever. Especially the never-ending drab and desolate landscape dotted with Bedouins on eternal wanderings with their caravans. What a tough existence these hardy desert nomads lead as they move with their herds from pasture to pasture and tent camp to tent camp, always in search of food for their animals. The women were a haunting sight as they wandered along the road loaded down with bundles of firewood, jugs of water and life's many necessities.

As expected, the northerly winds grew stronger and more constant the further north we went. A group of sailors ahead of us were weather-bound for ten days in an isolated marsa in Egypt, where the military would not allow them ashore. Fortunately, we were never holed up for more than four days at a time. The delays were far from boring. In Marsa Amid, we anchored close to a rundown desalination plant. The guard, who was two metres tall and very black, sat, doubled over for hours on end in the shade of his lean-to overlooking the bay. What was he thinking all day, we wondered? What did he think of the modern boats in the middle of his domain? We would have given anything to read his mind.

On a walk along the dykes and salt flats, we ran into some men at a maintenance yard. They had converted a container, which had washed ashore, into a shelter by cutting openings for windows and doors. Inside were a couple of bunks, a table made from a crate and some ancient cooking utensils. A well-worn prayer mat lay on the floor. "Kaffee?" The man pointed at a soot-covered pot. "Shukran! Shukran!" we replied in our best Arabic. But they were short of water. The fellow disappeared and returned with a juicy watermelon instead.

Two of the men were Christian, two were Muslim. The older Muslim had a dark spot on his forehead, a visible sign of having touched the ground in prayer five times a day throughout his life. "Haj," the younger Muslim declared, nodding respectfully at the older man. He looked very poor. However, as his title and the white crocheted cap he was wearing indicated, he had successfully completed his required pilgrimage to Mecca, and was therefore highly respected by his fellow Muslims.

What is the tall and handsome watchman thinking all day as he stands guard by his shack overlooking the bay?

Sudan is the largest, but one of the least developed plagued by civil war, drought and famine. Even so, everyone we met during our 2-week visit exuded a certain dignity and pride.

In order to make some headway, we tried to do an overnighter. It became an uphill battle. The winds grew more and more fierce as night progressed. Seas became confused. Before long, we were hammered by waves, which soaked us to the bone. Soon, a thick layer of salt covered Nor Siglar. The sheets became stiff and awkward to handle. Conditions were atrocious. We had never experienced anything like it. After 20 hours of bucking into the rough seas, tacking and beating hard on the wind, we could only record 40 nautical miles. "A night to remember," Martin noted in the log when the nightmare was over. "A night to forget," I countered, bone-tired.

We soon learned that if a fresh breeze were already blowing at sunrise, we would have a full gale by ten. So the best tactic was to start before daylight and cover as much ground as possible before the wind piped up. This way, we could get safely behind the reef and anchor early while the sun was still high in the sky and the visibility good. The charts were poor and rarely corresponded with the GPS, so we had to keep a good lookout to be able to estimate the depth from the colour of the water. We learned to note our GPS-positions on the way in, so that we could retrace our course on the way out in darkness the next morning.

Sailing north in the Red Sea against strong winds and steep seas in a challenge we shall never forget.

We clawed our way north to Khor Shinab, one of the most spectacular anchorages in the Red Sea. The inlet wound its way like a snake over 20 km into the Nubian Desert, where it opened up into a basin surrounded by hills, sand and rock as far as the eye could see. There was no sign of life except a few egrets and the trails of caravans in the distance. We hiked the ridges, wandering from cairn to cairn in the 35-degree heat. The view of the khor was amazing.

Anchored all by herself, Nor Siglar was reflected in the mirror of the calm, crystal clear water. The corals were clearly visible from the 200-metre peak above. The area was rich in fossils from the time the desert was under water. We would have liked to stay a while to explore. But the British aircraft carrier, Illustrious, which was participating in an exercise nearby, reported a low in the eastern Mediterranean. That meant a high in the Red Sea with periods of calm and a wind change to the south. It was a weather window we could not afford to miss. For it was impossible to know how long it would be till the next one.

We lucked out and motor-sailed for 42 hours in calm conditions all the way across the infamous False Bay to Egypt. At 23°30´ N, we crossed the Tropic of Cancer. For the last time, Nor Siglar bid the tropics adieu.

EGYPT - THE LAND OF PHARAOHS

The weather window generated an exodus of boats hoping to make a final dash for Suez. It lasted all of 48 hours. When it blew up again, we decided to seek shelter in Sharm Luli, our first anchorage in Egypt. It was a god-forsaken bay. All we could see ashore were some sinister-looking barracks partially hidden in the sand dunes. Martin's back was bothering him. This was definitely not a place to be stuck for any length of time. We would have to find a more civilized place. Safaga was only 150 nautical miles away. We had to make it there somehow.

Two days later, it calmed down enough that Martin thought his back could stand the overnighter to Safaga. We made great progress during the day. By evening, however, his back was so sore that he couldn't do his watches. To stay awake, I nibbled on cookies, drank buckets of tea and updated the log every hour. Nor Siglar was doing well. At breakfast, we only had 15 miles to go. But these turned into a nightmare. Suddenly, the wind veered to the north. In no time, we were blasted by 35- knot winds and 3-metre waves. Other boats turned back. But we were determined to make it. We knew Nor Siglar could do it. She excels in headwinds. We couldn't help but think of the misconception that sailing around the world is a downwind run. It simply isn't the case!

Fortunately, Martin managed to get on his feet to navigate us safely into the harbour. For I couldn't leave the helm for a minute in such treacherous and poorly charted waters. It took us seven hours to do the last 15 miles! But we made it. "Al-hamdu lillah!" Thanks to Allah – and to Nor Siglar!

It was incredibly windy in the anchorage. We worried about dragging and going aground. Kind cruisers helped us put down a second anchor. They also helped us bring jerry cans of water and diesel from the shore. We got soaking wet and cold on the rough dinghy rides. Frequent sandstorms covered the boats in dust. Even though we kept the hatches closed, the fine sand still found its way down below. The solar panels had to be washed every day. Otherwise, they didn't produce enough energy.

Mosque near Port Said.

Martin's condition reminded us of the time 3.5 years ago when he ended up having a back operation in Morocco. At that time, his doctor urged him to quit sailing. Since then, we have almost sailed around the world! Now he was totally immobile again. If we could only make it to Israel! Lying helpless in a bleak and windswept anchorage in Egypt was very depressing. It was hard to see our friends come and go while we had to stay behind.

While Steinar Kopperud from Maria Two kept Martin company and looked after our boats, his wife, Birgitta and I took a trip to Luxor and the Valley of the Kings where we were overwhelmed by fabulous treasures, temples and tombs from Egypt's glorious past. The burial chambers of the pharaohs were exquisitely decorated with hieroglyphics and fresco paintings. Tut Ank Ahmon's tomb contained valuable art and everyday items. His coffin was pure gold. It was astonishing to experience the dramatic contrast between the life we imagined in the temples millennia ago and that of the people living in the region today.

Back on Nor Siglar, Martin's back showed no improvement. I found an internet-café and contacted my brother Knut, who is an orthopaedic surgeon. "You just have to take your time and hope for the best," he said. "There is not much else you can do." Although he didn't have a miracle cure to offer, his moral support was comforting. So I made many trips to the café. Unfortunately, it was also a popular shisha joint frequented by the local men. Puffing away on their gurgling water pipes, they clearly enjoyed watching female tourists sending their emails to distant lands. It was not very pleasant to feel their piercing eyes on my back. In fact, Safaga was the only place on our travels where I felt harassed; especially walking down the street alone. And that was often while Martin was sick. Therefore, Safaga is one of the few places in the world that I really dislike. So when I lost a filling one day, there was no way I would go to a dentist there. Martin made me a temporary filling, which we hoped would last till Israel. What a pathetic pair we were! We couldn't really complain, though. For we have been quite healthy throughout the trip. Apart from our bad backs, of course, and a few cuts and bruises every now and then.

The doctor was right. After a 3-week rest, Martin was well enough to continue. The timing coincided with the arrival of our friends Shayne Dunlop and Gail Davies, who came to sail with us to Israel. Together, we set out for Suez, 200 nautical miles to the north. But this stretch, where the Red Sea narrows into the the Gulf of Suez, is considered to be the toughest part of the inland sea, offering a whole range of challenges: abandoned, unlit oil rigs cut off at sea level, unmarked reefs, large fishing fleets conducting unpredictable manoeuvres and, of course, fierce headwinds. Despite the busy traffic in the Strait of Gubal, we crossed the shipping lane and made our way through a maze of oil platforms marked by flickering flames, to the Sinai Peninsula, where the wind was supposed to be weaker. It had taken us four days to get this far. Now, we wanted to reach Suez at any cost and ran the engine at full speed. In the strong headwinds and steep seas, it burned much more fuel than usual. So when we only had ten miles to go, we ran out of diesel! We couldn't believe it. What next? A fellow sailor appeared out of nowhere and gave us a couple of cans.

Our challenges were not finished yet. For as we were about to enter the Suez Canal Yacht Club, we were clobbered by a khamsin – a terrific sandstorm packing 50-knot winds. So we had quite a struggle before we could throw our mooring lines to the "Prince of the Red Sea", supposedly the only honest agent in all of Suez. Our Red Sea experience was over.

We only had time to visit the museum in Cairo and to take a camel ride around the Sphinx and the spectacular Pyramids of Ghiza before embarking on the Suez Canal. The canal, which opened in 1869, is 193 km long and 11-12 metres deep. Initially operated by an international company, Egypt took over the administration in 1956. After the Six-day War of 1967, it was closed until 1975. War memorials, military paraphernalia, floating bridges and docks were among the haunting sights of the muddy waterway.

There are no locks in the Suez Canals - so it looks more like a long ditch. The transit, which took two days including a layover on Lake Ismailia, was a real test in patience and fortitude. Our pilot was greedy, aggressive and offensive. "Wife hospital four years!" he blurted out as he came onboard. He was really obnoxious and wouldn't leave Gail and me alone. It was extremely unpleasant. The pilot was more concerned with baksheesh than guiding us to Port Said. He kept harping about the bribe the whole way. Not only for himself, but for the police, customs officers and a variety of other colleagues as well.

The poverty, bureaucracy and finally, the bartering of the Arab world, got to us in the end, so it was heavenly to set out into the Mediterranean back to familiar waters and cultures again.

BACK IN ISRAEL – WE DIT IT!

Israel, May 9: Nor Siglar crossed her own wake from May 31 four years previous. Finally, we could call ourselves circumnavigators! We flew the flags from 76 countries and island nations as we entered Ashkelon Marina, where they recognized us from the East Mediterranean Yacht Rally four years ago. We received a champagne welcome and lots of attention. Even from the media. It is quite an event to complete a circumnavigation in Israel. Another highlight occurred on May 17, Norway's Constitution Day, when we had the

Meeting Shimon Peres at the Norwegian Embassy in Israel.

honour of meeting Shimon Peres at a reception in the Norwegian Embassy. Fortunately, Martin was wearing a jacket and tie for the occasion. Only the second time in nine years!

Nor Siglar was caked with salt and orange grime, her sheets stiff and her sails dirty. After a gigantic cleanup and a visit to the dentist, we moved on to Herzlia Marina a day sail away, where an Israeli friend, Itay Singer, whom we met in Fiji, gave us another royal welcome together with his family and friends. The kindness extended by the Singer family was in sharp contrast to what was happening around us. Israel was in the process of withdrawing its troops from Lebanon, an activity we could both hear and see from the marina, which was located below the flight path of gunship helicopters bringing soldiers home. May 14, Israel's Independence Day, was marred by suicide bomber attacks in Hebron, which caused several deaths. Places we had visited last time were not only unsafe but inaccessible as well. We were fortunate to have seen so much at that time. Security was strict everywhere. At the post office, we had to show proof of ID to send a package. Guards posted outside buildings and malls performed full body checks. In Israel, they are more interested in searching people's bags, briefcases and backpacks before they enter the shops than after!

"There is no point giving Arafat a finger," our friend, Itay declared. "He will take the whole hand! He simply doesn't want us here." As we were ready to leave, he gathered a group of friends at their favourite restaurant in Tel Aviv for a send-off party. The mostly Jewish clientele and Palestinian staff seemed to get along well. They were laughing, joking and teasing one another. Little did they know that the area would be haunted by suicide bombers in the very near future. For the negotiations between Israel and Palestine at Camp David were going nowhere. And with the announcement of an independent Palestinian state in September, the conflict was about to escalate and reach catastrophic proportions.

Martin's back was still giving him trouble. For a while, it didn't look like we would be able to continue. But after a few weeks of R&R and VIP treatment in the luxurious marina, he felt better. We decided to give it a try. We were two weeks behind schedule and had to keep at it if we were going to make it across the Bay of Biscay and the North Sea before the autumn storms set in. Our journey through the Mediterranean had to be more like a delivery trip than a cruise, with only short stops for bunkering and re-provisioning. That was fine with us. For we had sailed the Mediterranean twice before.

The first leg turned into a bit of a surprise. We had expected a relatively easy 3-4 day passage to Crete. But we didn't end up there at all! Gale force headwinds and short steep seas so typical for the Mediterranean forced us to do a lot of tacking. One day, our course took us to Libya in the south; the next day to the Peloponnesian Peninsula in the north. It was a real slog. In the end, we gave Crete a miss and carried on to Malta instead. The "short" 3-4 day trip turned into a 12-day non-stop passage of 1,100 nautical miles! So the Indian Ocean wasn't our last longer crossing after all!

The inner basin of Valetta, Malta's impressive harbour.

In Valetta, Malta's impressive fortress city, we only took time to shop for fresh food, fill diesel and water. In fact, we were so anxious to get going that we simply forgot to check out! It was the first time that happened on the whole trip! It is the norm all over the world to clear in and out on arrival and departure. We were already well on our way to Sicily when Valletta Port Control called us back. We were tempted to ignore the order. However, it was too risky and we turned back. And that was a good thing. If we had continued and been caught, we would have received a fine of US$2,000. Besides, the police were looking for three heroin smugglers from Libya who had escaped from a local prison the night before. So Nor Siglar was thoroughly searched before she was allowed to resume her voyage to Sicily, where we had to seek refuge from a storm approaching from the Balearics further west.

The Mediterranean is known for its "feast or famine" conditions, i.e. too much or too little wind. This time, we experienced mostly calm weather. But since Martin's back was still bothering him, we didn't mind. Under the circumstances, we were better off running the engine in calm weather than battling a gale on the nose. Our faithful "Mr. Perkins" purred like a cat for six days in a row all the way to Formentera, where we stopped for fuel. And the engine kept it up for four more days until we reached Gibraltar, where we arrived safely exactly one month after leaving Israel.

Only 1,800 nautical miles to go! What a relief! Our joy was short-lived. While ashore changing money, an unwanted guest had snuck aboard. We found him hiding in the forepeak. We caught him off-guard and the thief had not had time to steal anything. What he did manage, however, was to ruin our evening. Instead of celebrating the halfway point of our last leg with a nice dinner out, we ended up at a police station under the famed "Rock" delivering a report until the wee hours.

It only takes an hour by air from Gibraltar to Casablanca, so we treated ourselves to a quick visit to "our family" in Mohammedia who were so kind to us when Martin had his back operation. We stuffed our backpacks full of clothes and things we knew they could use, and that we didn't need any more now that we were going home. It was an emotional reunion and we had many heart-warming moments together. Our Muslim friends still mean a lot to us. The two little boys are like our grandchildren now. In a way we have "adopted" them.

Back in Gibraltar, we realized that we didn't have any charts to get us to Norway. We had sold them! When we left Halden six years earlier, the idea had been to sail back to Vancouver. We had not intended to return. However, plans change. Our cruise kept expanding and now we were back. In order to avoid a third Atlantic crossing, we had decided to end our odyssey in Norway. A fellow sailor kindly lent us the charts we needed. We were ready for the homestretch.

HOMEWARD BOUND
GIBRALTAR – NORWAY

We had been worrying about the exposed coast of Portugal with its strong prevailing northerly winds. Our rough journey south, in a following gale and high seas was still vivid in our minds. Martin's back was still sore and we were grateful to Pieter Jongeneel for coming to give us a hand again. This time, however, the weather gods were kind and gave us exceptionally favourable conditions.

As Nor Siglar sailed out into the Strait of Gibraltar, hundreds of dolphins came charging after us. Maybe all the bad luck, which we had been experiencing the past year was over? For dolphins mean good luck, and that is exactly what happened. First, we motor sailed on glassy calm seas for three days all the way to Bayona on the north coast of Spain. Then, we had a pleasant crossing of the Bay of Biscay in a fresh breeze from the southwest. It was so stable that we could have all our meals at the cockpit table. Unbelievable but true!

Near the Isles of Scilly, we crossed our old course from the Azores to Norway. That time, we had sailed up the English Channel. It was an experience we did not care to repeat. This year, having made such excellent progress, we had time to take the Irish Sea and the Caledonia Canal instead, a route we had enjoyed on our way south four years ago.

In Howth Marina north of Dublin, a young Norwegian couple recognized us from our articles in the sailing magazine, Seilas. They had just completed the first month of their blue water cruise. It was touching to see them filled with excitement and expectation in anticipation of the biggest adventure of their lives. We were nearing the end of ours. Saturated by impressions and events, we willingly shared our experiences and ideas.

Some of the nicest memories from our circumnavigation were created by these surprise encounters. It was so exciting to hear: "Wow! Isn't that Nor Siglar?" All over the world, we met sailors who had read our articles. "Anne and Martin! Thanks to your inspiration we are embarking on our dream!" a countryman called in passing, as he was heading south to warmer climes.

Our journey continued through the Crinan Canal, a neat "do-it-yourself" experience where we operated eight manual locks on a narrow 18 km canal, which meandered through a peaceful and pastoral countryside. The Caledonia Canal took much longer. It was 100 km long with 29 serviced locks and ten swing bridges. We spent five days on this beautiful waterway, winding our way through the Scottish Highlands past Mt. Nevis and across lakes and lochs where we scouted in vain for the legendary Loch Ness monster.

Even before leaving Gibraltar, we started receiving e-mails indicating that preparations were underway to celebrate our arrival. It was, of course, nice that people wanted to make a fuss over us. However, that meant having to give them an exact time of arrival well ahead. And that was difficult. Deadlines and itineraries were some of the things we had learned to leave behind us. However, all went according to plan. Our good luck was holding and the homestretch went beyond expectations. Even the North Sea was benign.

We easily met the deadline. In strong winds and overcast skies, 15 sailboats from the Halden Yacht Club met us at the famous bridge on the border between Norway and Sweden to escort us the last few miles to the King's Quay. Images from our landfall seven years ago flashed through our minds. Again, a large crowd had turned out to welcome us.

But the only person I saw was my mother. Now, 95 years old, she had followed us on a map above her bed throughout our voyage. No wonder she was the one to receive the most attention from the media who had arrived to record the event. It was not every day circumnavigators came home to Halden. There were lots of well-wishers and speeches, which culminated in the Halden Yacht Club awarding us a life membership. It was a touching and thoughtful moment.

There was no end to the attention. For me, however, most important of all was that my mother was still with us and able to be present after all these years. Martin had lost both his parents while we were away. Naturally, my mother was happy to have us safe and sound at home again. So were we. And we were relieved that we didn't have any more mishaps at the end of our voyage.

A big moment: Nor Siglar ends her around-the-world adventure in Norway.

Our long honeymoon was over. But the festivities were not. Two weeks later, we continued up the Oslo Fjord to Steilene Lighthouse, where the Chief Editor of Seilas, Henrich Nissen-Lie, came onboard Nor Siglar with a huge bottle of champagne. Sailors from the Royal Norwegian Yacht Club escorted us the last few miles to Dronningen, the Queen's Quay, where once again, we received a royal welcome. Also meeting us were Michael and Gillian West of Khamsin, neighbours from Spruce Harbour Marina, who had left Vancouver on the same day as we did. They had left Khamsin in Barcelona while they took a trip through Europe by land. Their surprise presence was a heart-warming finale to a big adventure.

"It sure doesn't look like she has sailed around the world!" were some of the comments from the dock. Nor Siglar certainly had. We had logged 56,000 nautical miles – approximately 2.5 times around the world at the equator. Obviously, Martin's diligent maintenance program had paid off.

We had become incredibly fond of Nor Siglar. What a versatile lady! Not only is she a trustworthy offshore vessel that brought us safely from port to port across the big oceans in all kinds of conditions. She was also our home – our one and only home - for 15 years. Now, we are going to give her a well-deserved rest in "the old country" where we will be using her as our floating summer home for years to come. Although we are returning to Vancouver to live, we intend to come back to our dear Nor Siglar and explore some of the most beautiful cruising areas in the world - in our land of birth. We have saved the best for last.

BACK ON TERRA FIRMA

When we set out on our blue water voyage, we had only planned to be away for a few years. We never dreamt that we would be gone so long. But it turned out to be much more than a sailing adventure. It became an enormously educational, rewarding and at times, a rather trying experience. And while we saw many beautiful places, it was the people we met along the way that gave the circumnavigation real meaning.

We also experienced the delight of bonding with fellow cruisers, brushed up on history and language skills and learned about other cultures. We came to know and understand lifestyles completely different from our own and learned that it is possible to live quite happily in a variety of ways in this complex and fascinating world. Now that we are back, it is reassuring to feel that this is where we belong. This is where we want to be. We have never been tempted to settle down on an island in paradise. Family and old friends mean much more to us than endless summer and exotic places.

So what have we learned from our adventure? It has taught us respect for people from different backgrounds, cultures and religions. We feel that we have become more tolerant and understanding. We have discovered an inner strength we didn't know we had. And we have learned to appreciate the small things in life. We witnessed how people from other cultures live more simply than we do. Now, we intend to do the same. It remains to be seen how long this new awareness will linger.

We have also seen with our own eyes how people all over this astonishing globe of ours have the same basic needs. Regardless of racial origin, culture, religion and environment, everyone needs air, water and food, shelter, clothing and last, but not least, Love. And all parents wish a better life for their children.

When we follow the news around the world nowadays, we feel more engaged than before somehow. Events far away seem more real now that we have been to so many of the places that make the headlines. Things appear more vivid when we can picture the locations in our minds. Before, they were nothing but a distant name on the map. We can better visualize conditions in conflict areas. And our thoughts go to the people we met there. Images come to mind. One thing remains a mystery for us, though: why is there so much misery in this world where we have met so much kindness?

Now that our circumnavigation is over, we are left with many different feelings. First, there is a sense of relief; a relief that we made it home safely. At the same time, we feel a certain vacuum. A very special lifestyle is over. We feel a bit restless, a bit lost. The future is like an open book. But we anticipate new challenges. An exciting part of the cruising lifestyle is that you discover new qualities about yourself. So now, we would like to explore some of those dormant qualities. We will embark on other projects and adventures. It is time for a change. We look forward to life on terra firma again.

Above all, it is nice to come home and feel that East and West, Home is Best. Still, the Dream will be with us forever.

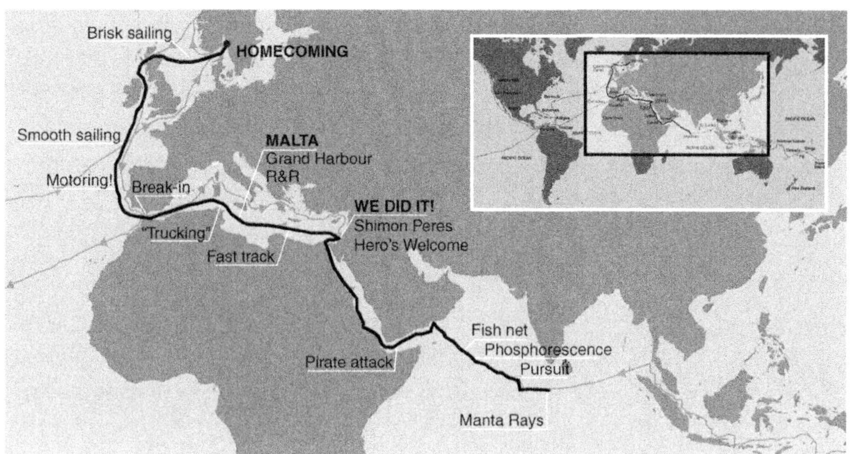

The end of Part 7 of the "9 Years on the 7 Seas Adventure", also published in print and as an eBook with the title

Closing the Round-the-World Circle

ABOUT THE AUTHORS
ANNE E. BREVIG AND MARTIN VENNESLAND

Anne grew up in Halden, Norway as a country girl on a farm. She always dreamt of seeing the world and began her adventures with life as an au pair, studying languages in Switzerland, Germany and the USA. In New York, she embarked on a career in international shipping and later became comptroller of a large Norwegian shipping company's Vancouver offices. When Anne met Martin at the age of 38, she was completely new to sailboats.

Having grown up inland, she didn't learn to swim until she was 16, was afraid of the water and became seasick easily. Anne never thought in her wildest imagination that one day she would exchange her comfortable life ashore with the often extreme challenges of life at sea – a decision she has never regretted!

Martin was born with salt water in his blood. He grew up by the tang of the sea in the small village of Sagesund on the south coast of Norway and has sailed all his life. The dream of travelling to exotic and distant shores on his own keel took shape at an early age. As a young man he emigrated to Canada to become a professional forester.

When taking early retirement to venture offshore, Martin was head of one of Canada's largest forestry consultingfirms. An avid outdoors person, he is happiest in the mountains, at his woodlot tending his cedars and Douglas firs or sailing on the high seas.

Nor Siglar in her element

ABOUT THE YACHT NOR SIGLAR

When choosing Nor Siglar, which means Northern Sailor in old Norse, we looked at practical points like size, strength, comfort, standing and running rigging, keel and rudder configuration, sailing ability and, of course, logical safety factors like cockpit draining, size of winches, hatches and windows etc. We did not wish to take a doctor's degree in dynamics or physics to be able to sail a boat around the world, and after having done so, don't think that is necessary either.

After having looked at a variety of sailboats, we finally chose a modern production boat constructed of hand laid fiberglass for the following reasons:

In contrast to the traditional full keeled, heavy displacement designs, we thought a lighter displacement, high performance cruiser-racer would give us superior sailing ability, higher speed and greater comfort. The size would be easy for a middle-aged couple to handle, while providing ample interior space and stowage, and still be large enough for a sea kindly motion.

The low maintenance aspect of a fiberglass boat was a major factor in the decision making process. It is a well-known fact that offshore cruisers spend a lot of time on maintenance and repair to keep their vessels seaworthy. Therefore, keeping these chores to a minimum is very important so that R & R, "Rest & Relaxation", doesn't always turn into a "Repair & Reprovisioning" ordeal instead. Who wants to spend hours on end varnishing wood and fixing hot, leaky teak decks when there are beautiful anchorages and unique cultures to be explored?

With a few exceptions, we have been very satisfied with NOR SIGLAR. Sailing-wise she has performed well in all conditions, which we have encountered. The light displacement, high ratio main and fin keel make her very fast in light winds. She also sails very well high into the wind, which we have found to be extremely important. Contrary to common belief, sailing around the world is not all downwind sailing. This is wishful thinking. Time and again, we have experienced conditions with wind on the nose where it should have been on the stern, even in "so-called" trade wind areas. Gone are the days of predictable weather patterns. Weather systems all over the world are no longer what they used to be.

VESSEL SPECIFICATONS

NOR SIGLAR

Gib'Sea sloop built in 1985
by Gibert Marine, La Rochelle, France

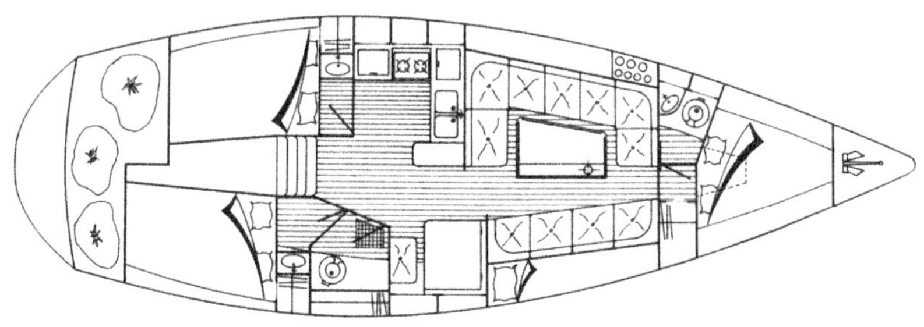

SPECIFICATIONS:

Total length (LOA): 40.4 ft

Hull length (HOA): 38.1 ft

Water line length: 31.8 ft

Beam: 12.5 ft

Draft: 6.5 ft

Mast height: 57.1 ft

Weight (displacement): 17,309 lbs.

Ballast (keel): 7,100 lbs.

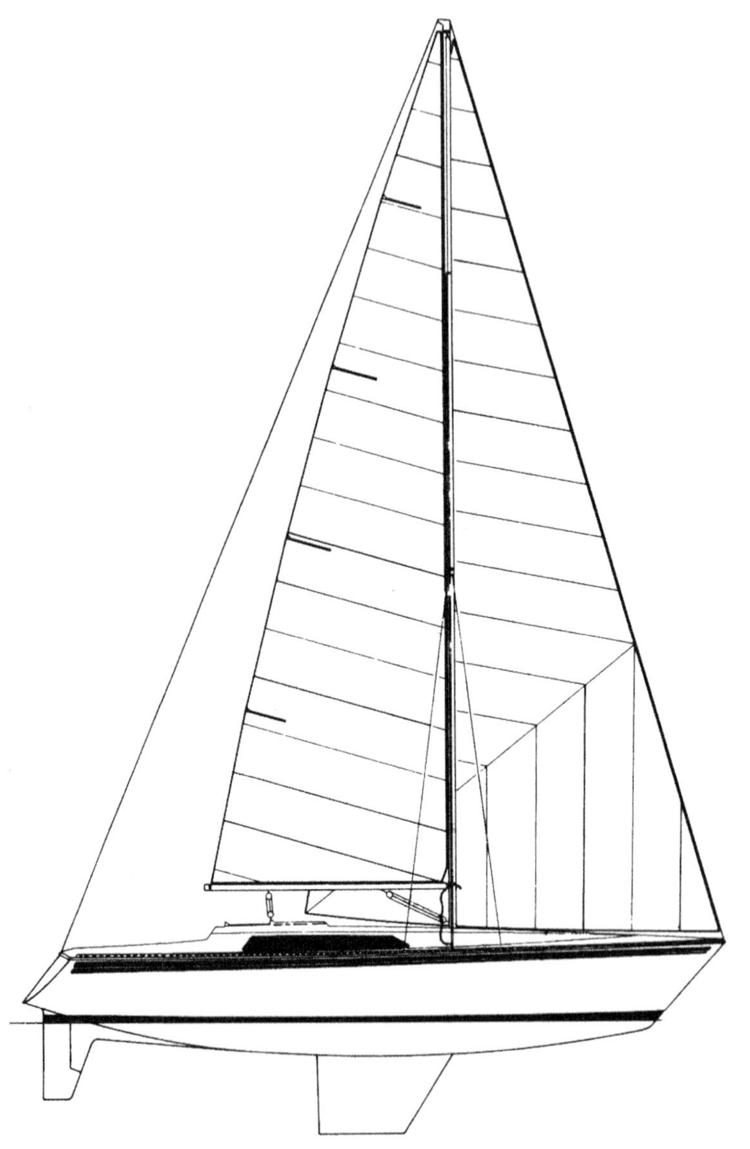

SAILS:

Main sail: 355 sq. ft

Cruising spinnaker: 678 sq. ft

No. 1 Genoa (130%): 473 sq. ft

No. 2 Genoa (110%): 398 sq. ft

No. 1 Stay sail: 237 sq. ft

No. 2 Stay sail: 129 sq. ft

Storm jib: 75 sq. ft

Engine: Perkins 4.108 – 50 HP

Fuel tank: 160 litres

Water tanks: 325 litres (1 x 200 l, 1 x 125 l)

EQUIPMENT

STANDARD EQUIPMENT (delivered with the boat):
Fridge, 2-burner propane stove with an oven, pedestal compass, wheel steering, outside bilge pump, 4 electric faucet pumps, 7 Barlow winches (2 self tailing), manual windlass, 1 battery, Perkins 4.108 50 HP engine.

ADDITIONAL EQUIPMENT (acquired later):
110-volt shore-power with charger and 240-volt transformer, house battery, AC/DC inverter, 4 solar panels, wind-generator, wind-vane, electric windlass, digital volt- and ampère meter, battery monitor, water-maker, hot water-heater, diesel-heater, propane system with 2x20-lb. tanks, roller furling on forestay and cutter-stay, collapsible mast steps.

NAVIGATIONAL AIDS:
2 GPS instruments (1 mounted/1 hand-held), 2 sextants with almanac and distance tables, 2 wall-mounted clocks, 1 barometer, 1 radar, 2 binoculars, 2 handheld compasses, foghorn, depth-sounder, wind-speed indicator, knot-metre, charts, reference books and cruising guides world wide.

COMMUNICATIONS EQUIPMENT:
2 VHF radios (1 mounted/1 hand-held), 1 SSB/HAM radio, 1 automatic antenna tuner, 1 AM/FM radio with CD and cassette players, 2 Walkmans.

SAFETY EQUIPMENT:
EPIRB (Emergency Position Indicating Radio Beacon), 6-person life-raft, emergency grab-bag, man overboard pole with light, life ring, life sling harness with line, rescue strobe lights, flares and flare gun, 3 safety harnesses, 6 life-vests, jack lines for safety harnesses mounted on deck, radar reflector, power searchlight, loudhailer, wire-cutter and axe, 3 fire extinguishers, buckets and 3 bilge pumps (1 electric/2 manual), conical plugs adjacent to all sea cocks.

SELF DEFENCE EQUIPMENT:

2 baseball bats, mace, hand-held electric "tazer", companionway alarm. No weapons.

GROUND TACKLE:

1 30 lb. Bruce (80 ft. chain/300 ft. line), 1 50 lb. Northill (205 ft. chain/200 ft. line), 1 30 lb. Danforth (25 ft. chain/200 ft. line) and 1 10 lb. Grapple for the dinghy

DINGHY:

1986-1994: Zodiac 10 ft. rigid bottom rubber dinghy with a 9.9 HP outboard engine
1994- Avon Rollup R 2.85 metre rubber dinghy with a 5 HP outboard engine

SPARES:

Engine parts as recommended in the Perkins Manual, tiller, propeller, whisker-pole, standing rigging, automatic antenna tuner, sheets and halyards, blocks and tackles, nuts, bolts and screws, batteries, light-bulbs, plastic hoses, electrical wiring, spare parts for the heads, sail repair kit with extra canvas.

MISCELLANEOUS:

Tools for electrical and mechanical repairs incl. blocks of wood and plywood sheets for potential damage to hull and hatches, extensive first-aid kit with a multitude of medications; fishing equipment, folding bicycles, scuba-diving equipment, cameras, computer, printer, electric sewing machine, vacuum cleaner, water filter, fuel filter with water separator, multimetre, fans, sun-shower, jerry cans, flashlights, headlamps, signal flags, guest flags, gifts, trading items and the usual personal and household effects.

For more details, see the Seven Seas Adventures website:

www.sevenseasadventure.com

GLOSSARY TERMS

Abeam: At right angles to the keel of a ship
Bilge: The lowest inner part of a ship's hull
Bulkhead: A structural wall which divides the vessel into compartments
Celestial Navigation; Taking positions by measuring the angle of celestial bodies above the horizon using a sextant and then calculating the vessel's location with distance tables and a nautical almanac
Channel 16: Emergency channel on VHF radio
Cockpit: A recessed part of the deck in which to sit and steer
Cutter Stay: An inner forestay for a smaller sail
Dragging: When an anchor slides along the bottom
EPIRB: Emergency Position Indicating Radio Beacon
Forepeak: A space (normally a cabin) in the bow of the vessel
Furling Gear: Equipment used to enable sails to be rolled on a stay or boom for storage
GPS: Global Positioning System uses satellite signals to pinpoint locations
Gybe: To change course in a following wind. Sails are moved from one side of the boat to the other. An accidental gybe is when this is not accomplished in a controlled manner. It can be a dangerous manoeuvre.
Halyard: A rope or wire for hoisting sails
Head: Ship's toilet
Lazy-jacks: Lines to contain the mainsail while it is being lowered
Lee Cloth A canvas secured at the side of a berth to keep the occupant from falling out when the boat is healing over or rolling from side to side
Leech: The trailing edge of a sail
Lee Shore: Windward side of a coast or shore
Lee Side: Side of the boat away from the direction of the wind (Leeward)
Lie a Hull A technique used in heavy weather with all the sails down and the tiller lashed to leeward

Life Line: Lines secured along the decks of the boat to prevent people from falling overboard
Mayday: International distress call
Port Side: The left hand side of a boat when looking forward
Preventer: Line leading forward to hold the boom at right angles to the boat when going downwind to prevent a gybe
Pulpit: Railing around the bow of the boat
Quarter: Area between the beam (midship) and the stern of a vessel
Reach: Sailing with the wind on the beam with the sail approximately halfway out. Can be a close reach, beam reach or broad reach
Reefing: To reduce the size of a sail
Running: To sail with the wind behind the boat
Sheet: A line used to adjust the sails
Shrouds: Wire supports on either side of the mast
Spreaders: Short struts between mast and shrouds to add support to the rig
SSB: Single Side Band – short-wave radio
Starboard: The right-hand side of a vessel when looking forward
Stay: A wire, supporting the mast fore and aft
Stern: The rear part of a boat
Tacking: To change course when sailing against the wind
Traveller: A sliding fitting which travels on a track, used to alter the sheeting angles of a sail
Turnbuckle: A mechanism to tighten shrouds and stays
VHF: Very High Frequency radiotelephone used over shorter distances to other vessels or land based stations
Waypoint: A planned crossing point between a certain degree of latitude and longitude
Wind Vane: A device that automatically steers a boat at a preset angle to the wind

Whisker Pole: A pole used to hold out foresails when sailing downwind Windward Direction from which the wind is blowing.
1 nautical mile (nm): 1,852 metres (6,076 feet)
1 knot: 1 nautical mile per hour
1 degree of latitude (°): 60 nautical miles
1 degree of longitude (at equator): 60 nautical miles
1 minute (') of latitude: 1 nautical mile (60' in 1° latitude)
Circumference of the earth at equator: 21,638 nautical miles / 40,075 km

BEAUFORT WIND SCALE

Beaufort Windspeed Description: - Force - Knots

0: - *0* - **Calm**

1: - *1 - 3* - **Light air**

2: - *4 - 6* - **Light breeze**

3: - *7-10* - **Gentle breeze**

4: - *11-16* - **Moderate breeze**

5: - *17-21* - **Fresh breeze**

6: - *22-27* - **Strong breeze**

7: - *28-33* - **Near gale**

8: - *34-40* - **Gale**

9: - *41-47* - **Strong gale**

10: - *48-55* - **Storm**

11: - *56-63* - **Violent storm**

12: - *63+* - **Hurricane**

MORE ADVENTURES ON THE SEVEN SEAS

If you have a computer with access to the Internet, you can read a "Flip-book" (a Flash plugin is required), based on the full-colour illustrated print version of "9 Years on the 7 Seas", as well as the Seven Seas Adventures Series, 7 books based on this book.
The Series is available in print as well as eBooks in many file formats.

The books in the Seven Seas Adventures Series are not just any old travelogues for adventurers. Rather, it is a collection of highlights from encounters with "ordinary" people from different cultures and backgrounds who live a life much different from what most of us are used to. Anne and Martin certainly learned that what we take for granted is an elusive dream for others.

The books "answer" a multitude of questions posed by travellers in general as well as prospective offshore sailors:

Read - and be inspired by how Martin, head of one of the largest forestry consulting firms in Canada and Anne, comptroller of a large shipping company, cut the ties and left their secure jobs and comfortable lives ashore to follow their dreams. Nine years and more than 56,000 nautical miles later, they had survived serious dangers, break-ins and a dramatic grounding, escaped close encounters with pirates, witnessed life-saving bravery and enjoyed heart-warming personal meetings on all five continents.

Get additional reviews and background information, browse image galleries and slideshow presentations, listen to interviews with the author (audio files), read updates and get optional downloads and much more on the Seven Seas Adventures home page –

www.sevenseasadventure.com

A CIRCUMNAVIGATOR'S FAQ

Read all about how we Planned, Executed and Survived our Around-the-World Adventure

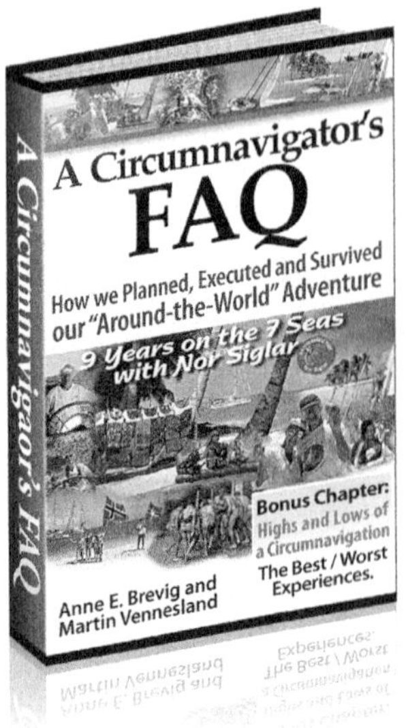

ISBN-13: 978-1494313753
ISBN-10: 1494313758

"Do you have any favourite places?" "Were you ever in danger?" "What would you do differently?" "Were you ever sick?"

These are but a few of the many questions Norwegian-Canadian couple, Anne Brevig and Martin Vennesland were often asked after they had finished their 56,000 nautical mile circumnavigation immortalized in their immensely popular book, "9 Years on the 7 Seas with Nor Siglar".

Time and again, when promoting their bestseller at boat shows, slide shows on-board cruise ships and a multitude of nautical and cultural organizations, people would invariably ask the very same questions. Hence the idea to collect the most frequently answered ones in a handy little FAQ-book. And here it is: "A Circumnavigator's FAQ", a book chock full of information, which will be useful to sailors and discriminating travellers alike, especially to those who yearn to get off the beaten track far away from the traditional tourist routes.

Here you can get straight answers from a couple who sought freedom from the everyday grind by cutting all ties and set sails for the unknown to live their dream and explore life on the other side of the horizon. During their once-in-a-lifetime fabulous, but also challenging adventure, which was filled with drama and excitement, strange and enchanting encounters, heartwarming hospitality and places of breathtaking beauty, they visited 76 countries and island nations covering a distance equaling 2.5 times around the world at equator. So now you are about to read an abbreviated version of the wisdom gained by these two experienced globetrotters who lived 15 years on their 40-foot sailboat, nine of them offshore.

Not only to they share valuable, real-life tips and ideas on how to enjoy the unknown and avoid dangers, but they also offer life-tested advice and recommendations.

One of the most Frequently Asked Questions was: "Do you have one all-important advice to other travelers?"

Read the adventurous couple's answer to this - and many other questions in this book, which cover the topics of Planning, Executing and Surviving a Around-the-World Adventure.

We met people from all corners of the world, experienced the delight of bonding with fellow cruisers, brushed up on history and language skills and learned about other cultures. We came to know and understand lifestyles completely different from our own and learned that it is possible to live quite happily in a variety of ways in this complex and fascinating world

Anne

Printed in Great Britain
by Amazon

52871472R00203